TAKE MY BODY AND FIX IT!

The Tastes of Western Spas

A Cookbook & Guide

by

Sonnie Imes

To all who seek a balance in their lives

TABLE OF CONTENTS

RECIPES

INTRODUCTION

If you have only dreamed of the spa vacation—massage, hot pools, pampering of your tired and aging body—and thought it beyond your means, thumb through this book and your dreams will suddenly take on the aspect of definite possibility. The world of spa vacations is accessible, varying in cost and regimen, and easily available for a day, a weekend, a week, a month at a time. The resurging interest in spas during the 80s has fostered many a new spa, which means the competition is stiffer than it used to be, and the spa-goer is the beneficiary.

In the West alone—California, Arizona, Utah, Colorado, New Mexico, British Columbia, Hawaii, Mexico—await dozens of spas that are just your idea of what a spa should be. Rugged and rustic, like the Hills? Elegant and sophisticated? There's only one Golden Door, and after reading about it, you may decide this famous world-class spa is just your cutglass goblet of carrot juice. Do you need a strict and regular course of rigorous training to get in shape? Read the National Institute of Fitness chapter. Or are you more inclined to a daily massage, an herbal wrap, a lazy swim, a nap and a good meal? Then you may prefer a Resort Spa.

From the 24 spas included in this book, you'll discover which spas treat stress, which spas have the best low-calorie cuisine, which spas take you on 6 a.m. walks in the desert, and which spas will give you a complete physical. You'll find that you can spa in the city, in the country, or in the outback of civilization. You'll become familiar with spa terminology—hydrotherapy versus thermal therapy, thalassotherapy versus fango treatment or Vichy therapy...not to mention mud packs, salt-glo rubs, loofah treatments, Scotch hoses, Swiss showers, aromatherapy, herbal wraps. And of course the traditional massages, facials, hair treatments, manicures, pedicures, and saunas.

5

You'll learn that you can be gregarious or reservedly into yourself. You can sign up with a companion or go it alone — no stigmas for the single. In many cases, you can go to the spa, and your companion can play golf, or shop, or lounge all day long.

One of the reasons I pursued this book is because I am an avid cook and a dedicated recipe collector. Over the past decade I have published 10 cookbook/guides, from Lake Tahoe restaurant fare to ocean-going cruise ship cuisine. The spa scene in the 90s concentrates heavily on good food, on nutritious, low-calorie, healthful dishes that are as delicious as any butter and cream based French sauce. Being able to duplicate these recipes at home has been a big incentive in my pursuit of Western spas; there are recipes from each spa chef, most of them creative food geniuses. Many of their recipes contain the ordinary ingredients of common entrees and desserts we know and love, the healthful aspect being that often they are simply prepared differently. Although exercise may be what you think of when you think spa, eating has become one of the prime highlights — eating well of course, eating things prepared in such a way that if you follow up with them at home you'll never have to diet again. There are spas where the concentration on diet may turn your life around — complex carbohydrates rather than sugar, minimal amounts of fat, sodium, and sugar — a deprivation that after a few days you realize makes you feel like a million bucks.

In a world as frantic as ours, a spa vacation can take on the overtones of those long, lazy days of childhood where time moves slowly, and the important things in life revolve around playing outdoors, running just for the joy of it, swimming with your friends, reading a book in a hammock under the mulberry tree. There are spas like this, where getting rid of the stress of modern-day life is the reason you're there. Classes in stress management abound, along with lessons in visualization (picturing yourself happy, relaxed, successful). You can sign up for biofeedback, hypnotherapy, yoga, Tai Chi, deep relaxation; you can take time for an acupressure massage, reflexology, self-hypnosis, meditation. Some spas concentrate on this kind of recovery—the mind as well as the body. Others offer only a few classes.

Some spas offer clinics that will help you quit smoking, control your rocketing cholesterol, or deal with a specific medical problem.

There are also spas where fitness is the most important word, and the toning of the body is what life is all about. Every kind of exercise class is available—jogging, walking, Jazzercise, calisthenics, water sports and water exercise, tennis, racquetball, weight rooms equipped with Nautilus or Universal equipment. You can sign up with a personal trainer and figure out the ideal program to lose a couple of inches from your waist; or you can choose at random and sample them all.

If you like, you can sign up at a spa where one of the activities is shopping in the nearby city. Or you can choose the spa that is miles from everywhere and to call home you have to use the phone in the spa office. Some spas take you on tours of the area—a busride to Indian ruins, a trip to historical sites. At some, you can ride a bike into the hills or into town; at others you'll get to hike to the top of a waterfall or into the bottom of a canyon. You can choose a spa that takes fewer than a dozen guests at a time or opt for the huge complex that discretely houses hundreds.

As you can see, spa-ing can be just about anything. And it is always such a treat—it is indeed one of the things you can do for yourself, if only for a day or a weekend, that you'll neither regret nor forget. Away from real life, in a setting that was built to pamper and aid and influence you to live your life with respect and responsibility, it is possible to get your life in order, to get priorities back on track, to come out not only looking better but feeling better.

Although several spas cater to the rich and famous, there are so many spas now within a comfortable price range that spa-ing has indeed become a vacation choice of the middle class...and from my point of view, it's due time. As we plunge toward the 21st century facing so many problems, a spa vacation may become one of the remarkable things that can truly help us, give us time out to reflect on our actions, offer us an opportunity to change selfish and indulgent lives for an unselfish life-style. It may sound silly to say that pampering could lead to a better world...but the pampering within the majority of today's spas is of a kind that nurtures and makes individuals comfortable with nurturing others; it is of a kind where we learn to take care of ourselves rather than expecting others to do it for us. Whenever you get an opportunity to renew and balance your body, your mind, and your spirit, take it; it may not change the whole world, but it will definitely change yours, for the better.

Enjoy Western Spas. I hope it leads to the perfect spa for you, or to the perfect half dozen. To your body, mind, and spirit...

bon appetit!

DESTINATION SPAS

The idea of a destination spa is that you have everything at your fingertips, and at the best of them you'll want for nothing. Encapsulated within the grounds are not only the requisite spa facilities such as pool, Jacuzzis, dining establishments and sleeping accommodations but many extras as well: bathrobes, hair salons, boutiques, talented specialists in dozens of therapy treatments ranging from acupressure to yoga, and always, outstanding spa cuisine. Within minutes of most destination spas you will find special recreation possibilities — golf, tennis, horseback riding, nordic and alpine skiing, excursions, and historical-site hiking.

Destination spas will often give you a physical examination as well as take into consideration your medical history and diet before setting you up in a program designed just for you and your particular health problems.

Camaraderie is a byword at the destination spas. Everyone is the same — you don't need to worry about what you look like and there is no need to impress anyone.

It's a good feeling to know that you are considered special, valuable, and that you will be healthier, probably slimmer, and in almost all cases, happier with a few days or a week of rigorous spa-ing under your now-skinny little belt.

CANYON RANCH

Canyon Ranch in Tucson, Arizona is not only a spa for your body, but one for your mind and spirit as well. I returned home raving about this spa, feeling a great sense of well-being after my visit.

It's no wonder, because Canyon Ranch maintains a philosophy that everyone can take charge of his or her health and well-being and make fitness fun and habit forming. They really care about you, taking that spa-inspired "zest for living" home with you.

Owner Mel Zuckerman opened Canyon Ranch in 1979 after turning his own life around by losing 30 pounds and bringing his asthma, high blood pressure, and ulcers under control. Zuckerman says, "Wellness is not a destination, it is a journey."

A week at Canyon Ranch is a good start to that journey. The 70-acre resort offers all the fitness activities that any spa-goer could imagine, plus extras such as racquetball, tennis, squash, and bicycling. There are more than 50 fitness classes every day, ranging from hard aerobics for the advanced athlete to "Flugels," a type of aquacise course where you wear inflatable leg and hand devices for maximum water resistance.

Spa treatments are also abundant, including herbal wrap, aroma wrap, and salt treatment. Another treatment I hadn't found at other spas is the clay treatment. Canyon Ranch says the "blend of healing clay and southwestern herbs draw impurities from your skin while you relax wrapped in warm, dry fabric. A soothing herbal steam bath continues the detoxification process."

But while Canyon Ranch's fitness and spa services are dynamic and numerous, it is its educational programs that make this spa different from others. Those programs will delve into each individual's personal problems, whether medical, mental, or behavioral, and then a specialist will help the guest sort out how to deal with these challenges in a healthy manner. One physician told me, "We're very interested in teaching our guests how to take the healthy lifestyle home with them."

I took one of these educational sessions and learned a lot. Jean Pierre Marques, who conducted hypnotherapy, gave me post-hypnotherapy suggestions after putting me into deep relaxation. He showed me how to stop worrying if I awake at 2 a.m. (about how to get to my next spa visit and if this book was coming along on schedule). It was interesting and effective — I could get back to sleep with ease.

Canyon Ranch's specialists will help stressed-out guests, ones who want to stop smoking, those who have a compulsive eating disorder, or arthritis, and people at high risk for heart attacks, among other subjects.

The ranch also has special sessions such as the Executive Health Program, Corporate Health Enhancement, Mind Fitness, and the Lighter Living Program held in the Ranch's Life Enhancement Center, a mini spa for small groups with common goals. The latter program takes people who are 30 pounds or more overweight and puts them in a special area so they don't have to be intimidated by skinny little people. (Most spa-goers already have healthy bodies and aren't overweight, although those with weight problems were the founding mothers and fathers of the spa movement 40 years ago.)

Whatever aspect of your mind or body that needs fixing, Canyon Ranch can help you mend it at the spa, but more importantly, inspire you to continue this healthy lifestyle at home.

THE LOOK OF THINGS

Canyon Ranch is a sprawling complex with guesthouses scattered about the cactus-covered grounds. Walking the distance from your guesthouse to the spa activities is part of the program.

The guesthouses are single-story adobe cottages accented with red-tiled roofs in the Spanish tradition. There are 67 standard cottages, 45 deluxe cottages, and 41 luxury suites. All the rooms have cable television, alarm clocks, and telephone.

Located in the canyons outside of Tucson, the spa has three main focal points — the clubhouse, the spa building and the Health and Healing Center.

The clubhouse, with high-beamed ceilings and massive stone fireplaces, holds the dining rooms, guest services, library, lounge, and evening programs.

The spa facility is a huge center with seven gyms, locker rooms, aerobic and strength training rooms, racquetball, handball and squash courts, offices for health and fitness assessments, and complete beauty, massage, herbal and skin care departments. Outside are tennis courts, a basketball court, and a 13-station exercourse.

Consultations for nutrition, health, behavioral sciences, and natural healing are held in the Health and Healing Center, which also houses the medical offices.

Nestled among landscaping that features waterfalls, tropical plants, streams, cactus gardens, and fountains are four swimming pools — three for exercise and one for relaxing with a book or lazing in the hot Arizona sun.

Everywhere are stations with water, lemonade, orange juice, and other drinks to quench your thirst, but I guarantee this healthy lifestyle will keep you thirsting for more.

HOW TO GET THERE

Once you make reservations at Canyon Ranch, you are in the capable hands of a staff that will take care of you from A to Z. A program advisor calls before you even get to Canyon Ranch to recommend services and offer advice, or if you have a question call (602)-749-9000, ext. 433. You need to also return the medical questionnaire before your visit.

I liked the way Canyon Ranch asks guests to call (800)-742-9000 and give them your flight arrival information. Also, the staff can arrange for the airline you're flying on to serve you a vegetable platter or a healthy alternative to flight food if you tell Canyon Ranch 24 hours in advance.

There was no confusion upon arrival at Tucson International Airport, and any stress melted away when a staff member met me at the Information Desk in the airport's lower level baggage claim area.

Use the baggage tags Canyon Ranch sends you to speed up the departure from the airport. Canyon Ranch is 21 miles or a half-hour's drive from the airport.

For reservations call the toll-free number (800)742-9000 in the United States, or (800)-327-9090 in Canada, or write Canyon Ranch at 8600 E. Rockcliff Road, Tucson, AZ 85715.

SURROUNDING AREA

I could have taken a trip outside the spa by signing up for the "Supermarket Survival" class which teaches guests how to shop with health in mind. But to me, a supermarket is old hat whether it is in Tucson, Arizona, Wichita, Kansas, or my hometown of Incline Village, Nevada, so I didn't opt for this class.

Don't worry. For those who want to sightsee in the area, Canyon Ranch is most helpful. The staff will call a taxi or arrange a rental car, set up tee times at nearby golf courses, or book a horseback riding trip through one of Tucson's five surrounding desert mountain ranges.

Canyon Ranch also has a few side trips available which leave right from the ranch. These outings include birdwatching, a shopping/cultural trip to Nogales, Mexico, and a visit to the Arizona-Sonora Desert Museum.

This museum has been called one of the top 10 zoos in the United States, but it is more than a museum or a zoo, it is a "living" example of the desert. It features the plants and animals unique to the Sonora Desert, such as the saguaro cactus which is found nowhere else in the world but the Sonora Desert around Tucson and the Mexican-American border.

WHAT'S INCLUDED IN THE PRICE

Canyon Ranch is a moderate to expensive spa, depending on what time of year you visit and how many "extras" you add to your package.

All the packages include accommodations, three meals a day, use of all spa and resort facilities, fitness classes, sports activities, recipe demonstrations, and all presentations by medical, fitness, and stress-management experts.

The packages don't include gratuitities. A 17 percent service charge is added, which covers tips for all the staff and cost of medical services such as blood pressure checks, cholesterol screens, weight and body measurements, and first aid for minor injuries.

I went to the spa nurse to find a cure (is there such a thing?) for my cold and she set me up with medicine for no charge. It was nice to have that service available.

Canyon Ranch has four, seven and ten-night packages, as well as a nightly rate. Each package offers a certain number of specialized services free before the spa begins charging extra for these consultations.

For example, the seven-night package includes two professional health consultations and five personal or sports services. From the professional health services, you can choose biofeedback, hypnotherapy, nutrition consultation, stop-smoking consultation, attitudinal healing, and personal growth consultation among others. For the personal or sports services, spa guests have a choice of massages, herbal wraps, facials, make-up consultations, manicure and pedicure, haircut, shampoo, and private racquet lessons.

Aside from these spa packages, Canyon Ranch has several specialized options throughout the year such as a hiking week which includes six all-day hikes, six massages, and one herbal wrap.

Deposits are required but will be refunded if the package is canceled 14 days in advance. Canyon Ranch accepts credit cards, checks or cash. No one under 14 years old may participate in the programs.

CLOTHING AND WEATHER

Tucson is known for sun, sun, sun. Those of us in colder climes dream of winter holidays in a warm place, and with 360 days of sunshine, Tucson fits the bill. Its summers can be much hotter, but June, July and August also mean cheaper rates at most Southwest resorts. Tucson's desert dryness does make the heat more bearable in the summer than heat in a humid area.

If you are visiting from November to April, bring sweaters, sweatshirts, jacket, gloves, scarf, cap, and windbreaker because early mornings and nights can be cold here (it's the way of the desert). If you are visiting from April to October, a windbreaker and casual summer clothes are fine. Of course, whatever time of the year you choose to visit Canyon Ranch, bring swimsuit, shorts and t-shirts, warm-up suit, leotards, tennis or golf attire, various sorts of exercise shoes, and casual clothes for the evenings.

Canyon Ranch supplies each guest with a terry cloth robe and thongs. When these get wet or dirty, just exchange them for clean ones. The locker rooms are also equipped with blow driers, curling irons, razors and shaving cream, tote bags, sunscreen, and other sundries. There's even sunscreen available next to the swimming pools.

Other items you might want to bring include sunglasses, hat, racquet sports equipment, camera, pocket radio. A digital alarm clock is in every room.

A TYPICAL DAY

There is an eight-mile walk on Saturdays. Every day there is a choice of one- two- three- or four-mile walks. Classes at Canyon

Ranch begin at 6:30 a.m. in the spring, summer, and early fall, and at 7 a.m. in the winter. I opted for the three-mile walk at 7 a.m. From then on, there are several fitness classes every hour as well as spa treatments and educational seminars. The variety of opportunities are mind-boggling, but the orientation, advice from program and fitness supervisors, and a daily schedule help keep things running smoothly.

I took time out from the hectic fitness schedules to do my own thing: to learn how to ride a mountain bike after years and years off any kind of bicycle. An instructor went with me for the lesson and we had a blast riding over desert paths for an hour.

The ranch recommends that everybody's daily schedule include two aerobic classes, one flexibility class, one muscle toning or strength class, a relaxation session, and one educational/specialty option.

Every class is identified by its type and its level of difficulty. The educational options were for all levels and included back care, breathing, and introductions to cross training, circuit weights, aerobic exercise equipment, and free weights.

For example, I did my walk and then participated in the jump-rope class, pool aerobics, rhythms (a dance class), meditation, aqua trim, and volleyball games.

In between all this exercise, each guest can schedule body and beauty treatments. If you can find the time, there are several special classes throughout the day, some of which are free.

For example, on the Wednesday during the week I visited, there was a desert museum trip from 8 a.m. to 1 p.m.; a "lunch and learn" cooking demonstration at 12:15 p.m.; a lecture called "Assessing Your Risk For Heart Disease" at 1 p.m.; a presentation from 1-1:30 p.m. about Canyon Ranch's membership programs; a cooking class from 3-5 p.m.; a session on "Managing Your Food Habits" from 4-5:30 p.m.; a lecture by a dietician for women on calcium and osteoporosis at 4 p.m.; a massage workshop from 7:30-9:30 p.m.; and a lecture by a holocaust survivor at 8 p.m.

As the man who gave me a tour of the grounds said, there's certainly no reason to mope about looking for something to do at Canyon Ranch.

EVENING PROGRAMS

Canyon Ranch's specialists come out of their offices during the evenings to conduct several kinds of seminars giving guests plenty to learn here once the sun goes down.

These free programs cover topics ranging from "Do You Have Fat Blood?" to "Financially Fit: Maximizing Your Investments." At least once a week, a 12-step meeting is held for those in Alcoholics Anonymous, Overeaters Anonymous, Narcotics Anonymous, and other similar organizations.

Not all the seminars are related to nutrition, stress-management, or lifestyles, either. There are cooking classes, pottery workshops, and even bingo sessions.

Of course, if the day has worn you out, there is a nightly movie showing in each cottage.

THE STAFF

The staff at Canyon Ranch is something special. I saw gardeners clipping off dead leaves so people don't have to look at anything ugly at all. I also heard of maids leaving little notes of congratulation to people trying to kick the smoking habit when they notice no more cigarette butts in a room's ashtrays. The staff really listens, giving a sincere impression that they care about the guests well-being.

Besides this attitude, the staff is well-trained in every aspect of fitness and health care. Listen to this: There are two medical doctors, nine nurses, three exercise physiologists, four dieticians, 45 fitness instructors, nine tennis pros, four racquetball pros, and more than 50 massage therapists; and there are bellmen at the airport and maids for every room.

Canyon Ranch considers 250 its optimum number of guests, but there may be a few more or a few less when you visit. There are always 600 staff members. That's better than a 2:1 ratio and, with the high level of staff expertise, that ratio is stacked in the guest's favor.

FOOD

I sat down for dinner at Canyon Ranch and a menu was handed to me. What? Menu choices at a spa? This was a different sort of menu, though; instead of prices it had calorie counts. So, do I choose a cheese enchilada for 165 calories or a California tuna salad for 275 calories? You guess.

Calorie control is achieved at Canyon Ranch through portion sizes. Women who are trying to lose weight are advised to eat 1,000 calories and men 1,200 calories. They try to keep you eating 60 percent carbohydrates, 20 percent protein and 20 percent fat. A vegetarian option is available at every meal, which can have four or more choices.

The most popular beverage here is water, and guests are encouraged to drink eight 8-oz. glasses a day. Otherwise, hot or cold herbal teas are available, as well as lemonade and orange juice. Everything is decaffeinated, including the coffee, and alcoholic beverages are a no-no. Smoking is not permitted except in non-public outside areas.

Of course, Canyon Ranch uses no preservatives, no additives and only whole grains and fresh fruits and vegetables.

A neat thing about Canyon Ranch is its daily "Lunch and Learn" session in a demonstration kitchen. Each day chefs show how to cook a different item off the spa menu. In the demonstration kitchen there is a whole wall full of spa recipes that anybody can pick up to take home.

If you want to continue to lose weight once you get home, a spa dietician will help set up a weight-loss program and an exercise physiologist will set up an exercise schedule for you.

If you are from the east, Canyon Ranch in the Berkshires is the first major coed health and fitness resort to open year-round in the Northeast. It is essentially the same experience with obvious environmental differences.

SUMMARY

Canyon Ranch is considered by aficionados to be the premier experience. Everything is simple, but there is no stinting on anything. The encouragement of life-style change in eating and exercise habits is without doubt the most valuable part of a Canyon Ranch experience.

CANYON RANCH

One of the many exercise classes offered

MEADOWLARK

Health takes on a different meaning when one walks through the gates onto the grounds of Meadowlark. At this 20-acre estate in the Californian desert town of Hemet, your traditional ideas about health are challenged.

Here, health is not an endless series of abdominal exercises or sweating in a high impact aerobics class. It is not mud baths or a discouraging body composition test.

Health at the Meadowlark Center for Health and Growth begins in the mind and is manifested in your attitude and your body.

This holistic center is a retreat where you can go to get your head together. When I left Meadowlark, I felt a catharsis of my former ways of thinking. That's why I call this a spa for the mind. And I loved it.

It was founded in 1957 as a nonprofit organization, which it still is today. In 1958, the doors opened at the Meadowlark Center with founder Evarts G. Loomis, M. D. as its mentor and executive. Considered a pioneer in holistic health practices, Evarts built Meadowlark as a place where the process of healing is promoted and the principles of health in body, mind, and spirit are taught.

This center combines group teaching sessions and individual spiritual and psychological counseling with a wholesome diet and a daily exercise progam. At the end of the week, the staff hopes that you feel better, in mind and body.

Those with medical problems will have recognized physicians available at the Holistic Medical Center to help them in the healing process. The staff talks about former guests who have come complaining of backaches or other ailments and have left improved.

I was just one of the 3,000 people who have visited the resort during its 27-year history. There are seldom more than 25 guests each week, although Meadowlark can accommodate conferences of 50 people.

During the week's activities of lectures, classes, counseling sessions, and exercise, the primary focus is to get the participants to use their minds to have a healthy body. Meadowlark does that by introducing new concepts in group classes. Those classes include psychosynthesis, biofeedback, dream interpretation, meditation, and fasting, among others. There are also opportunities to delve deeper into a particular subject, such as special sessions on Sacred Books, Contemplating the Masters, and the I Ching.

If this sounds a little on the spiritual side to you, don't be taken aback. I found it very refreshing and not overwhelming. It really was like a cartharsis to go to Meadowlark and that's a good feeling.

Along with extensive renovation, future plans are for an emphasis on inviting authorities on health to visit and teach at Meadowlark plus adding more athletic activities.

Guests, like me, can discover what holistic health means and how to apply it to our lifestyles.

THE LOOK OF THINGS

Meadowlark is situated on 20 acres enclosed by walls that give it the feeling of a safe haven from the rest of the world. I found the comfortable green lawns with bushes and trees relaxing and noticed small secluded areas with lawn chairs artfully arranged for private tete-a-tetes.

White buildings are scattered throughout the compound with the Main House and the Holistic Medical Center the largest buildings. The main grounds hold a clay and art room, sun porch, library, living room, and a small nondenominational chapel.

The guest rooms are spread out around the Main House and are set up for doubles, private rooms, or rooms with a shared bath. The accommodations were pleasant: My room was decorated in a blue and white color scheme with white wicker furniture.

Exercise facilities include a brand-new exercise center and a spa. A tiled, heated swimming pool, as well as a parcourse fitness system. There are many scenic areas for jogging and bicycling.

The buildings at Meadowlark were first erected in 1914 with a movie star owning it until 1927. Stables and a racetrack were built during this time. Movie mogul Louis B. Mayer and his brother Jerry, owned it for a time until 1945. Dr. Loomis, Meadowlark's founder, bought the complex in 1958 as a place to espouse his holistic views.

HOW TO GET THERE

Meadowlark is located in the desert town of Hemet, close to Palm Springs. The nearest airport is Ontario International. For transportation to and from Meadowlark, call Inland Express at (714) 626-6599 when your flight times are confirmed. If it is necessary to come into Palm Springs, call Meadowlark to arrange for transportation. There is a charge for the service.

Reservations need a $100 deposit and can be made by calling (714) 927-1343 or by writing Meadowlark, 26126 Fairview Ave., Hemet, CA 92344.

Check-in times are 3-7 p.m. and check-out time is 10 a.m.

SURROUNDING AREA

It's unlikely that you will have much time to investigate the desert around Hemet, but if you add a few days to your trip before or after a week at Meadowlark there is a lot to see around Palm Springs. This resort town was discovered by early Hollywood stars and has since become known as a place for the rich to play. The two-mile-long El Paseo Drive in Palm Springs is the Rodeo Drive of the desert.

Aside from the attractions of shopping, restaurants, golf, and tennis, the desert around Palm Springs is a botanical delight. There are several parks, museums, and reserves that showcase the palms, cacti, and flowers of the Southern California desert. For example, the Thousand Palms Reserve highlights a native stand of giant Washingtonian palms.

WHAT'S INCLUDED IN THE PRICE

Meadowlark is a nonprofit holistic center and, as a nonprofit organziation, the rates are very inexpensive. The weekly rates include room, meals, and the Meadowlark Program.

The Meadowlark Program included in the weekly cost is mostly class sessions with several people in them; any individual sessions entail additional costs.

These services and any services such as the biofeedback, homeopathy, acupuncture, Chinese herbalist-acupuncture, and nutrition counseling at the Holistic Medical Center are extra.

Beauty salon services are also extra, as well as the spa's highly touted polarity therapy (a balancing of the body's energy by using some Swedish massage, reflexology, and acupressure points). Other costs that can add up are individual psychological or spiritual counseling, yoga, or life change therapy.

CLOTHING AND WEATHER

Meadowlark is in the desert with the desert's extremes in temperature. It can be very hot in the day and then cool down quickly at night. No matter what time of year, bring a jacket for night.

Don't worry about dressing up too much; the staff is concerned about your inner health.

Towels for the pool are available, but you will need to bring just about everything else including toiletries such as shampoo and creme rinse. There is a guest laundry room.

There are no televisions in your room, so you might want to toss a book or two into your suitcase too.

A TYPICAL DAY

When I arrived we were told what was in store for the week. Such things as dream interpretation, guided imagery, an inspirational hour, putting color to work and a class called Qikung (life energy practice).

Aside from these classes (which were new and unusual to me), there is a big board with all the topics for personal consultations and the people who give them. Guests can sign up for whatever type session they want. I tried polarity massage and it was wonderful.

In a typical week, each day's highlights might follow something like this: Sunday, orientation; Monday, a walk, fasting explanation, guided imagery class; Tuesday, fitness parcourse, yoga, and putting color to work class; Wednesday, a walk, Qikung, and a codependency class; Thursday, a walk, yoga, and a nutrition session; Friday, a walk, swimming exercises, and a re-entry (into the regular world) class; Saturday, aerobic exercises before leaving.

Each day there is an inspirational hour at 4 p.m. Also, you can make your typical day untypical by asking for a Nepalese necklace to wear. It signifies that you are having a day of silence.

An exercise room is open from 7 a.m. to 5 p.m. with a trampoline, stationary bicycles, and exercise tapes. Using the swimming pool, hot spa, jogging track, parcourse, bicycles, and walks are up to each guest to schedule into their day.

EVENING PROGRAMS

There is a program each night, sometimes with different staff members, other times with an expert brought into Meadowlark. While I was there, the staff told me that they want to start bringing in authors, physicians, and people holding doctorate degrees to lead workshops and evening and weekend sessions.

Some of the current programs include a night of sharing with staff members; the personal healing power of Art and Color; improvisations by guests. There are also movies and videotapes for some of the nights.

THE STAFF

On board at Meadowlark are a yoga instructor, polarity therapy and massage therapists, color therapist, meditation instructor, and two art and color therapists.

FOOD

The vegetarian food is very good and prepared with health in mind. It was so good that I had a difficult time going on a fast, but did a three-day fast anyway.

Fasting here is promoted, but it is done carefully and with daily dietician overviews. Fasting groups meet each morning for a review. The dietician on the Meadowlark staff helps those who may not need to fast—or should not fast—find other ways to reduce weight.

There is a transition diet that is made up of fruit and vegetable juices. Another way to cleanse the body is to eat only vegetables, fruits, and juices.

A Meadowlark study found that after a two-week session, of those who fasted, 82 percent were better physcially, 92 percent had increased emotional well-being, and 92 percent were more mentally alert.

But even if you don't fast, the food is low in fat. Herbal tea, fruit, and nuts are always available on a help-yourself basis.

SUMMARY

Meadowlark believes if the mind is well, the body will be well also. Many of the more traditional spas are now focusing on stress reduction and how to relax, but Meadowlark with its holistic approach is way ahead of the pack, having taught it for three decades. Most of the guest were not spiritual to start, but left with a new point of view on spirituality.

GOLDEN DOOR

Open the delicate, rice-paper shoji of your room in the Golden Door spa and you are opening a door to peace, serenity, and a week of worry-free living.

One of the first personal fitness spas in the United States, the Golden Door has achieved in 32 years a reputation as one of the best spas around, if not the best. Spend a week here and the reasons why are abundantly apparent.

There is a quiet order to life here in the Japanese-styled surroundings that is very soothing. It is not only the fitness classes, the massages, and the nutritional diet that makes a guest feel like a million dollars. Each guest is treated as if he or she is worth a million dollars.

The Golden Door isn't just for the rich and famous, but it certainly is the lifestyle of the rich and famous, including breakfast in bed if you want.

The staff tells you on your first day, "Let us take care of you. Don't have any worries at all, you don't have to worry about scheduling or anything. You're just here to enjoy."

The enjoyment is a seven-day program designed to help you change your lifestyle to exercise a little more, eat a little better, and take some time out to let go of your worries and pamper your soul. Alex Szekely, the son of the founders and the current president, says the spa is a school of life that teaches you what you can do when you go home, physically and mentally. It is also a simpler lifestyle at the Golden Door with 80 percent of the spa's food organically grown on the premises. Alex believes this lifestyle makes people healthier and happier.

His mother, Deborah, founded the Golden Door on this tenet in 1958 after she and her husband, Professor Edmund Szekely, started Rancho La Puerta (see the chapter on Rancho La Puerta in this book) as a health retreat in Mexico.

The couple met in Tahiti after Deborah's vegetarian mother brought her to the South Pacific island during the Depression. Rancho La Puerta was such a success that people asked Deborah to build a little more glamourous retreat in southern California.

She did, but the Golden Door is not just a haven for Hollywood stars.

It is expensive, but it is not snobby and the staff are down-to-earth, truly caring people. The average age of the guests is 45-50 years old for women and 50-55 years old for men. There are eight weeks just for men, five weeks for couples, and the rest of the year is exclusively for women, including a couple of holiday weeks, a mother/daughter week, and an Inner Door week that focuses on strengthening the mind as well as the body.

Speaking for its reputation, the Golden Door has an 80 percent return rate and relies on word-of-mouth with no advertising.

Deborah Szekely opened the Golden Door near Escondido, California between San Diego and Los Angeles in 1958 and moved it a few miles down the road in 1975. Before she moved the spa, she traveled to Japan to design the new spa in the Japanese tradition of practicality, aesthetics, and symbolism.

What turned out works so well that it has a life of its own. The Golden Door may expand some programs and add a few massages, but it basically plans to abide by its motto: always better.

A little of the magic the Japanese believe is innate in every object found its way into the Golden Door, and it rubs off on the staff and guests.

THE LOOK OF THINGS

In Japanese gardens it is customary to design the largest stone as the temporary Omiya (honorable house) for the gods. The Golden Door's prayer rock has evolved as the spa's symbol of strength and well-being. Fittingly, it was also the cornerstone from which surveyors mapped out the buildings for the Golden Door.

The main building is designed after a honjin, which is a hospitable Japanese inn. It is a low, graceful building with an Oriental roof; it opens up onto one of the Golden Door's four courtyards. The Bell Courtyard has a 300-year-old temple bell and houses both a boutique offering only Japanese clothing and a small library.

There are 39 guest suites which purposely limit the number of guests at the spa. Even during couples' weeks, each guest is given his or her own room except on rare occasions for special requests. I stayed in the villa, which is really Deborah's villa and a place she might one day retire to — if she ever retires. I loved it, but it was a little far away, so I had a security guard walk me there at night.

All of the accommodations have Japanese sliding shoji doors with views of ponds and gardens. Each guest house has an individual tokonoma, a decorative shrine to the gods on a platform with fresh flower arrangments.

The gardens are carefully manicured and feature gates, stones, creeks, waterfalls, ponds, flowers, and grass. Japanese gardens are practical, aesthetic and symbolic gardens, and at the Golden Door there is a Sen, or Water Garden; Sen-Yi or Lake Garden; Dry, or Sand Garden. In one of the garden's ponds, the famous koi fish go about life in a fish heaven.

The fitness gyms — Dragon Tree and Bamboo — are made just for fitness (the Dragon Tree has Hoggan Camstar weight equipment) and the tennis courts are lighted. Two outdoor pools are available as well as a bathhouse, beauty rooms, jogging trail and a family-therapy pool.

A solarium, vegetable gardens, and a private hillside for walks complete the facilities.

The Golden Door's $15 million facilities feature $1 million worth of Japanese art, including a stone lantern collection valued at more than $500,000.

HOW TO GET THERE

The Golden Door's staff will pick you up at the San Diego airport if you call ahead with flight times. Meet your Golden Door driver at the Travelers Aid Desk in the baggage claim area. The spa staff suggests arriving between 1 and 6 p.m. by air or between 3 and 6 p.m. by car. The program lasts until noon the following Sunday.

For reservations call (619) 744-5777 or write Post Office Box 1567, Escondido, CA 92033. A $1,000 deposit must be made within 14 days of reservations or the reservation will be cancelled. Credit cards are not accepted.

SURROUNDING AREA

You never walk past the outside gate here so the surrounding area doesn't really matter, but I'll satisfy your curiosity. It's an isolated place, probably 20 minutes to get to a 7-Eleven, but you don't even need that.

The Golden Door is eight miles north of Escondido, 30 miles north of San Diego. The land it sits upon was once sacred to the Indians. It became the Deer Springs Ranch and remained as a working ranch for nearly a century. Then a horticultural experiment station was built to develop new strains of camellias and proteas. The Golden Door increased the holdings to 177 acres when it built there.

The surrounding agricultural area is known for citrus and avocados and is now going toward kiwi and other extoic fruits. At the Golden Door there are 425 citrus trees, 22 acres of avocados, one acre of kiwi fruit, and an orchard of varied fruit.

CLOTHING AND WEATHER

When you pack to come to the Golden Door, don't bring much. All your clothes are provided except underwear, nightgown, socks, and sneakers. Bring a couple of swimming suits and if those two are wet at the same time, the staff will dry out a swimming suit in its bathhouse. A warm jacket is a good idea for winter evenings, even if it is sunny Southern California.

The spa gives you shorts, t-shirts, warm-ups, windbreakers, raincoat, terry cloth robe, slippers, and a kimono. For dinner at night, you wear your robe, kimono, or shorts.

Everyone dresses in the same clothes so you don't have to make any choices. What they are trying to do is take all the decisions away from you and do your thinking for you so you relax. It's called spa brain.

You don't dress in what you wear at home, so just bring an overnight bag, your personal toiletries and cosmetics (although you probably won't use them), and clothes for the plane ride home.

There is a daily laundry service, as well as a twice-weekly dry cleaning service.

All the amenitities are included, even a toothbrush and toothpaste.

WHAT'S INCLUDED IN THE PRICE

It is expensive, but it is all-inclusive. All accommodations, meals, massages, facials, fitness classes, everything is included in the package price. The packages are seven days long from Sunday to Sunday.

The only things not included are private tennis lessons and private consultations. Also, the San Diego County hotel tax will be added to the bill. There are some extra charges for specialized beauty treatments like acrylic nails or permanents.

A TYPICAL DAY

A highlight of each day was the hour-long massage in my room, as well as the facial in the beauty room. It's very euphoric and sleep inducing. I found myself drifting to sleep in the chair during the facial.

The massage and facial are daily extravagances. The rest of the day is divided into more body treatments and exercise. But after an initial consultation, when you tell your personal fitness instructor your body type and your athletic interests, a daily schedule is made up for you and given to you on a "fan."

The success of the fan agenda is that you don't have to think or make a choice. You can turn off your mind, rejuvenate, and relax.

If you don't like your schedule, it can be changed too.

There's enough personal attention to your schedule that the staff knows if you haven't been around for a couple of hours.

The day starts with a morning hike with five fitness levels. After breakfast, I had a back warm-up class at 8:30 a.m., followed by water exercise. Then I would have some type of beauty treatment before lunch. In the afternoon, I had a swimmer's workout and the women's aerobic circuit, before a body treatment and yoga. Just before dinner was a wonderful massage.

The day-to-day exercise schedule doesn't change, but the pace of each class is stepped up daily. Golden Door exercise classes are composed of 16 regular classes like body shaping and aerobics and 10 specialty classes like Tai Chi or Jazz Dance.

The Golden Door is adding more treatments which will use home-grown herbs and special oils for the wintertime. A warm body scrub with a spicy smelling oil and organic mud from Austria is one of the treatments planned.

The skin care products are made especially for the Golden Door and are always less than three weeks old so the ingredients will stay active and preservatives won't be needed.

On Saturday, a makeover is given, as well as a wash and set or blow dry. Hair styling is also available for an extra charge and it is a nice way to finish off the total look, courtesy of the spa.

EVENING PROGRAMS

After dinner there are lectures on various things like meditation, nutrition, and the Inner Door (right brain, left brain functions and how to be more creative). During the week I was there we also had a cooking class and a class on prayer arrows.

After the lecture, a nightcap consisting of a dip into a steaming hot whirlpool and a short massage is suggested for those who need help sleeping. Who needs sleeping pills?

There are televisions and VCRs in both guest lounges.

THE STAFF

The staff to guest ratio is three to one, but the staff to guest involvement is more than that. I don't think they are so interested in making money as they are in making changes in your life. They stress daily that this is a school to manage your life differently when you go home.

I really felt sincerity here; it's like a big family. The general manager, reservationist, and maintenance supervisor have been at the Golden Door for years. It is an exciting atmosphere and a family one.

Each employee is given a $500 education allowance a year to further his or her specialty. For example, a massage therapist could go to a seminar on massages.

At the Golden Door there are 22 fitness specialists, each with a university degree, 16 beauticians, 12 people in massage, kitchen help, a chef and a full-time nutritionist.

FOOD

The food is presented beautifully. I was on 900 calories a day and I wasn't hungry. Although it is spa cuisine, what makes it different is that 80 percent of the ingredients are organically grown on the Golden Door property.

The gardens at the Golden Door and its sister spa, Rancho La Puerta, cost about $150,000 a year to maintain and are actually more expensive for the spa than buying vegetables. But the vegetable gardens are a priority because they are organic, simple, and home-grown.

A breakfast menu was given out at the beginning of the week and a typical breakfast was poached egg with whole wheat toast and garden fresh salsa served with "Golden Door" bran breakfast cereal. Lunch is served on a tray poolside.

Each day lunch and dinner menus were distributed. A lunch might be Caesar salad (30 calories) and Steve's Whole Wheat Pizza with Roasted Peppers, Mushrooms and Spinach (190). Dinner might be Mixed Garden Greens with an Italian Herb Vinaigrette (40) and Vegetarian Parsley Crepe with Grilled Vegetables, Wild Rice and Bean Sprouts (175). Dessert was watermelon (40) one day, but also a chocolate square another day.

Low calorie hors d'oeuvres and nonalcoholic cocktails precede the dinner.

The morning snack is potassium broth and crudites; in the afternoon a fruit concoction is served.

Red meat is never served. Tea and coffee are allowed, and smoking is permitted only outdoors where other guests do not gather.

The Golden Door offers a "Virtue-making diet" on Mondays. It is several beverages and snacks brought to you every two and a half hours, including a citrus drink, sunflower seeds, almond milk, gazpacho, carrot-apple juice, pureed vegetable soup, and lots of herbal tea.

The liquid diet is an entire day experience to give the body "needed time out." A dieter is supposed to slow his or her pace, take a couple of short walks, and spend 30 minutes sitting in silence.

SUMMARY

The Golden Door focuses more on inch loss than weight loss. It is all-inclusive and you will find that decision making is almost at a stand-still so you just focus on yourself. It's so serene and the setting is calming. A week at the Golden Door is a ticket to peace of mind and body.

CAL-A-VIE

In a scrub-brush valley outside San Diego, there's a spa that has collected the best of Europe's therapeutic treatments and combined them with good old American fitness. It is called Cal-a-Vie. It merges the American approach to fitness through diet and exercise regimes with the European emphasis on skin and body treatments.

This is a spa for those who want to be pampered - but not too much; who want to lose weight — but care more about excess inches; who favor healthy eating — but demand that their food be tasty. Cal-a-vie will make you feel invigorated, spoiled, beautiful, and healthy by the time you leave. And if you don't mind drinking tons and tons of water, you'll enjoy yourself too.

Cal-a-Vie's health philosophy follows the premise that we are all affected by stress and pollution and by the accumulated by-products of metabolism, all of which can create toxic conditions in the body.

Cal-a-Vie's programs are designed to rid the body of these toxins through the following: 1) exercise, which neutralizes stress-related hormones and speeds up detoxification through respiration and perspiration; 2) nutritious, light cuisine — a diet low in fat and sodium, high in complex carbohydrates and fiber, which serves to cleanse and restore the system; 3) water, which dilutes, then flushes the impurities from the body and 4) therapeutic treatments including massage, hydro and aroma therapy (and more), which help to induce the relaxation response and move toxic materials that accumulate in tissue and lymph.

The ever-present water is actually Vittel mineral water from France, and bottles of it can be found wherever you turn. The staff suggests that you drink it upon rising each morning and continue drinking it throughout the day to help in the detoxification process (it works as a diuretic). A recommended one liter per day as well as copious amounts of spring water should be consumed. As we exercise and perspire, the water flushes toxins, rehydrates the tissues, and replaces minerals. The frequent call to nature diminishes as the bladder adapts to the increased fluid consumption.

I began to feel like a sieve, and didn't really like waking up three times a night for the bathroom run. What's more, the Vittel water or fruit juices at Cal-a-Vie are served at room temperature, without ice, to be more gentle on our digestive systems.

But the other ways Cal-a-Vie strives to rid us of toxins can be delightful.

For example, thalassotherapy: In this treatment, the staff massaged my entire body in a sea water, seaweed, and clay combination and then wrapped me in a thermal blanket for 20 minutes. The seaweed wrap is designed to rebalance body chemistry and stimulate the metabolism by replacing lost minerals and pulling toxins through the skin. After a shower, they ordered me to relax (oh well, I can manage) on a table, then wrapped me in a mylar film and added a heating element in order to stimulate perspiration (an artificial fever therapy if you will) to complete the detoxification process. This treatment helps rebalance body chemistry, stimulate body function and get rid of toxins through the skin, besides making you feel great.

Cal-a-Vie exudes peace and serenity and sports a staff dedicated to its customers and the spa mentality. Attention to details, right down to the net bag it provides you for your personal laundry, is why Cal-a-Vie has become a spa for those who demand excellence, from movie stars to business executives to ordinary people like me.

There are all-men's weeks and all-women's weeks, as well as a couple of weeks just for couples. During the co-ed weeks, men have use of the whirlpool and sauna from 6-9 a.m., women from 6-9 p.m. The rest of the time the sauna and whirlpool are co-ed.

Cal-a-Vie was founded by a man who has owned and operated five hospitals and numerous health-related facilties in Southern California for the past 25 years. Before opening Cal-a-Vie in 1986, William Power researched European and American spas with his wife, Marlene, for more than a decade. Their concern for health and fitness, and their demands for ultimate spa treatments, led to Cal-a-Vie—a joining of American and European traditions.

THE LOOK OF THINGS

Like its philosophy of the best of American and European spas, Cal-a-Vie is an elegant continental community surrounded by a rustic western valley near the town of Vista, California. Just 45 minutes from the San Diego airport via a scenic, winding road, Cal-a-Vie is protected by a security gate and 125 acres of land where nothing encroaches on the view.

Here 24 individual cottages are laid out in European style, looking like a Mediterranean village with their terra cotta roofs, wide wooden plank doors, and window boxes of geraniums. Rock ponds, gardens full of star jasmine, and wine barrels filled with potted plants provide lush landscaping. A waterfall cascades into the swimming pool.

Each room is decorated in country French style with a large chifferobe, bureau, closet, and a bathroom equipped with amenities such as cotton balls and swabs, shampoo, creme rinse, hand cream, shower cap, etc. There are telephones in the rooms; television is located in a common room.

All rooms have a security alarm system and an emergency button if a client should need assistance.

Each guest has his or her own villa, and even if you come with a mate, you stay in your own place — a way to purify your thoughts as well as your body, I guess.

SURROUNDING AREA

Cal-a-Vie is set in what might be called California's spa country. Nearby neighbors are the famous Golden Door and La Costa. The temperate climate has made this country a recreational delight specializing in leisure. Close by is the Vista Valley Country Club where golf and tennis are available. Tennis lessons can be taken with the resident pro, and golfing green fees are added to your spa bill.

WHAT'S INCLUDED IN THE PRICE

I didn't need to bring much to this spa for a week because just about everything I could need was included in the package. Aside from all the toiletries, Cal-a-Vie provides any clothing you'll need for the week, and it is laundered daily. Also, any of your own clothing will be laundered free of charge within 24 hours of pick-up.

The sessions begin Sunday afternoon and end the following Sunday morning, and a maximum of 24 guests will attend. Complimentary transportation to and from San Diego International Airport is available.

During the week, spa guests are entitled to three facials, one hair and scalp treatment, two hand and feet treatments, five massages, one thalassotherapy treatment, one body glo treatment, one aromatherapy massage, one reflexology foot massage, two hydrotherapy treatments, numerous exercise classes and finishing beauty touches.

Every detail is provided at Cal-a-Vie, but it is provided at a high cost. Cal-a-Vie is on the high end of the spa scale and could be termed expensive. Tipping is not necessary and isn't expected.

A non-refundable deposit of $1,000 is due upon booking. If you should need to cancel (at least 30 days prior to your visit), this deposit will be applied to other sessions within one year.

For reservations, call Cal-a-Vie at (619)-945-2055 or write 2249 Somerset Road, Vista, CA 92084.

CLOTHING AND WEATHER

Cal-a-Vie provides a warm-up jacket, two sets of sweats, shorts, t-shirts, robes, bath shoes, and rain gear. Guests need to bring leotards (it's so much easier to see what exercise movements your legs are doing in leotards than in sweats), pajamas or nightgown, swim suits, hiking shoes, gym shoes, and gym socks.

Bring white-soled tennis shoes if you're planning on playing tennis.

Dress is casual and, although Cal-a-Vie is a glamorous resort, it's not unusual to go to lunch in a bathrobe because you just finished a spa treatment.

People usually lay aside the Cal-a-Vie garb at dinnertime and dress in their own clothes, but again, it's casual.

You really don't need to pack heavy here because you don't need a lot of changes. If anything is forgotten, and if Cal-a-Vie doesn't have it, the staff will buy it when they run errands on Tuesdays and Thursdays. For anything you take a liking to at the spa, including skin and beauty products and clothing, Cal-a-Vie will take an order and mail it to your home.

Rain wear and a windbreaker are really all the bad-weather gear a guest needs; it's more than likely you won't need any at all. Weather is ideal year-round with temperatures about 85 degrees in mid-afternoon. Occasionally, it'll be chilly in the mornings, but not enough to deter an invigorating walk at 6 a.m.

A TYPICAL DAY

The week of stress reduction, relaxation, weight control, and toning begins with a personalized fitness evaluation. The fitness director asked me what my fitness level was, did I have any meal preferences, did I want to reduce or maintain my caloric level, what was my medical background and what kind of massages did I like (any kind!). This information, plus a treadmill stress test, was fed into a computer and the result was a personalized printout on my overall fitness, my basal metabolic rate, and the percentage of lean body mass to fat. This also provided me with the number of calories per day I should consume to safely and healthily lose weight.

From that initial evaluation, my schedule for the week was set up and all I had to do was follow instructions on the daily cards, which are shaped like fans. On a typical day, the wake-up call was at 5:30 a.m. Rising with the sun, we took an invigorating walk covering 2 1/4 miles in 45 minutes. You can choose an advanced hike or a moderate walk on a nearby golf course. After the walk, we were measured, weighed, and our blood pressure taken.

Breakfast was Kashi, a mixture of nine grains and seeds. If you don't immediately dive into exercises after the 7:30 a.m. breakfast, a pleasant morning room for reading or watching television always has coffee and tea set up.

At Cal-a-Vie, mornings emphasize fitness, whereas afternoons are devoted to health and therapeutic treatments. A 30-minute body awareness class after breakfast shows what muscles do what and where they are, which is good because during the next hour, you'll use those muscles in an aerobic class. Then all those weary muscles are stretched and pulled every which way in a "Shapes" class.

At 10:50 a.m. (a time of day I came to look forward to), the staff serves a revitalizer. This delicious drink is a mixture of vegetables that have been simmered with a low sodium V8 juice. It is served hot and suppresses the appetite while supplying energy.

After the revitalizer break, I went into the gym to work on different aerobic circuit training and Nautilus machines, the Stairmaster, and the exercise bicycle. Other ways Cal-a-Vie gets our blood pumping during the morning is through an abdominal class, water exercises, and even a rousing game of volleyball. Water volleyball here was a real hoot and I had a great time playing. My team won, despite our dubious water antics.

In the late morning and afternoon the pace slows down and everyone concentrates on rest, relaxation, and those wonderful treatments. I am a massage junkie, and the massages at Cal-a-Vie were superior in every sense. At home, a massage is a mere tickling compared to the way the masseuses here really pummel your muscles. The massages are both Swedish (Western deep muscle) and Shiatsu (Eastern acupressure). They are not the pampering type of massage—those muscles are worked!—but boy, you feel good when it's over.

Aside from regular full-body massages, the specialized treatments at Cal-a-Vie are wonderful and highly scientific.

Besides thalassotherapy, hydrotherapy, body glo, and aromatherapy are offered. The hydrotherapy tubs are imported directly from France and give you a multi-jet treatment while a masseuse rubs your shoulders. The water contains lyophilised (freeze dried) sea water with minerals and perhaps a dash of rosemary, pine, thyme, or cypress.

A body glo is a one-hour treatment that removes dead skin cells and readies your body for aromatherapy massage. This massage is a stress reducer as well as a - there's that word again — detoxifier. Essential oils are chosen for each individual. For example, geranium oil is a natural astringent and is good for those with troubled skin, whereas lemon grass will invigorate and balance the body systems. Cypress juniper fights cellulite and water retention to help you slim down, and the blend of immortelle and lavender helps prevent aging of the skin. Cal-a-Vie's founder calls aromatherapy "the Rolls Royce treatment in skin care."

Then an assortment of facials, head and scalp massages, foot massages, and hand and feet beauty treatments bring out the best in each guest. The hand treatment includes exfoliation to get rid of the dead skin and a paraffin dip to rehydrate the skin. On Saturday, a nail and toe polish is added so you're looking sharp when you go home the next day.

Most of these treatments utilize seaweed, sea water or a variety of herb and flower essenses. It all sounds relaxing and pleasant, but after a nutrition class and dinner, I was exhausted and ready for bed at 9 p.m. After all, getting beautiful and slimming down is hard work!

EVENING PROGRAMS

In the evenings, the staff taught us fitness, nutrition and, low-calorie cooking. In the nutrition class, I learned that complex carbohydrates (expecially the unrefined, whole foods like brown rice, legumes, potatoes, vegetables, etc) are the best foods because they digest slowly, sustaining us for long periods and because they "burn clean," leaving only carbon dioxide and water as waste products.

I also learned that, as an added bonus of eating whole foods with all the fiber, you actually use calories digesting it. This is thermogenesis. On the other hand, concentrated simple sugars with white sugar at the top will quickly turn to fat because they go directly into the blood stream and the body can use only so much sugar at a time. Another culprit is fat. Only 3% of the fat you take in at a time gets used, the rest is stored as body fat for later use.

Another fun program was a cooking class given by chef Rosie Daley, who was trained by Cal-a-Vie's famous former chef, Michel Stroot. Stroot is acknowledged as the United States' leading expert on light and healthy food preparation and it is his recipes that appear in this book.

Daley, an exceptional chef in her own right, eagerly learned Stroot's secrets. She has been cooking for 16 years, working in a number of San Diego establishments and honing her skills as a chef of natural, fresh cuisine. Adapting her knowledge to spa cuisine was an easy step for her. Daley is also an artist, maintaining a studio where she designs fabrics and jewelry. This talent is evident in her plate presentation, which is always an exquisite balance of form and color.

She is as much loved by the guests for herself as her food. With her beautiful visage and perky, youthful personality, Daley wins the guests over during the cooking class, instructing us to use Canola oil, as well as olive oil, for cooking (they are more heat resistant than the poly-unsaturated oils) and to try to use organic vegetables whenever possible. She mentioned that organic lettuces have flavors of their own, but that lettuce from stores tastes like water.

49

THE STAFF

There is a ratio of four staff members to every guest at Cal-a-Vie, and these are versatile people. The highly trained staff members lend their expertise in a variety of ways. Someone who gives you the thalassotherapy treatment may also be skilled at foot reflexology and massage. Each staff member contributes multiple talents to the spa program, forming a serviceable team that helps to create the positive, restful atmosphere that Cal-a-Vie is noted for.

FOOD

Master Chef Michel Stroot has brought his "Cuisine Fraiche" to Cal-a-Vie and it is healthy gourmet. This chef was taught in the kitchens of Europe where heavy sauces, gravies, and butters are revered. But an 11-year stint at the Golden Door changed Stroot's philosophy toward food, and now he says he'd never go back to that type of cuisine he found in Europe.

Cal-a-Vie's dietary philosophy is concerned with nutrition and health, not only with reducing calories. By cutting fats and avoiding red meat and fried food as much as possible, a balanced menu is established which includes 58-68% complex carbohydrate, 10-12% protein and 20% fat.

All this nutrition talk makes for extremely tasty food. I knew I would like Cal-a-Vie after the first night's dinner - swordfish with lots of vegetables and a tofu-based cheesecake for dessert. Women are given about 1,000-1,200 calories a day and men are allowed 1,200-1,400 calories per day for reducers. This calorie count includes the mid-morning and afternoon "revitalizers" as well as the evening hors d'oeuvres. A lower calorie diet is available, but not encouraged. Cal-a-Vie supports the idea of small, regular, low-fat, nutrient-rich feedings throughout the day, coupled with exercise (both of which significantly raise the metabolism) as an efficient means of losing weight. The goal is to convert fat into lean muscle mass, not simply to shed pounds.

An example of a dinner menu includes onion-broccoli-rosemary baguette, mixed green salad with lemon dressing, pilaf of grains, stir-fry of oriental vegetables, chicken breasts in papillote, scallop brochette, pears and pernod.

I was lucky enough to visit Cal-a-Vie during Thanksgiving. We had the most tender turkey I've ever tasted in my life. The entire Thanksgiving dinner was 450 calories and it included wild turkey and stuffing, brussel sprouts with grapes, sweet potatoes, garden greens and sprout salad with hot ginger dressing, and a delicious butternut squash pie for dessert to round out this sumptuous repast. It was a Thanksgiving to remember, and so much healthier than our traditional American dinner.

SUMMARY

Expensive, exclusive Cal-a-Vie is the epitome of spa experiences. From the toiletries in the rooms to the healthful haute cuisine, this spa puts you in mind of a four-star hotel.

CAL-A-VIE

Exercise begins each day with a brisk, early morning walk through Cal-a-Vie's tranquil hillsides

BERMUDA RESORT

It seems outlandish with all the health spas cropping up throughout the nation that there are only a few spas where an overweight person can go.

Health spas in the United States began as "fat farms" but have evolved into places of pampering and fitness, even concentrating on stress reduction. Today, many health spas won't accept people who are 20 percent over their ideal weight, and those who are severely overweight don't have a chance of getting into most spas.

However, the Bermuda Resort in Southern California's high desert Antelope Valley is filling a niche for those who are overweight but want the pampering and fitness aspects other spas specialize in.

Bermuda Resort's programs range from a three-day weekend shape-up to a year's worth of long-term reducing. In the resort's newsletter, Shapely Times, one woman explains how she is losing 120 pounds in a year at Bermuda Resort while also attending Antelope Valley College nearby.

According to the general manager, a marketing study reflected the need for a spa that will take overweight people, so in 1988 the resort planned to emphasize its reducing program. He said some of his guests come to Bermuda Resort after going to other spas and feeling uncomfortable about needing to lose weight among "the beautiful people."

These people also want the pampering, the specialized fitness classes, and the motivational lectures while they lose weight. And the average weight loss here is one quarter to one pound a day.

I call this spa one of my "Be-Back" spas because it is one that I would like to return to. In fact, most of its customers are repeat business. The average age is 45-65 years old and 98 percent are women.

Bermuda Resort can accommodate 85 clients but will accept more customers who stay at motels next door in Lancaster, California. Groups are welcome here and usually receive some type of discount. Children are discouraged unless they come with their parents during one of the spa's family weeks.

The resort itself is like a revamped motel and not nearly as fancy as some other spas. More than 25 years old, it began as a reducing resort run by a medical doctor. At that time fasting was the rage and the physician oversaw a seven-day medical fast for his clients. This fasting fad peaked in the 1970s, filling the spa to overflowing.

Now, Bermuda Resort averages about 45-55 people at one time and concentrates on fitness, healthy eating, and keeping weight off by changing lifestyles. It may not be the fanciest resort, but its program of "fun, fitness and reducing" more than makes up for that.

THE LOOK OF THINGS

Bermuda Resort has kind of a motel feel to it. However, its facilities are right up there with other spas: two heated swimming pools, a large gymnasium currently under construction, indoor and outdoor Jacuzzis, coed and private saunas, lighted tennis courts, a pampering/massage building, half-mile fitness course, and an exercise room holding Nautilus and other weightlifting equipment.

The swimming pools are indoor and outdoor with the indoor pool holding aquatic exercise equipment and the outdoor pool sporting floating sundecks, lawn chairs for relaxing and sunbathing, and an outdoor Jacuzzi.

The half-mile fitness track runs alongside a lake that has become a gathering place for ducks and birds. Green grass and trees cover the 10 plus acres of Bermuda Resort.

The gymnasium has 11 new Nautilus machines, as well as a treadmill, Stairmaster, and five bicycles. Ping Pong, badminton, tennis, volleyball, and basketball courts are located on the premises.

A large new gymnasium with a special wooden floor for exercising will complement the current smaller gym aptly named the Skylight Room.

The accommodations are pleasant, each with a private bath, dressing room, air conditioning, color television, and patio area. Telephones are in the rooms. Most of the 37 rooms overlook the outdoor pool.

Guests are paired with roommates, but if you don't get along with yours, you are free to find a better match. The rooms have been recently renovated to look more light and airy.

The dining area, with its wicker chairs and well-presented tables, makes those 900 calories per day more enjoyable than a regular old cafeteria style gulp and run. The food is served and presented like in a real restaurant.

HOW TO GET THERE

Guests can fly into airports at Los Angeles, Burbank, Palmdale, or Long Beach to ultimately reach Southern California's Antelope Valley. By driving time, Bermuda Resort in the city of Lancaster is an hour away from Los Angeles, up in the desert mountains.

There is a commercial shuttle service to and from Los Angeles International Airport (LAX) that leaves many times every day. The cost is minimal and reservations are suggested to assure a seat. They can be made by calling (805) 945-2LAX.

The shuttle goes to Palmdale, Lancaster, Acton, and Newhall and leaves from the red bus stop signs on the center islands in front of each terminal at LAX. Passengers should arrive 15 minutes early. Be aware that the shuttle service will charge a few dollars extra for more than two bags and for things such as golf clubs and bicycles.

A complimentary shuttle is available from the local airport in Palmdale. Make the arrangements with Bermuda's staff prior to arriving at that airport.

If you are renting a car, the resort is an hour's drive from LA by Highway 5 north (Golden State Freeway) or by Highway 405

(San Diego Freeway) to Highway 14 north (Antelope Valley Freeway) and exiting on Avenue L.

When making flight arrangements, keep in mind that check-in time is 2 p.m. and check-out time is 12:30 p.m. Guests can arrive early for lunch at noon with advance notice. For reservations call (805) 942-1493; or in California call (800) 328-3276; or write Bermuda Resort, 43019 Sierra Highway, Lancaster, CA 93534.

SURROUNDING AREA

The Antelope Valley was once full of history makers: Indians, miners, settlers, and farmers. To experience part of that history, visit the Antelope Valley Indian Museum or the Tropico Gold Mine.

But today, it is fast becoming the next "Orange County," as it grows into a haven for commuters from Los Angeles, with only an hour's drive into the city. The growth is just incredible here.

Perhaps the growth is because the smog of LA doesn't reach Lancaster, or maybe it is the dry sunny weather or the scenic desert hills that get dusted with snow each winter. If you want to see the Los Angeles County countryside, Bermuda Resort has bicycles available for no charge.

Tennis and golf are plentiful here. The resort provides tennis racquets and balls and gives twice-weekly lessons through a local tennis pro. The pro will also come in for private lessons for a fee. The courts are lighted until 10 p.m. The staff will make golfing arrangements for you at one of the nearby golf courses.

Bowling is available just north of Bermuda Resort, hardly even a drive. Other activities in the surrounding area include cherry picking in Leona Valley, touring St. Andrews Priory — a working Benedictine Monastery in Valyermo — visiting Red Rock Canyon or the annual Antelope Valley Fair.

WHAT'S INCLUDED IN THE PRICE

A stay at Bermuda Resort is inexpensive and even more so if you stay in a double or triple room. Sales tax and a hotel/motel occupancy tax are extra. When making reservations, the spa requires a deposit of $100. Gratuities are voluntary.

The price includes acommodations, three meals, all drinks from a dietetic beverage bar, every physical fitness program, social activities, entertainment, and use of all facilities.

Optional services include the "pampering" such as reflexology, Swedish massage, Accumassage, Vibro-sauna, tanning bed, private tennis lessons, facials, pedicures, manicures, and services from a full-service beauty salon. For these options, it's a good idea to set appointments when making your reservation.

Bermuda Resort has three spa packages: the TGIF package for three days and two nights (includes facial, massage and reflexology, vibrosauna, accummassage or tanning bed); the Sleek in a Week package for seven days (several massages, facials, pedicures, manicure, scalp and hair treatments, tanning bed); and the Slim and Fit package for 30 days with all of the extra massages and services plus four free days.

In addition, it is less expensive for the regular guest to buy massages, body composition tests, and health analyzations in a package rate. All packages must be paid in advance.

CLOTHING AND WEATHER

Bring casual clothes as well as your sportswear for exercising because there are evening programs and organized shopping trips where you might want to wear something other than sweats. Some also dress casually for dinner.

The elevation is 2,350 feet above sea level, and despite being a desert, the area does experience a change of seasons. In a high altitude desert environment, it's a good idea to bring a sweater or jacket for cooler evenings.

Don't forget swimming suits. I always like to bring two so I have a dry one if I go to two water exercise classes in a day.

Bring all your toiletries; nothing is provided here as far as shampoo, conditioner, razors, etc. Bring it all.

There is a coin-operated laundry for self washing, or laundry bags are left in the rooms for one-day dry cleaning. Safety deposit boxes are available too.

A TYPICAL DAY

This is a self-motivation spa. The staff outlines the numerous exercise classes, entertainment, fitness consultations, and pampering massages, but it is up to each guest to make his or her own schedule. You figure out what you want to do and then do it.

No part of the program is mandatory, but if you want to lose weight and get into shape, the more you participate the better. Bermuda Resort has a three-part program to lose weight: aerobic exercise, behavior modification for a permanent lifestyle change, and menus that meet the guidelines of the American Heart Association, the National Cancer Institute, and the National Cholesterol Education Program.

The resort also features several activities that are fun (like shopping trips and dance classes) and several ways to pamper yourself such as massages, facials, and saunas.

Fitness testing is one of the first things you'll do at Bermuda Resort, and there are a number of different tests.

The "Microfit" test is a computerized system which measures all the major components of fitness, including body fat, body weight, heart rate, blood pressure, flexibility, strength, aerobic fitness, and more. While you're doing all this, a little man on the computer screen keeps you entertained. The "Bioanalogics" test measures metabolic rate, body fat, and pounds of fat and lean body mass.

After your testing, it's up to you to choose which exercise classes you want to take. In a typical day, the schedule might look like this: 7-9:30 a.m., morning weigh-in and breakfast; 9 a.m., stretch class; 10 a.m., Move-n-Lose, a non-impact aerobics class, or Sit-n-Fit, a workout while sitting in a chair; 10 a.m. to noon, exercise consultation; 11 a.m., Trim-n-Tone or Aqua Aerobics.

Noon is lunch; 1:30 p.m., shopping trips on Tuesdays and Thursdays; 2 p.m., Bench Robics, working the legs and the rear end; 2:30 p.m., Group Personal Training, a circuit training program; 4 p.m., yoga; 5 p.m., guest orientation; 6 p.m., dinner.

One of the exercise programs the staff is really excited about is the Bench Robics, which uses one minute of bench stepping to three minutes of body sculpting, all set to music. Also, the Ultimate Fat Burner combines 20 minutes of Bench Robics with 45 minutes of Group Personal Training to really burn calories.

Massages are held from 9 a.m. to 5 p.m. daily and the options are Swedish massage, reflexology, Accumassage, and Vibrosauna (sort of a tank that massages you while you enjoy dry heat). A full-service beauty salon offers pedicures, scalp massages, manicures, facials, hair treatments, and styling.

EVENING PROGRAMS

Each night something is planned, ranging from motivational lectures to bingo games to live entertainment. The week I was at Bermuda Resort, the lectures included the "Missing Link," "Compulsion over Eating," and astrology and psychic subjects. Movies are shown each night, too.

THE STAFF

As part of the current general manager's goal to make Bermuda Resort a top quality spa, he has boosted his professional staff with a registered dietician, added exercise physiologists, a motivational counselor, licensed cosmetologists, and beauticians and certified massage therapists. A new chef has been hired who is also a nutritionist.

The staff is enthusiastic, professional, and sensible. Bermuda Resort also adds more staff help during weeks when there are more clients at the spa, so there is always a good staff/guest ratio.

FOOD

The three meals each day are kept to an average of 900 calories and they are excellent. The food is great, well-presented, nutritious, and tasty.

The meals are about 25 percent protein, 50-60 percent complex carbohydrates, and 15-25 percent fat. Whole grain cereals, pasta, baked products, rice, vegetables, and fruits are staples here. Several of the main dishes are vegetarian.

Also, raw vegetable snacks are served twice daily. Guests are encouraged to eat these because the raw vegetables are supposed to help raise the metabolism and promote weight loss.

This spa will allow you to drink calorie-free beverages such as coffee, tea, diet soft drinks, and water all day long in order to get at least 64 fluid ounces a day.

SUMMARY

Bermuda Resort has a lot of different things to offer. It gives you your freedom but stimulates you to participate in its exercise programs and diet as well as the pampering. I felt lots of good vibrations and a great sense of camaraderie among the staff and guests. I hope to "Be-Back."

BERMUDA RESORT
Warming up by the pool and fountain is a great way to start any day

CARMEL COUNTRY SPA

If the idea of going to a spa to lose weight intimidates you, the casual, down-home atmosphere at the Carmel Country Spa could be the choice for you.

You can lose weight here - and the staff will help you do it — but the program isn't an inflexible, regimented schedule of diet and demanding exercise. Also, this spa doesn't cater to the rich and famous, just ordinary folk.

The commonsense philosophy of the Carmel Country Spa stresses proper eating habits and exercise, with everything in moderation. A wide variety of people visit this spa, folks from 18 to 80. The maximum number of co-ed guests is 45 at a time, and the length of stay can go from one day to months.

One of its most illustrious graduates was a 32-year-old Southern Calfornia man who lost 250 pounds in 240 days.

The Carmel Country Spa is in the Monterey Peninsula's Carmel Valley, not far from sun, surf, and shopping. It is far enough, however, to be away from the tourism-emphasis of Monterey and bucolic enough for a guest to focus on relaxing and losing weight.

There is more of a feel of a "fat farm" to this spa. The beauty and spa treatments that resort spas specialize in are available but not as all important here. Exercise classes and a nutrious, low-calorie diet take high priority.

I enjoyed this kick-back spa because it is unsophisticated but friendly, somewhat plain but satisfying. It lives up to its motto of "Rest, Relax and Reduce" with a healthy dose of country hospitality.

THE LOOK OF THINGS

Remodeling continues on the 50-year-old facility that now houses the Carmel Country Spa. It was built in 1948 as a school, and the current owner, Frances Buller, bought the buildings and opened a health resort in 1978.

The accommodations consist of 20 basic, casual rooms that are very clean. Up to 45 guests can be housed, depending on single, double, and triple occupancies. The rooms are divided among four single-story buildings. Telephones are in the rooms; a 50-inch television is in the lounge.

All the spa-type facilities are available here: an Olympic-sized pool and hot spa, gymnasium with weight-lifting and aerobic equipment, beauty salon, massage rooms, dining room, etc. The heated swimming pool has exercise bars on the sides, and the gym has treadmills, rowing machines, exercise cycles, mini-trampolines, and a weight bench.

The grounds are landscaped with native bushes, trees, and flowers to give it a country touch.

HOW TO GET THERE

Plan to arrive early in the day; the main meal is served at 12:30 p.m.. It doesn't matter which day you arrive or leave, the program is ongoing.

If you are arriving or departing by airplane, the spa staff will make pick-ups or drop-offs for a moderate charge. Advance notice is required.

By car, the main highways to the resort are Interstate 5 from the north and Highway 1 from the south. Call Carmel Country Spa for a brochure that gives detailed driving directions to the spa. It is basically located near the upper end of the 15-mile-long Carmel Valley. The valley stretches from the Santa Lucia Mountains to the town of Carmel near the Pacific Ocean.

For reservations, write #10 Country Club Way, Carmel Valley, CA 93924 or call (408) 659-3486.

SURROUNDING AREA

Only a short drive from the Pacific Ocean, Carmel Valley is tucked away in the mountains near Carmel and Monterey. Scenic beaches are nearby, as are the quaint shops and sights of Monterey. On one of our "health" walks we retraced the former haunts of John Steinbeck, who wrote of Monterey in his book "Cannery Row."

Also in Monterey is the Monterey Bay Aquarium, highly acclaimed for its kelp forest exhibit (complete with sharks), its playful sea otters, and its hands-on exhibit for children to learn about tidal sea creatures.

For a fee, the spa staff will drive a guest to shopping or tourist sights.

WHAT'S INCLUDED IN THE PRICE

This is an inexpensive resort and the prices vary depending on the occupancy number in your room. The fee covers accommodations, meals, instruction, and activities. It doesn't cover any type of spa treatment such as hydrotherapy or massage or any type of beauty treatment from the salon.

This spa concentrates on weight loss through exercise and diet; therefore, fitness classes are included in a package, whereas a massage is not.

A deposit equivalent to one day's accommodation is required, and cancellations must be made 72 hours in advance to avoid charges. Check-out time is 11 a.m. The spa will charge for a half day if a guest stays later than the check-out time. Lunch on the day of check out is an additional charge.

CLOTHING AND WEATHER

Known as the sunbelt of the Monterey Peninsula, the Carmel Valley boasts 283 sunny days a year. The temperatures are in the low 80s in summer and in the 60s and 70s in winter.

The dress code is relaxed. On the list of things to bring, the spa suggests an exercise suit, leotard, warm sweater or jacket for evening, and two bathing suits. Bring golf and tennis wear if you want to play at a nearby course or court.

This spa provides no extras, so bring soap, shampoo, blow dryer, creme rinse, towels, robes — the whole works.

A TYPICAL DAY

A guest can pick and choose what he or she wants to do here — nobody is standing over you to follow a certain schedule. This spa does not run on a Sunday to Saturday basis. Guests can check in any day of the week and leave whenever they want.

There is an emphasis on fitness, and almost everybody participates in the daily morning walks. The first day, a Sunday, we drove to Monterey and walked around the Monterey Aquarium and Cannery Row area. This was in lieu of a walk at Pacific Grove Beach, which was cancelled due to a 14k run that day.

Another day's walk took us to Quail Lodge in Carmel, where we followed a three-mile path along the golf course.

After the morning walk and breakfast, exercise classes begin. Mostly aerobics, stretching and toning, the highlight is the "aquathinics" class in the swimming pool. Held twice a day, this class works your muscles in a fun and refreshing way. Hatha yoga is taught in the later afternoon before happy hour.

Spare time is available for individual workouts in the gym and personalized spa treatments such as massage.

A couple of the treatments unique to Carmel Country Spa are the Thermo-trim and the Salt Rub.

A Thermo-trim is a Scandinavian body treatment designed to get rid of cellulite. It's a heat therapy system that uses seven silicone belts equipped with thermal heating elements. These belts heat to 104 degrees to increase blood circulation in different areas of the body, which in turn increases the digestive process and raises the metabolism.

During a Salt Rub, a therapist pastes your entire body with a mixture of sea salt and safflower oil to cleanse the skin. I felt like a mackerel being salted and oiled and ready to be put in a can. Other spa treatments include a body wrap and a massage.

EVENING PROGRAMS

The evening programs are informative. They might be a lecture from an herbalist, nutrition tips from the chef, entertaining excursions to the beach for a sunset walk, or a visit to Cannery Row. The entertainment/lectures begin at 7 p.m. If there is nothing scheduled, a television, video library and assorted table games are available.

THE STAFF

Carmel Country Inn's staff includes experienced exercise instructors who motivate you to go that extra mile. The chef is willing to reveal all the kitchen tricks he has learned over the past 20 years of his culinary experience. He is also helpful about teaching nutrition in a down-to-earth way.

FOOD

Upon arrival at Carmel Country Inn, guests are put on a diet of 700-800 calories per day for women and 1,000-1,200 calories for men. Some modifications can be made to personalize a guest's diet, but overall, the meals are prepared with maximum weight and inch loss in mind.

First and foremost, the spa encourages guests to drink at least 8 glasses of water a day. The reason is that the water helps the body metabolize stored fat, get rid of waste, reduce fluid retention, and maintain proper muscle tone.

Breakfast, served from 7-9:30 a.m., is a mere 100 calories. Guests select four items out of a choice of grapefruit, orange, a glass of tomato juice, poached egg, and wedge of toast, but for maximum weight loss the staff suggests choosing only one item.

Coffee and tea are served, but with warnings for guests to try to minimize caffeine intake as it neutralizes iron and B vitamins.

At breakfast, three capsules are handed out: a multi-vitamin for mineral maintenance; licorice root for an energy boost; and LBSII (lower bowel sitmulant), which is the equivalent of one bowl of bran cereal.

Lunch, at 400 calories, is the main meal. A lunch one day was barbecued chicken breast, marinated vegetables, a huge salad, and lemonade made with diet 7-Up and lemon juice.

Guests have a choice of meat or fish for the main meal.

Happy hour at 5:30 p.m. is vegetable hors d'oeuvres and diet sodas on the rocks.

Dinner is usually soup, salad, and dessert. The soup, concocted from a low sodium chicken base and steamed vegetables, is just 30-40 calories. The dessert is surprisingly good considering the de-emphasis on sugar. The chef's secret is to use instant Jell-O with fruit for a filling, a satisfying and low calorie dessert.

In a nutrition lecture, he shared some of his cooking secrets, emphasizing that moderation is the key to weight loss along with exercise after meals. He stressed often that if we eat large meals at night, we had better take a long walk afterwards. Fat is made when people sleep on full stomachs.

Some of his secrets are:

Spray fish with seasonings and oil on both sides and grill it to keep it moist and tasty.

The trick to marinating is to cover the vegetables or meat with the marinade and then put plastic wrap over the top so no air can get in. Same with leftovers; plastic wrap directly on top of the leftovers will keep air out and keep them fresh.

His culinary/spa bible is the Nutrition Almanac, which he recommends highly for people who want to understand the basic elements in food and how they affect metabolism.

SUMMARY

Making Carmel Country Inn special are its country location, sunny weather, casual atmosphere, and relaxed exercise program. This health resort excels in its non-threatening approach to fitness and diet.

THE HILLS HEALTH RANCH

In a rolling wilderness of lakes, trees and hills, in a countryside of cowboys and corrals, in a historic setting of gold rushes and lumberjacks is a spa.

But it prefers to be called a health ranch.

The Hills Health Ranch takes all the history, flavor, and ambiance of British Columbia and packages it into a spa to create a unique fitness experience.

Moreover, it utilizes some of the best cross country skiing terrain in North America to turn it into a year-round resort.

When the owners, Pat and Juanita Corbett, decided to get into the spa business in the early 1980s, they looked around for something different. They found it in the Cariboo Gold Rush Country in western British Columbia.

The couple also wanted a resort with access to great skiing, so they built the resort from the ground up in a town known as 100 Mile House, which is often called Canada's "Whistler of Cross Country Skiing."

In the summer, The Hills has the flavor of a western ranch; in the winter it has the aura of a ski resort. Like Pat says, "We don't have sun and sand, but we have cowboys in the summertime and great skiing in the winter."

The Hills also has a strong spa program in conjuction with its winter and summer resort. This has resulted in a remarkable 80 percent return business. That's the highest of all the spas I visited.

Considering there were 3,800 people who visited The Hills in 1989, the Corbetts have a strong business going. It's no wonder — they treat their guests as if they are extra special, while the setting too is extra specially beautiful.

The story of what happened to my terrible, excruciating sinus headache while I was there conveys an example of the special treatment guests receive, partly because of the extraordinary knowledge of fitness and health the owners have.

Here I was in beautiful Canada, but my head was pounding and I didn't want to do anything except lie in bed in misery. Co-owner Juanita Corbett, who has had more than 4,000 hours of training in her fields, gave me a not-so-simple facial that worked miracles. She used a lot of eucalyptus and steam and then massaged my neck and shoulders to release sinus congestion. Then she did extended reflexology on my feet, and I swear my headache disappeared and didn't come back.

Juanita was a professional singer in Kentucky before moving to Canada. She sang at the Grand Ole' Opry before learning her specialized skills in facials, reflexology and health...and now, she can take your body and fix it!

In fact, it was her curiosity in spas that gave the Corbetts the idea to build this spa in 1982. After winning a free trip to anywhere in the world, Juanita chose a week at La Costa where both Pat and Juanita became gung-ho to build their own spa.

When The Hills Health Ranch opened in 1985, it was the only spa in Canada. It is still the only spa west of Toronto.

THE LOOK OF THINGS

It's not in the spirit of this ranching/western countryside to be opulent, so The Hills Health Resort opted for a country western decor.

From the highway gate entrance to the pictures on the walls, country is the theme here. Most of the furnishings are Victorian in the main house where the dining room, pool area, sauna, and exercise facilities are.

Also, on the grounds are a 2,500-square-foot aerobic studio, tanning booths, beauty salon, ski shop, and a 28-horse stable.

The pool area, decorated with wooden beams, greenery, and fans, holds two whirlpools and an indoor swimming pool.

The accommodations consist of 20 Swiss-style chalets made of wooden logs but with the space of a space-utilizing condominium. Each chalet contains a fully equipped kitchen, three bedrooms, a living room with color television, a dining area, and a bath. There's enough room to sign up with two other couples, but The Hills doesn't mind putting a single in a chalet.

In this country ranch setting, when you look out your window you see nothing but nature, mountains, forests, lakes.

Plans for this destination spa/resort are to build a 24- or 28-room hotel with a true country feel about it. That means a wrap-around veranda, big fireplace, and furniture that lends itself to the memory of the gold rush days. This would add to the spa's capability to service the groups and business conferences that are becoming more popular here.

HOW TO GET THERE

For a resort that is hidden away in British Columbia's vast reaches of wilderness, mountains, lakes, and hills, The Hills Health Ranch is fairly easy to reach.

At 290 miles from Vancouver, B.C., one can go to The Hills by airplane, highway, train, or bus. I took one of the six daily flights to nearby Williams Lake and for the return trip, I went the scenic route via B.C. Railway. If you were to drive, it's a five-hour trip from Vancouver.

Unless you make marvelous connections in Vancouver, you'll probably need to spend at least one night in the Pacific Rim city before taking a commuter flight on to Williams Lake, near the resort.

I stayed at the Four Seasons Hotel in downtown Vancouver, soaking up the luxury and service that only a fine, reputable hotel can provide.

The Four Seasons is very plush, and sits near the harbor smack in the middle of downtown. It is above the Pacific Centre Mall, which holds over 200 shops. From my room I could see the snow-covered mountains of British Columbia.

A health club at the hotel allows fitness-conscious guests to try out the indoor/outdoor pool, Jacuzzis and saunas, and the wide variety of exercise equipment.

After a night at the Four Seasons in Vancouver, I took the 36-seat Air BC commuter flight operated by Air Canada to the town of Williams Lake. We stopped for refueling at the historic lumber town of Quesnel. It was a comfortable, two-hour flight.

At the airport, nearly 60 percent of the time it will be one of the owners of The Hills who will pick up guests. But if not the owner, someone from the staff will drive you to the ranch from the airport. The charge is $25.

If you come by bus or train there is no charge for the shuttle service, for that is a 10-minute drive vs. an hour-long drive to the airport.

The scenic train ride on B.C. Railway's Cariboo Dayliner is offered three times a week from Vancouver. Only two hours more than the trip by car, the train travels through four regions of British Columbia and is a relaxing, awesome trip for the tourist.

To drive, take either Highway 1 or 97 from Vancouver.

If you arrive at an odd time for the daily classes, The Hills keeps its swimming pool and stationary bikes available throughout the day.

For reservations at The Hills Health Ranch call (604) 791-5225 or write The Hills Health Ranch, C-26 108 Ranch, 100 Mile House, B.C., V0K 2E0. The fax number is (604) 791-6384.

SURROUNDING AREA

The "ranch" is set on 380 acres in what is called Cariboo country. The closest town is 100 Mile House, getting its name from Canada's gold rush boom of 1858. It was originally a road-house 100 miles from where the Cariboo Wagon Trail began at a Native American settlement called Lilloet. The roadhouse, one of many called 50, 75, 100 Mile House, etc., served the adventurers on their way to the gold fields near Barkerville.

Today the area is a tourist destination with lakes and forests for campers, hikers, and anglers in the summer and skiing in the winter. The ski network The Hills is a part of boasts 200 km (125 miles) of groomed, dual-track trails throughout the town of 100 Mile House. Ski huts are interspersed throughout the trail system.

In the summer, there are two 18-hole golf courses within 10 minutes of The Hills. Other summertime activities include rafting, camping, and horseback riding.

WHAT'S INCLUDED IN THE PRICE

As a year-round resort that focuses not only on its spa but on other resort activities as well, The Hills has an abundance of packages — or you can try a la carte. All of the packages have inexpensive to moderate prices.

First, there are several spa packages ranging from two-day weekenders to a 10-day emphasis on weight loss.

The Weekend Spoiler Package includes exercise classes, a Saturday night hayride, a massage, meals, accommodations, and use of all facilities. Add a second massage, facial, manicure, and pedicure for the Beauty Weekender.

In the 10-day weight loss program, the package includes meals, accommodations, classes, two massages, facial, various health-oriented workshops, nutritional and lifestyle analyses, cycle tours, the sing-a-long party, workouts, and a fitness assessment.

However, the three different week-long spa specials are probably the most popular and you can begin your stay any day of the week you want. An Executive Renewal package basically covers everything: massages, facials, tanning sessions, hikes, health-related workshops and anaylses, a herbal wrap, food, and accommodations. The Inches Off spa package eliminates the beauty and body treatments, focusing only on the fitness activities, food, and accommodations.

And the "Try a Thlon" adds daily guided mountain bike riding, canoeing or rowing, and cross country hiking to the fitness regime.

For any of the six-night spa packages, a 5 percent discount will be given to each husband and wife signing up together.

Beyond spa packages, The Hills offers a reasonably priced downhill ski package including lift tickets at Mt. Timothy, cross country ski packages that include spa treatments and classes, and several different golf and horseback packages.

Hotel taxes and gratuities are not included in the packages.

There are no private phones in the rooms, so be prepared to use a pay phone if you need to make calls.

Check-in is after 2 p.m.; check-out is at 11 a.m. Spa holidays begin with dinner on the night of arrival and end with lunch on the day of departure.

Reservations are confirmed with $50 or 25 percent of a package's price, whichever is greater. Cancellations before 30 days results in a full refund; 50 % at 15-29 days and no refund for less than 14 days' notice.

At The Hills, couples or families can take different programs at the same time. A person can check in for extended stays if he or she wants to use The Hills in a "fat farm" capacity.

CLOTHING AND WEATHER

The change in seasons is great here, so be prepared for winter from October to May, or the shorter summer season from June to September.

The Hills Health Ranch advises its guests to bring aerobic shoes, walking shoes, sweatshirts, exercise clothes, loose comfortable clothing, bathing suit and large towel, thongs and a jacket. Of course, in winter, you'll need cross country ski apparel, sweaters, parkas, and warmer foot, hand and head gear.

It's been said that The Hills is where Spandex meets denim. This resort is not a luxury spa; it's a down-home casual kind of place. And bringing both your Spandex for exercise and your jeans for haywagon rides is a good idea.

Personal laundry can be done at the resort for $2 a load.

At a median 3,600-ft. elevation, The Hills can have hot sunny days in the summer and snow in winter. The area receives an average of 80 inches of snow a year.

A TYPICAL DAY

Here you are allowed "spa brain" although you don't have to do anything scheduled for you. Upon arrival each guest is given a week-long schedule of fitness classes, workshops, seminars, and pampering. If you don't like it, adjustments can be made, but the schedule is arranged so you don't have to think — just relax. That's called "spa brain."

I started each day with a power walk, which is more than a hike. We were encouraged to take long strides and swing our arms forcefully, kind of like cross country skiing.

After the walk and breakfast, fitness activities are held throughout the rest of the day. The class descriptions are self explanatory from their names: Above the Belt, Aquafit, Beginner Moves, Fat Burner, Below the Belt, Lower Back Focus, No Bounce, Sizzler, Power Walk, Stretch and Strength.

The weekend itinerary when I visited The Hills was as follows:

Friday at 7:30 a.m. — power walk, then exercise classes at 9, 10, 11, and 2, a fitness seminar at 3:30 p.m., and video night at 7 p.m.; on Saturday after the power walk I had two fitness classes in the morning and a hike at 1:30 p.m., stretch at 4:30 p.m., and a hay ride at 7:30 p.m.; on Sunday it was the same schedule with a socializer in the evening; and on Monday the fitness schedule was beefed up with classes at 9, 10, 11, 4:30, and 7, a hike at 2:30 p.m., and a nutrition seminar at 1:30 p.m.

Each guest is given a fitness assessment and a lifestyle questionnaire that analyzes body composition, muscular strength, muscular endurance and flexibility as well as exercise habits.

One of the favorite activities is the hayride, or in the winter, the sleigh ride. In keeping with the down-home western flair, the horse-drawn sleigh or haywagon (depending on the season) takes the guests to a teepee called Willy's Wigwam. There up to 30 people can sing along with country western songs and folk tunes, tell a couple of jokes, and enjoy country living.

If you aren't on a spa package schedule, you can choose from Alpine and Nordic skiing, horseback riding, fishing, hiking, mountain biking, and many other recreational activities. Rentals are available as needed.

EVENING PROGRAMS

Several seminars are scheduled during the day or in the evening with topics of fitness, nutrition, stress management, makeovers, and fashion.

Any night of the week you might find a country gospel singalong, videos, games (Win, Lose or Draw was a favorite), and wellness workshops. Then there is also the favorite twice-weekly pow wow at Willy's wigwam.

THE STAFF

I think the staff truly likes what they do and this shows in the way the entire operation is run. Juanita Corbett feels that her staff is one of the resort's strongest assets and I agree. The staff of 50 is caring, extremely helpful, and nurturing.

There are two trained medical staff, four certified fitness instructors, and the cross country ski instructors have trophies under their belts for Nordic racing events.

FOOD

In a survey, 96 percent of the guests rated the food at The Hills Health Ranch as good to excellent, and spa cuisine is included in this assessment.

The spa food is made up of 60 percent complex carbohydrates and 25 percent protein with a low fat intake. Salt, sugar, alcohol, and caffeine are eliminated and multivitamins and minerals are given three times a day by a nutrition counselor. The calories are kept to 1,000-1,500 a day. There are no choices in the spa menu.

Spa guests can eat in the dining room at individual tables, but most opt for the communal spa table. The dining area also serves regular food created by the resort's Swiss chefs.

There is no smoking in the dining area and there is a full bar on the grounds.

SUMMARY

I like the whole idea of a spa ranch and give credit to the Corbetts for pioneering the concept. I also think it would be the treat of a lifetime to come here for Christmas.

It would be a true old-fashioned Christmas, for you get to cut your own tree and take it back to your chalet by horse-drawn sleigh.

THE PALMS

When I went to The Palms at Palm Springs, it seemed as if half the people had already been to this spa at least once, or to its sister spa, The Oaks at Ojai.

The reason is that this is one place where a person can lose weight. One man told me that between the heavy exercise and the 1,000-calorie-a-day diet, he could lose one and a half pounds a day. His example is to the extreme, but during one month, the average daily weight loss ranged between .43 and .71 pounds per person. The average daily inch loss was between .36 and .75 inches.

How do they do it? Exercise, exercise, exercise.

This has been the key for Sheila Cluff's success with her two spas and her life as a health and fitness lecturer, author, and publisher. Coming from the East Coast many years ago, she got her start in Southern California before the fitness craze really hit.

In 1977, Sheila converted a 1920s motel in the resort town of Ojai into a health and fitness spa called The Oaks at Ojai. Its success resulted in her opening The Palms of Palm Springs right in the heart of this exclusive resort community.

She hasn't stopped there. Sheila also authored "Aerobic Body Conditioning," which explains a specific type of low impact aerobics using wrist weights to increase the intensity. She publishes the 55,000-circulation Spa News and lectures and speaks on her 30 years in the fitness business. She also travels the world with her business, Health Holiday Tours, taking people to the Caribbean, the Greek Isles, and Jamaica, keeping them fit along the way.

She is the energizer for The Palms and The Oaks, telling you to "Relax! Feel beautiful!" on your fitness vacation.

The average stay here is nine and a half days and some people will stay for three weeks in order to shape up their bodies. The Stop Smoking Program is a 21-day program that has an 85 percent long-term success rate.

This resort caters to women between the ages of 30 and 60; only 20 percent of its guests are men.

I liked being in the middle of Palms Springs with easy access to the shopping and the many restaurants. Of course, if you are going with a serious goal to lose weight, stay put at The Palms and follow its regimen of exercise and diet.

THE LOOK OF THINGS

It appears that a former motel was renovated to become The Palms spa. Some of the rooms were converted to massage therapy rooms, others were renovated to house the spa's guests. The clean white walls of the spa's buildings reflect the desert sun and contrast with the resort's green grass lawns and red-tiled stucco roofs. There are poolside rooms or bungalows with private patios. The maximum capacity for The Palms is 80 guests.

In the middle of the courtyard is a large swimming pool for lap swimming, water exercising classes, and for just cooling off.

The Palms sports a library, office, sauna, whirlpool spa, beauty salons, and a fashion boutique, as well as the in-house Las Palmas dining room.

A nice feature of The Palms is its activity board that is posted daily with all the exercise classes, the evening's lecture, the day's menu, and sign-up sheets to find partners for tennis, golf, bridge, or whatever.

HOW TO GET THERE

It is only five minutes to The Palms from the Palm Springs Airport. The best way to get here is to take a taxi. Palm Springs is also only a two hour drive from Los Angeles.

For reservations call (619) 325-1111 or write The Palms at Palm Springs, 572 No. Indian Ave., Palm Springs, CA 92262.

SURROUNDING AREA

Just a block away from The Palms is the main drag of Palm Springs and all its exclusive, and expensive, shops. This is where the movie stars play, and prices reflect that. Desert Fashion Plaza, where Saks Fifth Avenue, I. Magnin, and Gucci are located, is only a five-minute stroll from The Palms.

Palm Springs is not all shopping. You can try horseback riding, hot air ballooning, or a celebrity tour of 70 movie stars' homes. Everyone who visits Palm Springs should take the Palm Springs Aerial Tramway from the desert floor to the top of Mt. San Jacinto at 6000 feet; there is a 40-degree temperature difference from the city.

You can also bicycle, golf, and play tennis at various spots all over Palm Springs.

WHAT'S INCLUDED IN THE PRICE

This can be a moderately to inexpensively priced spa, if you don't add any extras such as massages or facials. The spa's price includes meals, accommodations, exercise classes, and lectures. It doesn't include massages or beauty treatments. But what is a spa without a massage? So once you add on these extras, I would term this a moderately priced spa.

It might be a good idea to call The Palms ahead and ask about any special weeks or promotions coming up. Sometimes there are promotions offering bonus time (stay two weeks and get the third week free), 25 percent discounts for friends, 50 percent discount for daughters staying in the same room as their mothers and so on.

There is a cancellation policy for massages and beauty treatments, so be sure to notify the staff if you can't make an appointment. Otherwise you will be charged for a massage you didn't get.

CLOTHING AND WEATHER

It's hot here: Even in May when I visited, the temperatures swelled into the high 80s. Bring outfits that you can work out in and still be cool. The Palms and The Oaks are informal spas. They want you to exercise, eat right, and feel great. They aren't concerned about appearances. You can wear shorts at dinner, or jogging suits, or whatever you want.

Bring swimming suits, robes or pool coverups, leotards and tights, and walking and hiking shoes.

If you are planning to go shopping in Palms Springs' sophisticated shops or out to eat at a fancy restaurant, bring a nicer, casual outfit.

In the wintertime, Palms Springs cools down at night and it's a good idea to bring a sweater or jacket for the evening.

Safe deposit boxes are available for jewelry and valuables.

A TYPICAL DAY

A day at The Palms begins at 7 a.m. with either a vigorous three-mile jaunt or a leisurely 1.5-mile nature walk. In my walk, we headed through town toward the mountains and paced ourselves through a residential area. It was invigorating.

Breakfast follows the walk and then the day's exercising begins. There is a different type of exercise class every hour and each lasts about 45 minutes. These classes are designed to increase and maintain flexibility, burn calories, condition the heart and lungs, and tone muscles. The spa staff recommends that each guest do at least one stretch, one aerobic, and one strength training class each day.

The staff also strongly recommends that each guest have a mini-physical by the spa's registered nurse before beginning an exercise program. The nurse will also chart your weight and inch loss during your stay at The Palms.

The classes taught throughout the day vary in their intent and intensity. They include a stretching and toning class, creative aerobics, aquaerobics, aquatoning, a challenging high impact aerobics class and body conditioning.

A session will teach you how to tone your body by using weight training equipment and there are other sessions that focus on beauty, such as a demonstration on skin care.

To calm down after a hard day's workout, a hatha-yoga class is held at 4 p.m. and a true spa "Happy Hour" serves fresh fruit drinks at 5 p.m. Dinner is at 6 p.m.

Massages are given by appointment on the hour from 9 a.m. to 9 p.m.; facials are given from 8 a.m. to 8 p.m. Other special services that you can arrange by appointment include a private fitness consultation, salon services, or a body composition analysis.

For variety in your daily exercise, public tennis courts are nearby as well as the numerous golf courses that help to make Palm Springs famous. Bring your own equipment, such as tennis rackets, golf clubs, or bicycles; otherwise you'll have to rent.

EVENING PROGRAMS

Each day the activity board tells what the evening program will be and it usually consists of a wide variety of instructive entertainment. One night we had a cooking demonstration that was given in a very professional manner. It was lively and informative and the hour and a half passed quickly.

The week I was visiting The Palms was a special session given by the Heart Association. The "Happy Heart Spa Cuisine Week" featured lecturers who told us how to live a healthy life without feeling deprived.

Aside from the lectures, The Palms has movies available each night as well as bridge and various board games.

THE STAFF

At The Palms and at The Oaks, the most notable and active staff member is the owner, Sheila Cluff. You call her a staff member because she doesn't seem like a typical hands-off owner. Sheila manages to oversee the operation of The Palms and The Oaks as well as teach 8 to 10 exercise classes a week.

She heads a staff of exercise instructors, masseuses, and cooks who specialize in spa cuisine. The two spas also use interns in recreation from area universities.

FOOD

Just 1,000 calories. That's all you will eat each day at The Palms. If you want to lose weight, you can at The Palms. Its fitness programs and its nutritious diet will combine to help you shed pounds. The spa stresses natural, whole foods, including fresh vegetables and fruits, low fat proteins, and whole grains.

The Palms serves no sugar, no salt, and no artificial sweeteners. Caffeine is frowned upon.

In a typical day, we would have a breakfast buffet with several kinds of cereal, fresh fruit, milk, and cottage cheese. The sit-down dinner might be lasagna, with cheesecake for dessert. Yes, that can be prepared in under 1,000 calories.

Guests can also ask for an alternative meal such as a high protein salad or a high fiber salad, depending on their needs. Also, if you are one of the lucky ones who doesn't need to lose weight, a baked potato or brown rice can be added to lunch and dinner.

In case the diet doesn't give you enough vitamins and minerals, a vitamin/mineral pack is handed out as a supplement.

SUMMARY

This is a well-established spa with a high repeat business. It isn't the most fancy or pampering spa you'll ever go to, but for good old fitness and diet, The Palms will fit the bill...and take off those pounds.

ROCKY MOUNTAIN WELLNESS SPA AND INSTITUTE

A week at Rocky Mountain Wellness Spa and Institute isn't just a vacation, it is an investment in your life. This spa offers a "for life" program — one that teaches its guests about living and how to live better. It is different from some spas because it focuses on total wellness, not just pampering or weight reduction.

Come here with an open mind and you will leave with a head full of knowledge on what makes your body tick. I learned so much in one week's time, from what types of food can cause allergic reactions in me to the mineral contents of my body. The spa staff, and its entourage of on-call experts, performed mineral and vitamin analysis as well as metabolism testing. They also took into account my eating habits, fitness level, my percentage of body fat, my resting and training heart rate, and then put all the pieces of my body puzzle together. I found out what pieces were missing and what pieces needed improvement.

The entire program at Rocky Mountain Wellness Spa and Institute is scientifically based and proven to work. It is also extremely individualized. Only 15 guests at a time stay at the spa, based in Steamboat Springs, Colorado, and each guest is given a personalized analysis of his or her health. Before I even arrived at Rocky Mountain Wellness Spa and Institute, I had to send in a hair sample and fill out a nutritional questionnaire.

A laboratory analyzes the hair and determines what metals are present in your body. People in the United States are increasingly taking in more and more toxic metals from such seemingly harmless substances as baking soda, underarm deodorants, aluminum cans, and cookware. The spa staff helps its guests learn how to combat this mineral toxicity, and also for each quest compiles a 35-page Nutritional Analysis, a guide on the individual's nutritional needs.

But this is a "wellness" institute and the entire program is not based on the physiological aspects alone. The Rocky Mountain Wellness Spa and Institute concentrates on mind, body, and spirit.

One of the major focuses is on reducing stress. Because it is "the silent killer," Rocky Mountain Wellness Spa and Institute has made stress reduction one of its top priorities. The institute's co-owner, Larry Allingham, says, "Teaching people how to reduce stress in their lives and still live and work in the fast lane is what we're all about."

Three methods are espoused by RMWS: auto-relaxation, progressive relaxation, and train-the-brain technique. The auto-relaxation technique "peels away layers of stress accumulated over a lifetime" through a 25-minute exercise. Progressive relaxation deals with reducing muscle tension and self-healing. Train the brain uses imagery and visualization to achieve inner peace. I am still using both methods in my everyday life — because they actually work!

This spa opened in 1983 as one of the first spas in the nation to combine wellness with weight loss and exercise. Its owners, Larry and Dorothy Allingham, were the epitome of stress for much of their adult lives. Larry was the owner of car dealerships in Kansas and had problems with smoking, alcohol, and stress. Dorothy drank, smoked, and didn't watch her diet. But in the early 1980s, the car dealership failed and the Allinghams lost millions in a few months.

They came to Steamboat Springs — where they owned some land--with $14 and the gumption to start a new life, one totally different from their former days of stress. They developed their budding interest in stress reduction, health, and nutrition. Larry earned a bachelor's in nutrition and started conducting seminars in wellness. As their philosophies became more fine-tuned, they created The Rocky Mountain Wellness Spa and Institute.

People in their 30s, 40s, and 50s are attracted to the institute, especially (do I dare use the term?) "yuppies" in high stress positions. The relatively new spa already has 20 percent repeat business.

I think the repeat business will increase as more and more people discover Rocky Mountain Wellness Spa and Institute, because after your week at the spa is up the staff doesn't just cut its ties with you. Two weeks later, the spa sent me a note with pictures of me at the spa and asked how I was doing. I was also told about its policy of encouraging former guests to call back anytime to ask about health problems or to get help with managing personal crises. The advice is free for the rest of your life.

Long after I've finished researching this book, I'd like to return and see if my wellness and fitness level is as good as I can get it. I know that Rocky Mountain Wellness Spa and Institute is the best in the business for telling me about the state of my wellness and fitness levels.

THE LOOK OF THINGS

The spa is located at the base of the Steamboat Ski Area, which has 21 chair lifts and is the fourth largest ski resort in the United States. The institute rents the clubhouse and suites of one of Steamboat's four-star condominium complexes. This eight-acre condominium complex has a rustic flair with high-beamed ceilings in the common rooms. The views from the dining room and the suites are of a serene valley framed by the jagged peaks of the Rocky Mountains.

The individual suites share a common room but have their own private bed and bath. There are a dining area, exercise rooms, and indoor whirlpool and sauna. The swimming pool is the indoor/outdoor type and there is also an outdoor Jacuzzi. A small library has more than 100 titles on related wellness subjects as well as a video collection and an extensive filing system for current articles on everything from "A, vitamin" to "zinc."

Outside is the fresh air of the Rocky Mountains, cool, clear babbling streams, wildflowers, and green meadows or fields of white winter wonderland depending on which season you visit.

HOW TO GET THERE

Steamboat Springs has an airport that is served by major airlines in the summer or by jet service during the winter. It is a short 40-minute flight from Stapleton International Airport in

Denver, Colorado, or it is a two-and-a-half hour drive from Denver on Interstate 70 and Highway 40.

If you are arriving by airplane, complimentary airport pickup is arranged if you call ahead with your arrival time.

Check-in is at 4 p.m., but if you arrive early you can go ahead and participate in the daily activities until your room is ready. Check-out time is 11 a.m.

For reservations, write Rocky Mountain Wellness Spa and Institute at P.O. Box 777, Steamboat Springs, CO 80477 or call toll-free (800) 345-7770 nationwide or (800) 345-7771 in Colorado.

SURROUNDING AREA

Steamboat Springs is a year-round destination resort that has made a name for itself in recreational activities. The green valley was once the summer stomping grounds of the Arapaho and Ute Indian tribes. They came for the refreshing summer days and the natural mineral hot springs.

Today, people come for hiking, tennis, golfing, mountain biking, kayaking, whitewater rafting, downhill and cross country skiing...and for the refreshing summer days.

In the winter, this is a ski town that averages 27 feet of snow a year. In the summer, the community of 5,000 residents hosts rodeos and chamber music festivals, softball tournaments and theater and dance productions.

There are also a variety of stores for the shopping nut as well as many artists' galleries and exhibitions. There are several shops and restaurants within walking distance from the spa; in fact, just a block away. Steamboat Springs also has a bus service that stops in front of the spa's condos and goes to grocery stores, movie theaters, shopping, and downtown Steamboat Springs. Taxi service is also available.

Just 30 miles away is Steamboat Lake State Park, and four miles outside of town is Fish Creek Falls, a fun place for a picnic.

One day we went to the mineral hot springs, which a tourist would have difficulty finding unless he or she was with a local or one of the institute's staff. After driving on a windy mountain road, we arrived at the hot springs. Soaking is available in three different baths that mix the fresh mountain water of the river with the thermal heat of the springs, resulting in the perfect temperature.

Surrounded by 150,000 acres of national forest land, one of Steamboat Springs' best offerings is its scenic beauty.

WHAT'S INCLUDED IN THE PRICE

Rocky Mountain Wellness Spa and Institute is an inexpensive spa that includes everything in one price. With all the extra tests (mineral analysis, metabolism testing, etc.) I thought there could be some hidden costs, but there aren't. The price includes all the laboratory work involved, the personal computer wellness assessment, meals, accommodations, cross country ski gear in the winter, bicycle rental in the summer, a spa cookbook, and all uses of the sauna and Jacuzzi.

Daily touch-up cleaning is done in each room, with a mid-stay thorough cleaning by the maid service. The rooms included in the price do share a common room; if you would like a private suite it can be arranged, but there will be an additional charge.

There are optional services available for an extra charge — manicures, pedicures, and body contour wraps. This wrap treatment, featured on the Phil Donahue Show, allows clients to experience tighter skin and an inch loss of one to five inches in an hour. This is not an herbal wrap which can cause temporary water loss, the contour body wrap results in permanent loss of inches (unless, of course, you sneak out and eat three banana splits). Some people have lost up to eleven inches.

Aside from this extra cost, everything else is included in the price, including the 17 percent service charge and the 9.2 percent tax on meals and lodging.

Rocky Mountain Wellness Spa and Institute will accept personal checks, Visa, MasterCard or Discover. A deposit is required.

CLOTHING AND WEATHER

You are in the mountains when you visit Rocky Mountain Wellness Spa and Institute and you need to dress for any kind of weather. The best way to dress is in layers, whether it is summer or winter. Take a jacket, sweatshirt, and a t-shirt so you can add or subtract these layers as your exercise level and the day's temperatures dictate.

In the summer, bring hiking apparel. In the winter, bring something to go cross country skiing in, such as a warm jacket, mittens, hats, turtlenecks, and warm pants.

This is in addition to the usual spa fare of swimsuit, exercise clothes, sweat suits, and tennis shoes. Dress here is casual. I wore my warm-ups from morning to evening without changing for meals.

Other items to bring include a hair dryer (they are not available in the locker rooms), a wristwatch with a second hand, a camera, a lock (if you want to lock your exercise locker), and toilet articles. At 7,000 feet in elevation, you will need sunglasses, suntan lotion, and lip balm to protect yourself against the high altitude sunshine.

One more thing to bring—a long-handled natural bristle brush or if you prefer, a loofah sponge. What for? The spa advocates a dry brush massage technique for its health and beauty attributes. The process effectively exfoliates the skin, removing impurities and stimulating blood circulation.

Don't bother to bring a towel because there are plenty available in the locker rooms.

EVENING PROGRAMS

This is an "intellectual" spa and evenings are spent learning. The spa brings in experts each night to discuss a variety of topics, such as nutrition, stress, effective grocery shopping, fitness goals, self esteem, love, relationships, etc. During my stay, I learned about priorities, wellness lifestyles, nutrition, and stress. I also had a session with a chiropractor who talked about how easily our bodies get out of whack from daily life and working. He suggested using a slant board once or twice a day to bring blood to the brain and realign the spinal column.

The evening seminars are very informative, and with the spa limiting its sessions to 15 people, allows for individual discussion.

A TYPICAL DAY

A walk followed breakfast every morning, with a staff member accompanying me to the Steamboat Ski Area or around the grounds. Then stress reduction classes and exercise periods were held until lunch. Afternoons were filled with an outdoor exercise activity, individual consultations, and perhaps a massage or sauna before dinner. Seminars were held in the evenings to teach about different facets of wellness.

About three or four hours a day are devoted to exercise, which includes low impact or water aerobics, circuit training, stretching, fitness walking, body toning, or yoga in the mornings. In the afternoons, I went cross country skiing at Rabbit Ears Pass on the Continental Divide one day and mountain biking on a mountain road the next day. It was my first time cross country skiing and I loved it, especially knowing that the sport is one of the best all-around physical exercises.

If the exercise is too much or too little for anybody, the staff will adjust it to meet individual wants. There is also a downhill ski package available in the wintertime.

In between exercise, I had classes on meditation, stress reduction, and nutrition. The private consultations were fascinating, as I learned a great deal about my body. For example, I learned that my fat percentage should be lowered by 15 percent (and I thought I had been so good about my fat intake!)

In the late afternoon, I had massages and saunas. This is not a pampering spa for nails, hair, and body treatments. It is more of an active, learning experience.

My time was filled with all the activities available, but on one day I still had enough time to read and relax for an hour. There are televisions in the room, but the staff discourages guests from using them to avoid outside influences.

THE STAFF

The staff is young, enthusiastic, and professional. They are truly dedicated and enjoy their jobs. Each staff member brings to the program his or her own area of expertise, adding to the over-all wellness experience. A certified ski instructor took me cross country skiing one day and the staff chiropractor presented a "wellness lifestyle" seminar. By bringing in the best in their fields, RMWS keeps its guests well-informed and well taken care of. The Allinghams are also very visible and participate in the program.

Everyday a different staff member eats breakfast, lunch, or dinner with the guests to explain the program, answer questions, and continue the ever-constant process of teaching the guests about their health and mental welfare.

FOOD

The meals are excellent and the diet there is very cleansing. If that seems like an impossible combination, you just have to believe me. One night we had a mushroom pate and a ginger oriental dip with fresh vegetables, black beans with salsa, and a fresh grape sorbet. Amazingly, there was no sweetner or thickner for the sorbet.

Most of the meals are vegetarian and the spa does not serve anything with wheat, corn, dairy, sugar, caffeine, or chocolate. The reason for eliminating these items is to remove from the diet the substances most commonly linked to food allergies, and to cleanse the system. The spa will conduct allergy tests on guests to determine what they are allergic to and hence should avoid.

Distilled water is served to help rid the body of toxins and impurities. Once your body is back to normal, you can start to feel the healthy change.

Rocky Mountain Wellness Spa tries to limit the caloric intake to 1,000-1,200 calories a day. At 10 a.m. and 4 p.m. a juice is served to keep your energy up.

Sheri Stevens takes on the challenge of creating delicious, nutritional meals. She owns a catering business called a La Petite Cheri and caters for business meetings, weddings, romantic dinners for two, as well as the Wellness Institute. She earned certificates in French and Italian cooking from Ma Maison of Beverly Hills, but spa cuisine is as challenging to her as gourmet cuisine.

Breakfast is usually multi-grain cereals, breads, muffins, waffles, pancakes, and fresh fruit. Lunch is the main meal of the day, consisting of a variety of creative foods such as Indonesian stir-fry, lasagna with homemade marinara sauce, stuffed artichokes, and many other wonderful dishes. Dinner is homemade soups and salads. The spa uses a wide range of salad ingredients. To give you some ideas: romaine lettuce, spinach, green leaf lettuce, tomatoes, carrots, sprouts, celery, onion, avocado, cucumber, cabbage, nuts, sunflower seeds, raisins, jicama, cheese, broccoli, kidney beans, green beans, and pasta.

The spa recommends that before you arrive in Steamboat Springs you should try to reduce your intake of simple sugars, refined food products, caffeine, and fatty meats. This will make the transition to spa food easier.

SUMMARY

Each day was another learning experience and I was happy with the whole week. I learned things about my body — physically and mentally — that I will carry with me the rest of my life. And just knowing I have a place to call if I get severely stressed-out makes me less stressed already!

ROCKY MOUNTAIN WELLNESS SPA AND INSTITUTE
Ready to relax after a workout

THE MAUI CHALLENGE

The Maui Challenge is about the most exciting, invigorating, inspiring, fun, and adventurous way to get fit. It is not a spa in the sense that you soak in hydrotherapy tubs, count calories carefully, or hear numerous talks about self-improvement. But it is a spa because it shapes up your body while at the same time giving you a fresh new outlook on how to enjoy life and build self-confidence.

Those who like to label things call this a soft adventure. It is a cross between a health spa and an adventure destination program. It lets you rough it during the day and sink into luxury at night. The Maui Challenge is no risk, but high fun.

The Maui Challenge is a week-long course in the Hawaiian Islands where you get physically in shape by exploring the waterfalls, lava fields, beaches, mountains, and bays of Maui. The staff takes you to all the untouristed spots on the tropical island and then challenges your fitness through sport. Each evening, you can relax with massages, gourmet cuisine, Jacuzzi spa, and luxury accommodations.

If I had known beforehand that I would be swimming under powerful waterfalls and walking over rough lava beds, I possibly would not have gone to this spa. But having been there and done the "Maui Challenge" I feel better about myself, more confident in what I can undertake and more excited about life's opportunities.

Two of the main reasons for this fresh new outlook are Maui Challenge's "challenges" and its staff.

The challenges are daily hikes that will stretch your endurance and at the same time make you forget your physical pain by introducing you to Hawaii's scenic beauty and wonders. Most days are filled with hikes, although we enjoyed water sports one day and a fantastic catamaran ride and snorkeling trip another day.

The staff are loveable, excitable people who have a passion for what they do. As guides to Maui's experiences, they can also be trusted with your lives in their hands. One of our guides, whom we called a Hawaiian Sherpa, made me feel so confident that I would trust him to take me anywhere—even across a raging waterfall in a harness pulley. The staff was also acutely aware of each participant's strengths and weaknesses and would plan alternative outings for those who, for one reason or another, wouldn't enjoy a particular challenge.

For example, because I am afraid of heights, I and two others were given an alternative hike to do instead of the planned hike which scaled a high crater with switchbacks.

These guides became my best friends. They were crazy, silly, wonderful, and people I could trust. And because of that, I too, was crazy, silly, and learned I could trust myself to do things I hadn't dreamed of before.

The Maui Challenge was conceived by Debbie Sturgess, who made an adventure camp out of the things she likes to do herself and in the places she likes to live. She began "challenging" the public in the spring of 1987 and her program has received much acclaim since then. In a review of health spas, Cosmopolitan magazine lauded the Maui Challenge for its tough workouts and its cross training advantages.

"The Challenge concept combines the luxury of a spa with the physical and mental expression of outward bound programs and adventure travel," Sturgess explains. "Participants are not only stimulated physically, but educated and invigorated by the environment. It is a unique program—in fact, to my knowledge, there is no other program like it in the country."

Because of Maui Challenge's popularity, Sturgess has opened The Sedona Challenge near The Grand Canyon in Arizona. She also anticipates opening other challenges in different locations. The Maui Challenge is held once or twice a month, as well as on special occasions for private and corporate groups. A call to the Maui Challenge office can tell you what the scheduled dates are for the challenge each year.

The fun fitness vacations can accommodate beginner through advanced fitness levels. Because of the small size (only eight people at a time), the staff can gear its activities to each individual in a group.

I loved the Maui Challenge — its hiking, snorkeling, boogie boarding, and its staff. It was a hoot. Although it may sound more challenging than you think you want in a spa vacation, don't let the physical exercise scare you away. I urge anyone, from youngsters to seniors, to try the Maui Challenge. You won't regret it and the "challenge" will never be more than you can handle.

THE LOOK OF THINGS

It is a winding, narrow road from the airport to the village of Kailua that is your base for the Maui Challenge. The Hana Highway is a spectacular road that is so twisting it can take two hours to drive 35 miles.

The Challenge utilizes the Kailua Maui Garden Estate as its headquarters. The first thing you notice about the estate is its lush vegetation. Banana trees dot the grounds, while two peacocks strut around guarding the palms, flowers, and tropical gardens.

The Pacific Ocean is a mile away but seemingly close from the estate's vantage point. It can be seen shimmering in the distance from the rooms.

Guests stay in five different bedrooms located in either the main house or a garden apartment. The rooms are adequate. The Challenge will place its guests in the shared rooms and even if you come alone you will likely have a roommate.

A swimming pool, Jacuzzi, and barbecue are located on the two acre estate.

HOW TO GET THERE

When I arrived at the Maui airport, I was greeted with a traditional Hawaiian lei. The Challenge staff picks up its guests in a mini-van and drives us 20 miles to the estate. At the end of the week, transportation is provided back to the airport.

The Challenge weeks throughout the year are booked on a first-come, first-served basis and are limited to eight participants.

A $500 deposit is due when you make reservations for this moderately-priced spa vacation. The rest is due 30 days before arrival. You can call (800) 448-9816 for information or write The Maui Challenge, P.O. Box 5489, Glendale, AZ 85312 or call the Arizona office at (602) 878-7071.

SURROUNDING AREA

Maui is one of Hawaii's eight main islands, although the state encompasses more than 100 islands, reefs, and shoals. It is 20 degrees from the equator and was formed by volcanos spewing into the ocean and building up land masses.

The Challenge will provide plenty to do and see on the island of Maui, but if you have more time to spend on Maui there's more to experience.

Let the staff of the Maui Challenge introduce you to the magnificent Haleakala Crater, Maui's waterfalls and rain forests, and its beaches. If you have more time, try other tourist operators for dinner cruises on the Lahaina coast, luaus with South Pacific food and dances, or helicopter trips to Maui's waterfalls and valleys. It is not difficult to find these operators; just pick up any tourist brochure in the airport or at any tourist information center.

If you go to Maui in the right season (January to May), don't miss a whale-watching trip. There are several tours available to see the humpback whales, and the Challenge staff can guide you to the best tour operator—if they aren't taking you on a tour themselves. The humpbacks frolic in the channels between Maui and its neighboring islands of Lanai, Kahoolawe, and Molokai during their annual migration to Hawaii's warm waters.

WHAT'S INCLUDED IN THE PRICE

The Maui Challenge includes daily "outrageous hikes," accommodations, transportation to and from the airport, and three gourmet meals a day. All equipment, bicycle rental, windsurfing lessons, and water sports are included in the moderately priced program. The program also includes a day of sailing and a night of dinner and dancing. The Maui Challenge doesn't spare any expense in its activities. Airfare is not included.

Extra costs are massages, manicures, pedicures, facials, water skiing, tennis, and golf.

Laundry service is included in the package. You can leave your laundry each day at the foot of your bed and it will be cleaned by the time you return in the afternoon.

CLOTHING AND WEATHER

It's important to bring the right clothes to the Maui Challenge. If you don't, you could end up miserably wet and cold.

You will be climbing high mountains where the temperature drops and hiking through rain forests that will make you wet. Bring a windshirt and windpants because these are light but will keep you dry. The feather-weight jackets are good because they allow your skin to breathe, unlike conventional raincoats. Plastic raincoats seem too hot in Maui's tropical climate.

As far as shoes and swimsuits go, bring about three sets of each and be prepared to throw one away. If you bring an old pair of sneakers and an old swimming suit, you won't care if it gets muddy and ruined during a waterfall hike. The extra shoes and swimsuits are so you can be wearing a dry pair while the other pair dries out.

Make sure one pair of shoes is for hiking, with enough room in the toes for extended downhill hiking. Aqua shoes or something to wear on the beaches and reefs, and while windsurfing, are a good idea.

Other clothing should be jeans, t-shirts, extra socks, warm sweater, jacket, gloves, shorts, sandals, and a casual outfit for going out on the town Saturday night.

Miscellaneous items you should bring include sunscreen, sunglasses, toiletries, hat or visor, chapstick, insect repellant, and Neosporin or some other medication for your lava cuts. It's best if your camera is waterproof too.

Another good idea is to bring two baggies so on hikes you can put dry clothes in one bag and wet clothes in another.

Bring your own toiletries, towels are provided.

A TYPICAL DAY

Every day we woke up with a sense of adventure about the day's forthcoming activities. The staff sensibly started us out with a stretching session in the morning. Then the day's activities began.

The first day we took a three-mile, three- to four-hour hike through La Perouse Bay, which is named after a French explorer who anchored here and mysteriously disappeared in 1786. The hike entailed walking across Maui's most recent lava bed which flowed around 1790. The trail is well-defined but somewhat rough and, at one point, follows along the top of sheer cliffs cascading down to the ocean. It kind of spooked me, but the guides helped out, and I used a walking stick for confidence.

We sat in tidal pools that massaged us as the waves came in and out. We also snorkeled in the bay, did some rock skipping, and wandered along two beaches. On the little beach, bathing suits were optional, and we saw a lot of optionals!

On the second day, half the group tackled the Skyline Trail up Haleakala Crater while the other half took a rain forest walk.

The Skyline Trail hike begins at Poli Poli State Park and covers eight miles with an elevation gain of 3,800 feet. During my Challenge week, the group had to start three miles before the state park which made it an 11-mile trek.

The trail began in a redwood forest. As we continued up the crater the scenery looked more and more like the moon with tons of red lava rock. The first set of clouds we actually hiked above were white and fluffy and you could see through them to other islands. Then the landscape became more barren and the clouds thicker until at the top all we could see were clouds, red rock, and the sun.

At the top you can get on a bicycle after hearing a very stern lecture on safety and signing a two-page waiver. We donned raincoats and began the 38-mile ride down from Haleakala Crater. For the first 15 miles all you do is brake through the numerous hairpin turns and then you come upon pastures of cattle and plantations of sugar and pineapples. One word of advice – take pictures going up Haleakala, because you won't have a chance to take them on the way down.

The next day was a hike through the crater which for some was 12 and a half miles, but for me was a three-mile round-trip hike. We were at 2,000 feet in the tropical rain forest.

We put hiking aside on Wednesday when we spent the day windsurfing on Sugar Beach. Some of us took a catamaran ride with Captain Jerry, who took us to 15 knots and put the catamaran on one pontoon. We were vertical and he just kept us there like we were suspended in time and place. It was like a ballet.

We also learned to boogie-board on this day, hanging out in the water and waiting for the wave to take us into the beach.

On another day we hiked to the seven sacred pools of Hana and sat in a waterfall in O'heo Gulch. The 184-foot Makahiku Falls drops stunningly into a gorge below.

Finally, on the last night, we went out on the town to relive the adventures of the past week and share our experiences before parting ways the next day.

EVENING PROGRAMS

There are no evening programs other than enjoying massages, dining on gourmet meals, or relaxing in the hot spa. On the last night of the week, everyone went out on the town to a restaurant and those with enough strength went dancing. My group went to Mama's Fish House where we had excellent seafood.

THE STAFF

The hiking guides are all experts in Maui's history, flora, fauna, geology, and folklore. When hiking with these guides, you don't just go for the physical exercise. They provide you with an extensive education in Hawaiian natural history.

The guides are also very good about teaching you how to hike without getting blisters or running out of energy. They can inspire confidence in anyone to try nearly any kind of challenge.

They are also experts in their sport. One of the guides was a Sherpa in the Pakistani Himalayas for five years and a professional mountain guide for eight years. Another interesting guide came to Hawaii after directing films and teaching emotionally disturbed children in San Diego. He was also the aerobics instructor each morning and helped us get stretched out and supple for the day's activities. A massage therapist will come to the estate in the late afternoon to knead out all the tiredness.

FOOD

A private chef fixes nutritious meals for the Challenge participants three times a day. The cuisine aims toward gourmet vegetarian with lots of fish and poultry added. The staff frowns on cigarettes, alcohol, and caffeine drinks. With such a good workout each day, nobody was counting calories. The best part about this health spa is that we didn't feel like we had to count them. If you are working that hard during the day, it's OK to eat a little extra at night.

SUMMARY

The Maui Challenge is not for the weak or frail; it is not for couch potatoes. It is a week of adventures in a spectacular place that will give anybody a good outlook on life and increased confidence in themselves. This is an adventure in fitness, but it is also an adventure of the soul.

PLANTATION SPA

Parrots squawk. The scent of Plumeria wafts through the lush gardens. Pacific Ocean breakers pound in the near distance. This is Polynesian heaven.

The Plantation Spa on Hawaii's Oahu is a tropical paradise with a Swedish accent. That "accent's" name is Bodil Anderson.

A Swedish native, Anderson gained her spa experience in the famous health resorts of Sweden, then brought those techniques to Hawaii.

At the Plantation Spa, I enjoyed a soothing massage, I devoured healthy vegetarian fare after working up a hunger on a rain forest walk, and I relaxed under swaying palms with urging from a lilting Swedish voice.

Bodil believes that any spa in the world is a reflection of the person who runs it. As the owner of this spa, Bodil lets her personality shine through. She loves the outdoors, so rain forest hikes and beachcombing walks are part of the spa's itinerary. With youthful enthusiasm, she describes the spa's canoe trip on the final day as a way for guests to relive their childhood and experience the outdoors.

"A frog may jump in your boat and you get it out," she says with glee.

Relaxation is important to Bodil too, and she encourages her guests to calm down, sit and talk, do nothing. When visiting American spas, she found that some of them are nothing but classes, activities, and lectures that keep their guests always with too many choices to make. To her, it was stressful, so at the Plantation Spa she made sure we had time to relax. This way a person can unwind and get in a good, centering frame of mind.

"You should always have some free time to sit and read, write a letter, talk with people.

Bodil says she tries not to make her spa too much different from a guest's home, but here she won't succeed.

The Plantation Spa is truly Hawaiian and will never seem like the home I have in Nevada. It was formerly an old estate and a halfway stop for people traveling between Kahuku and Kaneohe in the early 1900s. The lush tropical gardens bloom everywhere, and green mountains rise above the land.

Anderson makes this spa truly fun and enjoyable. Others love it too, including stars Richard Chamberlain, Margaux Hemingway, Barry Williams, and Leslie Nielsen. The average spa-goers' age is in the 40s, and 80 percent of the guests are women.

It is Oahu's first health spa and its emphasis is on lifestyle changes, healthy eating, exercise and relaxation.

THE LOOK OF THINGS

The Plantation Spa, as its name says, is a refurbished plantation on the windward side of Oahu between the Koolau mountains and the Pacific Ocean. By coastal markers, it is located between the rock formations of Chinaman's Hat and the Crouching Lion Inn.

It is on the Kamehameha Highway, just across the street from the Pacific Ocean. The spa's activities are housed in the buildings of the old estate. The carriage house is a gymnasium. The orchid house has been transformed into a lovely massage and herbal wrap facility. The main house and cottage house provide rooms for the guests.

The Plantation Spa was opened in 1988 and is situated on seven acres of land. The spa itself is small and graciously Polynesian.

Its indoor/outdoor style of living, and the tropical lushness of the surrounding gardens make it a beautiful, relaxing place. A waterfall cascades into the swimming pool. Next to the pool is a Jacuzzi surrounded by ferns, flowers, and exotic greenery.

The Sauna awaits the guests in the Pavillion for a nice, relaxing break.

The cheery rooms are decorated in flowers and bright colors and have fantastic views of the countryside, mountains, or ocean. The remodeled orchid house is divided into four massage rooms that sport views of the ocean from their elongated windows. It is lovely because it is isolated and set back in the trees.

Future plans aim at enhancing the old estate even more with nature walks marked and gazebo-like treehouses built for peaceful contemplation.

HOW TO GET THERE

The Plantation Spa is in the Ka'a'awa countryside, not far from Kaneohe Bay. It is a scenic drive on the Pali Highway from Oahu's better-known tourist area, Waikiki. The spa is 24 miles from Honolulu International Airport and 26 miles from Waikiki.

The spa's staff will pick you up and take you back to the airport for a fee. Otherwise, rental cars and taxi service are available for travel to the spa.

Try to schedule your arrival between 2 p.m. and 4 p.m. on Sunday and your departure on or before 10 a.m. on the following Saturday. Check-out time is at 11 a.m. Also, if you want to be picked up by the spa staff, provide the flight information to them one week in advance.

SURROUNDING AREA

Oahu is Hawaii's foremost tourist island. It is heavily developed in some areas, such as Waikiki Beach, and therefore can provide the nightlife and entertainment some tourists seek. Local bus service can take you to all the tourist stops from Pearl Harbor to shopping centers to Diamond Head.

For peace, quiet, and beauty, the spa's backyard is really the best place to be. The rain forest is behind the spa and a beautiful (and public) beach is just a five-minute walk away. There is a beach directly across the street, but it is rockier than the public beach.

If you are coming a day early or staying a day late, consider renting a car and driving around the island. You can see the north shore where the surfers wait for the truly big waves, you can snorkel in the fish-laden Hanauma Bay, you can visit a pineapple plantation, or you can experience the Waikiki strip.

WHAT'S INCLUDED IN THE PRICE

The Plantation Spa is a moderately priced resort that includes everything in one fee. This means accommodations, three lacto-vegetarian meals a day, all exercise programs, hikes, activities and lectures, four massages and one herbal wrap, and European juice and broth fasts upon request.

It costs extra to have a pedicure, manicure, or facial.

The Plantation Spa requires a $500 deposit within 14 days of a reservation. To make a reservation, call (808) 237-8685, Fax (808) 947-1866 or write 51-550 Kamehameha Highway, Ka'a'awa, HI 96730.

CLOTHING AND WEATHER

This is a spa where you dress down, not up. Don't bring fancy clothes; don't bring jewelry. Bring Hawaiian attire, meaning swimsuits and shorts.

Bring your regular spa gear, such as shorts, T-shirts, sweat suits, tennis shoes, hiking bookts, lots of socks, and exercise clothes.

Bring your own hair dryer as well as your toiletries.

In my room, there was a robe for me to use. If you forget something, the spa has a gift shop that also carries the essentials.

I learned a Hawaiian custom at the Plantation Spa too, and that is to take off your shoes before entering your room, so if you don't like going barefoot bring soft slippers or socks.

The days are warm and tropical, but the ocean breezes cool down the nights; a jacket or light sweater would be a good idea.

A TYPICAL DAY

There is a sunshine program and a liquid sunshine program at the Plantation Spa. In case you don't know, liquid sunshine in Hawaii is the light sprinkling of rain that comes down in the afternoons while the sun still shines brightly. It sounds unbelievable, but it's true.

The Plantation Spa tries to offer a little bit for everybody — aerobics to hiking to lectures to massages. However, Bodil believes people should get out in nature more and she therefore schedules a lot of hikes and walks.

Wake-up every day is at 6:45 a.m. and the day begins with either yoga or a walk to the beach and around the countryside. Breakfast is at 8 a.m. followed by a workout that can range from aerobics, water volleyball, lap swimming, stretching, or "back and abs" exercises (that's back and abdominal). Another exercise featured here is hydrotone. When doing this water exercise, I put on water resistant boots and wore hand weights. Supposedly twenty minutes of hydrotone is worth an hour of heavy workout.

After a noontime lunch, the afternoons are devoted to relaxing, massages, herbal wraps, and low impact exercises such as stretching or toning. I had one of the best massages ever at the Plantation Spa. Besides being given in the beautiful orchid house, my massage therapist sure knew how to penetrate those muscles. At one point, she jumped up on the massage table in order to apply better pressure to my back. For such a little bit of a girl, boy did she pack a wallop.

Afternoon classes are given, and while I was there I attended a lecture on iridology, the science of understanding body conditions by evaluating the iris in a person's eye — very popular with guests.

Another class is "Cook's Helper." Instead of a traditional demonstration cooking class, this one puts the learners into the kitchen. A concoction of lentils, beans, and rice is prepared while every kind of vegetable imaginable is stir-fried in sesame seed oil in a wok.

Along with teaching the spa guests how to cook this nutritious meal, the spa staff also conducts a health food store seminar. Items from a health food store are brought in and guests are taught how to look at the labels to make sure what one buys in a health food store is actually healthy. You also learn how to sprout different seeds.

Dinner is at 6 p.m. and several evening programs are held afterward.

In addition to these daily activities, there are at least three special adventures for the spa-goers. One day the guests hike to Sacred Falls along a lush, tropical path that narrows into a wide crevasse in a mountain. A waterfall thunders down from the mountain into a cool pool that is a perfect swimming hole.

On the last day of the session, a canoe trip is taken up the Kahana River. This scenic trip has become everybody's favorite not only for the emerald forests that line the river but for the pure sport of rowing.

EVENING PROGRAMS

These evening programs are not just the usual (but informative) lectures on nutrition, positive thinking, stress management, health hints and self improvement; the Plantation Spa adds a bit of spontaneity and fun to its evening programs.

Once Jerry Coffee talked about his experiences as a prisoner of war in Vietnam and it was so moving that the spa convinced him to return to other sessions and speak. His tale of imprisonment and faith was inspiring. Other nights Hawaiian lei making or silk screening is taught. During a spa-type luau, the guests are entertained with hula dancing and Hawaiiana storytelling.

THE STAFF

There are nine employees on the staff including the adminstrative directors, massage therapists, chef, and exercise instructor. The spa's casual atmosphere spills over into its staff. They are fun, informative, and helpful.

FOOD

Vegetarian food is the bill of fare at the Plantation Spa. It is a lacto-vegetarian diet, allowing a few milk products. In fact, the milk products are rather creative — almond milk, soy milk, goat milk, and sesame milk, as well as yogurt and buttermilk.

They don't worry about counting calories, but they are calorie conscious. Everything is natural and made from scratch.

Bodil Anderson also believes in balancing the body's pH through eating. Too many foods high in acid can cause arthritis and osteoporosis, claims Dr. R. Berg of Sweden, although he admits it's an unscientific recommendation, but he claims we should always look at the positive result. Citing the book "Diet for a New America" by John Robbins, Bodil espouses eating more alkaline foods instead of acidic foods. Also some foods should be served with others to balance a body's pH.

Another cuisine aspect that is earning a reputation for the Plantation Spa is its European juice and broth fasts. A guest can fast one or more days under this method that allows them to drink a healthful broth and fruit and vegetable juices such as carrot, beet, mango, papaya, mountain apple, celery, and tomato. I didn't fast myself, but three other spa-goers did while I was there and had no complaints about the fasting fare. Their problems of minor headaches stemmed from a caffeine withdrawal, which just shows what we do to our bodies with sodas and coffee.

The broth, made of potatoes, leek, onion, parsley, and carrots, is supposed to be good for you as a daily drink and also to keep weight down, spirits up and very healthy, high in potassium & minerals and very alkaline.

For those of us eating rather than fasting, some dishes included papaya soup, tomato-avocado soup, carrot-rice loaf, potato casserole, ratatouille and Thai vegetable curry. Breakfast might be oatmeal, buckwheat, muesli, juices, and fresh fruit grown on the grounds.

Smoking and alcohol are not allowed during the spa week. Guests with serious health, drug, or alcohol problems are not accepted.

SUMMARY

Everywhere you turn on this old Hawaiian estate is lush, tropical foliage inspiring peace and relaxation. And everywhere you turn at the Plantation Spa is the Swedish mindset of health and fitness. The combination is truly delightful.

RANCHO LA PUERTA
The relaxing grounds at The Ranch in Texate

RANCHO LA PUERTA

In legendary times, Native Americans found magical healing on the flanks of Baja California's Mount Cuchuma — a mountain they called "the exalted high place." Since 1940, that mystical mountain has watched over Rancho La Puerta, a health camp turned sophisticated spa.

To me, the exalted high place reminds me of a summer camp where I sweat it out with the other happy campers who want their bodies to look fit, trim, and beautiful. After a week at this place, one of these happy campers even told me that they felt like a kid again — walking taller, feeling fitter, acting better.

The 150-acre Rancho La Puerta, set in the Sierra Madre mountains 40 miles southeast of San Diego, is a spa with a holistic approach. It meshes exercise and organic meals with stress-reducing activities like yoga and massages. An emphasis is also put on self-improvement and how to take home a healthy lifestyle.

There is no alcohol, no telephones in the rooms, no radio, no television at Rancho La Puerta. Smoking is frowned upon and banned from the spa buildings and dining room. But if you can live without these unhealthy vices, Rancho La Puerta has a 50-year track record of shaping up lives.

When I arrived, a courtesy van picked me up from the San Diego airport along with other spa guests and took us to the spa three miles south of the Mexican-American border. Once at the spa grounds, we were given free range of the six lighted tennis courts, six aerobic gyms, weight-training gym, four swimming pools, five whirlpool/jet therapy pools, three saunas, library, village store, volleyball court, men's and women's centers for Swedish massage and herbal wraps, and miles and miles of hiking trails.

THE LOOK OF THINGS

The Ranch furnishes flashlights so we could find our way at night to our individual rancheros, haciendas, or villas scattered on the grounds. Interconnected by brick sidewalks, Rancho La

Puerta can give the impression of a big Boy Scout camp. But unlike a Boy Scout camp, accommodations are much more luxurious than a tent.

Rancheros sport a studio bedroom and a bath while haciendas include a living room, fireplace, bath, and one or two bedrooms. The higher-priced villas offer a private pool, hot tub, sauna, kitchen, and dining areas. The villas offer more privacy and better views, but their distance from most of the activities also means more exercise whether you feel like it or not.

All the accommodations are decorated in a Mexican/Colonial style, emphasizing native arts and crafts and a seemingly boundless use of painted Mexican tiles.

But we didn't have much time to lounge in our haciendas. A full schedule of daily activities and evening lectures kept us busy, while facials, massages, herbal wraps, manicures and pedicures provided our pampering.

What I enjoyed the most was the peaceful atmosphere that prevails throughout the Ranch. I took the opportunity to take hikes around the beautiful grounds and soak up the serenity. Geographically, Rancho La Puerta has a great location and a lot to offer. Take the time to relax, because you can get caught up in the multiple activities offered every hour of the day.

I learned that Rancho La Puerta doesn't allow people to visit who have serious health problems or who are over 35 percent overweight (I made that cut-off). I can see why, with the myriad of activities to keep up with no one can be slow to the punch. Over 50 percent of the guests lose three pounds or more during the minimum week-long stay and 60 percent make return visits to Rancho La Puerta. It seems they discovered the secret of Mount Cuchuma, and so did I.

WHAT'S INCLUDED IN THE PRICE

When 17-year-old Deborah Szekely and her husband, Edmond, opened Rancho La Puerta in 1940 as the first fitness resort in North America, a tent was not included in the $17.50 weekly price.

Fifty years later, the Szekely family still operates Rancho La Puerta but its moderate price covers nearly everything, including accommodations.

Besides myself, I was assured that only 149 others would be at this sprawling ranch during the same week. Prices include three all-natural vegetarian meals a day, 40 different exercise, water, yoga, Tai Chi and other classes, evening lectures, films and games, supervised mountain and meadow hikes, and use of all spa facilities.

Treatments such as pedicures, manicures, facials, massages, and herbal wraps are not included in the price but are offered at very reasonable rates.

A deposit is required with a reservation and the full sum is due 30 days before arrival. Visa and Mactercard are accepted. There are minimal cancellation fees for two weeks notice and a substantial penalty for less than two weeks notice, barring a medical emergency. Guests must stay a minimum of one week, although some lesser stays may be arranged depending on space. Children under 6 are free, while those ages 7-14 have a reduced price. However, no babysitting is available.

All guests will need either a birth certificate, naturalization papers, valid passport or certificate of voter's registration for Mexican immigration.

CLOTHING AND WEATHER

There is an average of 340 sunny days a year at Rancho La Puerta, but a guest must also be prepared for a little rain in case he or she happens to visit on one of those 25 days of cloudy weather. Fortunately, none of those 25 days fell on the days I was at Rancho La Puerta, just a little morning drizzle one day.

At an elevation of 1,800 feet, Rancho La Puerta, like most of Baja California, has no sharply defined seasons. A dry climate prevails most of the year, neither too hot nor too cold. Because of this, many exercise classes are held outdoors year-round.

Bring exercise clothes—a jogging outfit, leotards, tights, shorts, t-shirts, and a bathing suit. Besides aerobic shoes (or the basic tennis shoes), bring a pair of shoes for hiking since it is a vital part of scenic Rancho La Puerta. Don't forget a supply of good exercise socks.

Because Rancho La Puerta is spread out, I learned that a gym bag or tote bag is a good idea (otherwise you may be carrying around a plastic bag with all your belongings in full view). At the beginning of the day, fill it with whatever you think might be necessary for that day's classes, massages, saunas, etc. It will save you many trips running back and forth from the spa buildings to your room. Zippered pockets on your jogging suit are also a good idea for keeping keys safe.

Casual clothes, even jogging outfits, are appropriate for dinner and evening activities.

A TYPICAL DAY

On Saturday evening, the day I arrived, the Rancho La Puerta staff outlined the various activities available and explained the Ranch's "Start-Up Spa Program" for those who have never attended a fitness spa or taken an aerobic exercise class.

For those with a little more exercise in their background, a list of the week's activity choices are given to you to pick from. All should make massage and beauty treatment appointments on this first day since the prime treatment times can fill up.

Early each morning, yoga is offered as an eye-opener and then dawn hikes are taken. These range from a three-or-four mile mountain hike up steep terrain to the gentle, two-mile meadow hike I enjoyed, as well as an advanced hike, breakfast hike, and meditation hike.

Breakfast is served between 7:30 and 9 a.m. and morning classes begin at 9, although a stretch and wake-up exercise class is offered earlier.

There are five or six different activites each hour and freedom of choice is an essential part of Rancho La Puerta. There is a selection of classes throughout the day geared especially for and limited only to men.

Morning classes (for everyone) include Body Awareness, Aerobics, Body Toning, Body Contour, Women's Aerobic Circuit, Waterworks, and the vigorous, painful, miserable, excruciating, but oh so good for you, Absolutely Abdominals. These exercises concentrating on the stomach muscles were the bane of my existence at this spa.

A yoga workshop, as well as morning and afternoon classes of yoga, focuses on the Hindu art of relaxation, breathing, and meditation.

Lunch, served buffet-style, is held from 12:30-2 p.m.

Afternoon classes, also held on the hour, include Bottom Line (for those muscle groups below the waist — hips, thighs and buttocks), All That Jazz dance class, Advanced Weight Training, Dumbbells, Back Care Workshop, Absolutely Abdominals, Aerobics and Stretch and Relax.

Hikes held in the afternoon include leisurely, short walks to a picnic site, a nature trail, the nearby river, or the Ranch's organic garden.

But not all of Rancho La Puerta is exercise, exercise, exercise. Mid-day lectures on nutrition, better breathing, and heart rates will teach you how to live the healthy life once you get home. A crafts class, such as Painting on Silk, is taught.

A warning: Don't completely fill your day with scheduled classes and lectures, take time out for massages, facials, herbal wraps, saunas, hot tubs, and other pampering. Take advantage of the $100,000 worth of new equipment in the weight-training gym or one of the four swimming pools and six tennis courts.

Rancho La Puerta recommends that a guest make time each day for cardiovascular workouts, strengthening and toning workouts, stretch and flexibility classes, coordination and balance sports such as dancing, tennis or volleyball, relaxation, lectures and, of course, self-rewards like facials, scalp treatments, and herbal wraps.

EVENING PROGRAMS

Evenings can be spent quietly reading, conversing, or catching up on the latest movies on video. But they can also be a time of learning, self-improvement and entertainment through the wide variety of guest speakers the Ranch offers each week. I really enjoyed speakers Lila Green and Cathy Sunshine who made a stop at the Ranch the week I visited.

Lila, who believes "laughter is the shortest distance between people," takes a light-hearted look at humor in everyday life. She is a humor consultant as well as a specialist in gerontology and she also gives a presentation on the British Royal Family. After all, Lila is a founding member of the Royal Society of Michigan and has been to tea at Buckingham Palace.

Cathy gave two lectures on managing change, making decisions, and balancing our lives, careers, relationships, and ourselves.

Other evening programs include crafts classes, such as the one on how to make folk art prayer arrows, and hilarious bingo games. During one of these rollicking bingo games, which are very funny and fun to play, I won a nice Mexican blanket.

THE STAFF

The ratio of staff to guest is about two-to-one at Rancho La Puerta, if all the staff from kitchen workers to physical fitness instructors are included.

Most of the fitness instructors are young, energetic Americans, many of whom have previously worked at fitness centers or obtained college degrees. The massage therapists are all Mexicans, a requirement by the Mexican government. And all of them are experienced and know the body's muscle structure and exactly what it's connected to from "the ankle bone connected to the shin bone connected to the knee bone...." Additionally, there is a staff of manicurists, pedicurists, hair stylists, facialists, and herbal wrap therapists.

Tipping is not included in the overall price and is expected. The Ranch hands out a sheet giving advice on the average range of tips for luggage carriers, maids, and kitchen and dining room staff.

Reservations may be made by calling (619) 744-4222 or (800) 443-7565 or by writing Rancho La Puerta, Inc., Post Office Box 2548, Escondido, Calif. 92025. The ranch's FAX number is (619) 744-5007.

FOOD

Can anyone be satisfied on a 1,000 calorie a day diet? What's more, it's a diet low in salt, preservatives (that means no diet sodas), cholesterol, and refined sugar.

High in energy, fiber, and complex carbohydrates, it's a diet that is primarily lacto-ovovegetarian.

It sounds scary and really unappetizing, but the Ranch's meals are truly delicious. But just to remind guests they are at a health spa, each item is marked with its caloric content. The staff urges guests to stick to only 1,000 calories a day, but we could have more if we wished. Breakfast and lunch are served buffet style, so you can have a choice of what and how much you take.

The Ranch frowns on anything artificial, so I would recommend bringing your own sugar substitute if you can't live without it. For sweetener at the Ranch, a little bit of honey is used.

A typical dinner was vegetable soup (60 calories), salad with cilantro dressing (40 calories), chile relleno (310 calories) and a cinnamon dessert (100 calories). Breakfasts forego bacon and eggs for healthier foods such as whole wheat breads, cottage cheese, fruit, and juices. Yes, butter is offered, but it is marked at 60 calories for only one pat.

Much of the vegetables, herbs, and fruit are organically grown at the Ranch. This includes 89 fruit trees, an apple orchard with 31 varieties, raspberries, strawberries, blackberries, boysenberries, many different melons, 40 kinds of lettuce, 40 kinds of tomatoes, 15 different winter squashes, 20-25 types of peppers, and 40 different herbs. For table accents, there are 120 varieties of cut flowers.

Besides feeding guests healthier food, the Ranch staff also tries to teach us how to eat healthier at home. A few tips: eat more fish and chicken, drink alcohol in moderation, serve whole grain foods for breakfast, look for baked or broiled items on restaurant menus, eat earlier in the evening, use less salt, substitute olive oil for other oils in salad dressings and cooking, and train those taste buds to like healthier foods.

SUMMARY

Luxurious, but oh so simple, Rancho La Puerta thrilled me with its lack of television, radios, and phones. Without these time-wasters, you have hours in the day to fill with hikes, exercise, good food...something to keep in mind once you return to "civilization."

VISTA CLARA SPA
A place to hear your thoughts

VISTA CLARA SPA

The chef at Vista Clara asked, partly to himself and partly to me, "How do I get the blue sky onto a plate?"

Anywhere else this might be considered an unusual question, but at Vista Clara the question seems perfectly natural.

Here, in this New Mexico spa, it is the ancient but ageless land that serves as the inspiration for everything from its cuisine to its philosophy.

At every step, a Vista Clara guest encounters the high desert landscape – the mystery left behind in Native American artifacts, pueblos and ruins, the changing dance of hue and light the sun performs each clear day. And it is this way on purpose.

In 1986, Chris and Carmen Partridge left their hectic lives in New York City for a vacation and decided life was worth a permanent reprieve from humankind's hustle and bustle. So they started Vista Clara (which means clear vision) on 80 acres south of Santa Fe, New Mexico.

Chris Partridge convincingly says that the surrounding area is what makes this spa different from the rest. It has its own magic, which makes Vista Clara a place you can really accomplish rejuvenation, he says. And, it happens very naturally.

I found myself wholeheartedly agreeing with a line in one of Vista Clara's brochures: "We found we could hear our thoughts far more clearly than before."

It is because of this stillness and relaxed ambiance that the chef can carefully consider how to mimic the desert colors including the sky – in his presentation of spa cuisine. For his art is cooking, and his goal is to present his preparations as if the plate were a canvas.

He is not the only one with a careful attention to detail and presentation; it is seen in the rest of the spa as well.

Vista Clara is a luxurious spa with a laid-back air about it. Its staff is attentive and professional, but they let the desert landscape here do the work of relaxation and rest.

With only 14 guests each week, averaging in age from 35 to 70, there is plenty of individualized attention at Vista Clara.

The Partridges are striving for excellence in this spa and want to concentrate not only on the mind and body but the spirit too. In a changing world, a traditional vacation is not always the answer when a person needs a "quick fix" of rejuvenation. but a spa is a vacation in a place like Vista Clara — a true rejuvenation. Here people can get back in touch with who they are...and get rid of stress.

Vista Clara, a relatively new spa, wants to keep this philosophy, even as its popularity pressures it to expand.

"We want to keep it small and overall it must remain a spa because the vehicle to accomplish rejuvention is the spa. We simply provide the environment; the guests make their own discoveries."

THE LOOK OF THINGS

Twenty-two miles from Santa Fe, New Mexico, Vista Clara is situated on a remote valley floor at the foot of the Sangre de Cristo Mountains. Canyons, mesas, even 1,000-year-old Native American petroglyphs can be explored here.

The spa itself emulates the traditional southwest adobes and utilizes Native American motifs in its buildings and its accommodations.

The guest hacienda has 10 suites with wood floors and ceilings, southwestern furniture, Persian rugs, and original art. They are luxurious rooms. Each suite has a sitting area, private bath, and patio. There are no televisions. Family and associates are advised not to bother a guest.

Each room opens out on the pool area and colonnade courtyard. This "Courtyard of the Deities" is used for special lectures and informal gatherings.

By the tiled swimming pool is a hot tub located especially so it overlooks the setting sun.

The Great Kiva is a focal point for many activities. In Native American cultures, the circular space was used for ceremonies, but at Vista Clara the kiva serves as the physical and aerobic conditioning complex, i.e. the gym.

Also on the grounds is a therapy center with four body treatment rooms, steam and sauna rooms; a Native American sweat lodge is within walking distance of the therapy center. For extra ambiance, teepees are set up at various locations on the grounds.

HOW TO GET THERE

A shuttle picks up all Vista Clara guests from the Albuquerque Airport at no charge. Vista Clara's shuttle will also take guests back to the airport for their trip home.

If you are driving, take Interstate 25 to Exit 290, get on Route 285 from Exit 290, drive to the Route 41 turn-off, take Route 41 to Vista Clara. It's about an hour-and-a-half drive from Albuquerque.

Guests should arrive between 1 p.m. and 4 p.m on Saturday and depart by 11 a.m. the following Saturday.

For reservations, call toll-free, (800)-247-0301; in New Mexico call (505) 988-8865 or write Vista Clara Health Retreat and Spa, at Box 111, Galisteo, NM, 87540.

SURROUNDING AREA

This is an area where many people take their vacations — summer and winter. Santa Fe is well known as a southwestern community for lovers of art and culture, as well as recreation.

Surrounded by two sets of mountains and bisected by the Rio Grande river, Santa Fe County ranges in elevation from 5,000 to 12,500 feet.

I spent one morning in Santa Fe. It's a different kind of city, very southwestern, with an emphasis on Native American culture. A plaza is at the heart of the town, and a church, just a block off the store-lined plaza, is the gathering point for locals and tourists alike. It is touristy as far as numbers of tourists go, but not filled with tons of souvenir shops.

Another side trip I did while staying at Vista Clara was to Galisteo, population 200. I went on a gallery tour of this artist community with Spanish origins.

Galisteo is only about one mile away from the spa, and Taos, known for its great downhill skiing and its Pueblo is two hours away from Santa Fe.

Also, out in the country of northern New Mexico are Native American cave and cliff dwellings, pueblos, Spanish missions and churches. Just one example is the Puye Cliffs, an abandoned 2000-room Anasazi village built between 1400 and 1450 AD.

Closer to Vista Clara, we took a hike to Native American ruins in the nearby Pecos Wilderness Area.

There's plenty to do in northern New Mexico; just check with the Santa Fe Visitors and Convention Bureau at (800) 777-CITY, and they'll send you a visitors guide of the area's sightseeing.

WHAT'S INCLUDED IN THE PRICE

Vista Clara has seven-day or three-day packages.

This is a moderately expensive resort, but a week-long package here includes everything: meals, accommodations, a personalized program of private exercise consulting and daily treatments, clothing (robes, towels, etc.), day trips to Santa Fe Plaza and pueblo ruins, and ground transportation.

These things are also included in the three-day packages which are held Sunday to Wednesday or Wednesday to Saturday.

Gratuities and taxes are not included in the package price.

A reservation is confirmed with a $1,000 deposit that can be applied to another week if you cancel 30 days in advance. A fee will be charged for missed individual spa appointments.

Vista Clara accepts traveler's checks, Visa, and Mastercard but doesn't accept personal checks.

Check-out is noon or a guest will be billed for an additional day.

CLOTHING AND WEATHER

Guests need only to bring an overnight bag with personal belongings. Shorts, T-shirts, robes, and sweatshirts are handed out at the spa.

But in your belongings you should include personal toiletries, sunscreen, lip protection, sunglasses, sun visor or hat, bathing suit, leotards, tights, workout socks, 3-5 pairs of hiking socks, good hiking or running shoes, aerobic shoes, and casual wear for evenings.

For fall and winter, bring coats, sweaters--in summer, extra T-shirts, and shorts.

Safety deposit boxes are provided, and the spa staff advises its guests not to wear valuables in the fitness and therapy areas.

This region of New Mexico enjoys 300 days of sunshine a year with moderate seasons. The elevation is high at 6,100 feet resulting in a dry, clear climate.

A TYPICAL DAY

The days are varied at Vista Clara and any kind of schedule will be interrupted by trips to Santa Fe, Galisteo, pueblo ruins, and other sightseeing.

When at the spa, the guests are given a personalized "active program" and a "passive program." The active program is hiking, workouts in the pool, low impact aerobics, Native American dancing, and other fitness classes and activities. The passive program leans toward facials, aroma wraps, body mudpacks, aromatherapy, yoga, Tai Chi, and a daily massage.

Anything could be scheduled, including aerobics, body sculpture, aqua aerobics, stretch and relax, Arroyo Fit (a cross-training fitness class), bench step, Clear Balance, Tai Chi.

The same goes for the body treatments, usually done in the therapy center. Guests have a choice of full body massage, body polish (a gentle process using an oatmeal, honey, and almond meal mixture to exfoliate, hydrate, and soften the skin), clay body mask (full body mask with earthen minerals and oils to aid the body in elmination of impurities and to stimulate circulation), European facial, deluxe facial with hand and foot treatment (even includes a rosemary leg massage), paraffin hand treatment or foot treatment.

Something different about this spa is its use of the native culture and land. Native American arts are part of the program here, too: you might find yourself being taught about the medicine wheel, drumming, dancing, or how to spend time in the sweat lodge.

Another day might mean a trip to Santa Fe for lunch, a walk, a body sculpture, or more free time. Additionally, hiking here is encouraged with or without a guide. Over the spa's 80 acres of land are several marked hiking trails leading to magnificent vistas, rugged terrain, high desert flora, and ancient petroglyphs. These hikes range from 25-40 minutes on average. More hikes in the Santa Fe National Forest and the Pecos Wilderness area can be arranged for those who want additional challenges.

In the future, the spa owners have plans to incorporate more activities such as cross country skiing and archery into its program.

But most of all, Vista Clara wants its guests to take some time out to listen to their own thoughts and rejuvenate.

EVENING PROGRAMS

With only 14 guests, Vista Clara fashions its evening programs after the desires of each week's participants. Having access to a wide variety of experts and specialists, Vista Clara will call on whomever the guests want to hear.

One of the favorite lecturers is a mountain man. The area's culture and history are also popular topics. A cooking class is held once a week as well as a slide show about Santa Fe set to classical music.

Having the flexibility to meet the interests of only 14 guests has resulted in the use of a wide variety of lecturers including psychics, dream therapists, Native American storytellers, futurists, local historians, and nutritionists.

THE STAFF

Vista Clara's staff is young, accommodating, and knowledge-able — it's easy to believe owners Chris and Carmen Partridge when they say the staff consists of the best people they can find.

FOOD

This is the best spa food I have tried. I don't know if it's the southwestern flair, the chef's incredible presentations, or the natural ingredients gathered from nearby farms and orchards.

Balanced nutritionally, the cuisine ranged in calories from 1200 to 1500 a day.

Just picking out a day, say Thursday, we had blintzes, lowfat cottage cheese or yogurt, and fresh fruit for breakfast; a fiesta salad or grilled vegetables and salad for lunch; and canneloni, mixed greens and strawberry margarita sorbet for dinner.

Weight loss isn't the intention of this spa diet. Natural and nutritional eating is the aim. Most of the vegetables, herbs, and fruits are organically grown in Vista Clara's own gardens and orchards, but then the chef will scour the countryside for the extra touches when they come into season, such as raspberries while I was staying at the spa.

Graham, the chef, likes to blend the indigenous ingredients like pecans, pinyon nuts, apricots, crawfish, and raspberries, and of course, chilies. He swears there are different types of chile crops, although a chile's hotness depends on its age and thickness. The older and thinner a chile, the hotter it is in your mouth.

After looking for the best ingredients, Graham then dreams up a recipe and a way to present the food on the plate. He'll look at a piece of Native American art and then try to copy it on the plate using spa cuisine, but he hasn't found an ingredient that could emulate the blue New Mexico sky. You can watch this creative chef at work anytime at Vista Clara. The open kitchen policy was set so guests could walk in and learn how to cook healthy food from Graham.

Neither smoking nor alcohol is allowed indoors at Vista Clara. If a person must smoke, he or she can find ashtrays outside.

SUMMARY

This truly is an enchanting place in the Land of Enchantment. The land of New Mexico does seem to have some sort of magic to it. Additionally, the low-calorie food here is the very best of all the spas that I visited for this book, and its presentation is art. The chef sees a picture in his head and puts it on a plate.

NATIONAL INSTITUTE OF FITNESS
The domed housing makes NIF unique

THE NATIONAL INSTITUTE OF FITNESS

The National Institute of Fitness in southwestern Utah is a true fitness vacation.

Its brochures advertise that with enough time people can lose up to 100 pounds here with the Institute's all-time record being a loss of 130 pounds. But it is also a vacation for fit or slightly overweight people with a schedule brimming with a vast array of classes for all three fitness catagories.

However, a person doesn't have to diet or starve or get too crazy to take off the weight. He or she just has to exercise.

Dr. Marc Sorenson founded the National Institute of Fitness in 1974, running it through hotels in such places as Phoenix, Park City, Utah, and Hawaii. In 1983, he and his wife, Vicki Sorenson, who directs the program, settled the Institute into a permanent home in Utah. Since then, their business has been increasing as fast as guests' weight has been decreasing.

Dr. Marc & Vicki Sorenson have published a popular book on weight loss called "Eat More, Move More and Lose More." This is really a serious weight loss/fitness center. Don't expect to be pampered, but do expect a staff to care about you and encourage you to better your fitness level and lose weight.

Many spas won't take overweight guests because of the medical risks involved. National Institute of Fitness will take overweight guests, and it is one of the few places that allows long-term stays. Many will stay for six months; one woman stayed a year.

The average stay is about four weeks, during which women lose around 12-25 pounds and men lose about 25-35 pounds. The average age of the guests is between 35 and 45, but you'll see guests anywhere from 30 to over 60 here.

Weight loss is the ultimate goal for most guests, but the spa focuses on fitness. Sorenson says that weight loss is a by-product of exercising and eating healthy. The body will take care of the weight loss if you're living right.

NIF has often been called the "walking resort" because the foundation of its exercise program is walking. Group walks are held every morning in Snow Canyon — a mysterious canyon of red sandstone walls, ancient lava flows, and remnants of Native American habitation.

Walking Club awards are handed out to those who reach milestones of 40 miles, 100 miles, 250 miles, and up to 2,000 miles. T-shirts, gym bags, sweatsuits and even walking shoes are presented as prizes. Besides putting in walking miles, the only stipulations are that you attend lectures and listen to the many postive action tapes at NIF.

NIF doesn't want to just have people lose weight during their stays; it also wants to educate its guests to form lifelong habits.

It is definitely an upbeat spa that is extremely clean, extremely tidy, and extremely organized.

Its worth is measured by the fact that physicians often refer their patients to National Institute of Fitness as well as attend themselves. Once an overweight person has tried and failed with crash diets and other zany food and exercise programs, the National Institute of Fitness can set him or her on a sensible path to weight loss and fitness.

THE LOOK OF THINGS

Snow Canyon, once a spiritual site for Utah's native Indians, is the centerpiece of this spa. The buildings, tennis courts, lodging, and swimming pool are located at the entrance to the canyon, but the heart of this spa's program is in the canyon itself. As a "walking resort," NIF plans most of the daily hikes to lead into its red-walled canyon.

It is a geological wonder, with red sandstone rocks scattered around ancient lava flows. There are more than 20 walks to various areas whose names provide descriptions: Indian Caves, Johnson's Arch, Indian Petroglyphs, Little Zion, Three Ponds, Santa Clara River, Lava Caves. The walks range in length from 1 mile to 21.1 miles, depending on the guests' fitness levels.

On one of my walks through the canyon, surrounded by mesas and red rock, it seemed as if the picturesque canyon was sculpted instead of formed by nature's forces of wind and water, or as if an architect took his hand to the canyon and designed it just so.

The canyon is made from prehistoric geological impacts, but the spa itself at the mouth of the canyon looks like a futuristic camp on Mars.

Most of the buildings resemble white spaceship domes with large windows opening out on the canyon and the desert. Situated on four of NIF's seven acres, the resort's complex includes an arrival building, lodging, an indoor heated swimming pool, an aerobics room/gymnasium, and a dining room and kitchen.

There are rooms for beauty salon services and makeovers as well as a workout room that houses free weights, a Nautilus-type system, exercise bicycles, cross country climbers, and Stairmasters. Men's and women's locker rooms, a first aid station, a laundry room, and a whirlpool also add to the complex. There are racquetball and tennis courts here too with free group lessons.

In the future, NIF plans to build a massive, five-story dome that will hold many of these facilities, freeing some of the older domes for much-needed lodging.

The spa has a shortage of private rooms but can accommodate a maximum of 115 guests through semi-private rooms that are either doubles or triples. The rooms are motel-like in appearance, nice but not luxurious. The resort is almost always filled to capacity.

I was impressed with the cleanliness here.

HOW TO GET THERE

The National Institute of Fitness is located in Utah's Color Canyon Country, an area of scenic wonders but also quite remote.

NIF is 300 miles from Salt Lake City and 120 miles north of Las Vegas, NV. St. George, UT is the nearest town.

There is airline service to St. George through Skywest Airlines, and airport pickup and return is included in the price of a stay at NIF.

If you drive, take Interstate 15 to St. George and exit on Bluff Street. Follow Bluff Street 12 miles north, enter Snow Canyon State Park and drive almost five miles to NIF.

For reservations call (801) 628-3317, (801) 628-4338 or (801) 673-4905 or write NIF at 202 North Snow Canyon Rd., P.O. Box 938, Ivins, UT 84738. The FAX number here is (801) 673-1363.

A non-refundable deposit of $100 is due with the reservation application, and the balance is due two weeks before arrival. Make reservations; The National Institute of Fitness is nearly always filled to capacity.

Transportation to the airport or bus depot for departing guests is available on Sundays only. Other arrangements can be made through the local taxi service.

SURROUNDING AREA

The southwest corner of Utah, where NIF is located, is called the state's Color Canyon Country. Dotted throughout the area are sheer canyon walls of red sandstone. In the canyon's depth is a geological history of lavas and seas, and a human history of Native Americans.

This is desert country, and that means mesas of interesting cacti, nights of starry skies, and a thermometer that gives its mercury exercise going up in the day and down at night.

Elevation is 2,800 feet at St. George, the small town nearest to NIF. On Sundays, many of the guests take the opportunity to explore the other canyons nearby, including the biggest canyon of them all, the Grand Canyon in Arizona.

Scenic American Tours will take NIF guests on a discount group rate to the north rim of the Grand Canyon for a full day of sightseeing. Other trips go to Pine Valley.

NIF also rents bicycles for those who want to combine sightseeing with exercise.

WHAT'S INCLUDED IN THE PRICE

This is one of the best deals for a fitness vacation in the United States. It is definitely a bargain spa. Don't look for chocolate-dipped strawberries at this no-nonsense spa but for the best value your money can buy.

I would term NIF inexpensive. The price includes three meals a day; all classes in exercise, nutrition, weight control, dance, and others; lodging with maid service; and use of all recreational facilities.

Plan on spending extra for Swedish massages, European facials, manicures, pedicures, hair styling, image consulting, private weight training, private tennis lessons, and use of the tanning bed. Those services must be paid for at the time they are given.

A guest may want to bring extra money for side trips, movies, horseback riding, and other entertainment outside the spa.

A $100 room and telephone deposit must be paid on arrival but is refundable when all bills have been paid at the end of the stay.

CLOTHING AND WEATHER

Southwest Utah is a desert climate with warm summers and mild winters. It accommodates all-year recreation and leisure activities.

The desert setting will bring a contrast of temperatures: very warm in the daytime but often downright cold at night. Bring a sweater or warmer sweatsuits for those chilly mornings, and lightweight jogging outfits, t-shirts, and shorts for working out mid-day. Swimming is a popular sport here, so bring a couple of swimsuits.

Dress is extremely casual. There is no need to wear anything fancier than shorts and a shirt to dinner although the last night of your stay is a "graduation" night and you might want to bring something casual-dressy for this event.

The only toiletry that is provided by NIF is soap, so don't forget your hair dryer, shampoo, toothpaste, and other toiletries.

A TYPICAL DAY

When I arrived at NIF, after the usual tours and familiarization lectures, I was given a fitness test that analyzed my body composition, weight, blood pressure, flexibility, and strength. From that I was put into the B fitness level, and all my activities for the week would come out of the B schedule. There are three fitness levels and the staff will graduate a person to a new level as fitness improves.

Walking is all-important at NIF and each morning begins with a hike. The A group takes a 1-3 mile hike at 6:10 a.m.; the B group a 4-6 mile hike at 6 a.m.; and the C group a 7-10 mile hike at 5:50 a.m.

I walked an average of six miles a day during my stay at NIF. We were encouraged to take walks on our own, too, while listening to positive action tapes on Walkman cassette tape players. Guests are asked to bring their own Walkmans, but the spa has tape players to lend out.

After the walks are aerobic, swimnastics, and weight training classes for each level until lunch is served.

Afternoons are devoted to more classes, ranging from race walking to aquadynamics to body conditioning.

Everybody halts their day at 2:30 p.m. for a lecture by Dr. Fit himself (Sorenson) or Dr. Ralph Ofcarcik, a nutrition specialist. A couple of the lectures while I was there were "The Effects of three Dietary Sacred Cows (Caffeine, Alcohol, Diet Sweetners)" and "The Effects of Diet and Exercise on Cardiovascular Disease." The two-week cycle of lectures mainly focus on fat control, nutrition, and fitness.

Exercise classes are again scheduled after the lecture until dinner, when things settle down for the evening program and bedtime.

NIF stresses that guests will have to work up to a constant exercise schedule as well as more mileage on the walks. I didn't feel pressured to attend all the classes, and I enjoyed picking and choosing which ones I wanted to participate in. But one warning when you pick and choose—participation is the key to losing weight.

EVENING PROGRAMS

Each evening, the guests are treated to a lecture-type program or entertainment, and a slow-stretch class is given afterward to prepare those tired muscles for bed.

I loved the cooking demonstration. The chef is not only a cook, but a comedian, and we laughed a lot while we learned. She used the oddest ingredients to make something healthy.

We also had a guest talent show one night and movies another night. The movie selection is basically PG. Another option some nights is a Snow Canyon slide show by a local naturalist.

THE STAFF

This staff really cares. Other places may say they do and admonish their staffs to put up that pretense, but I felt the staff at NIF truly was concerned about what was happening with me. It is one of the few places that I've felt this.

The director of NIF says she hires employees who are generally interested in the wellness of the guests first. She looks for people who are honest and good and then trains them if they need to be. As a result, she has built up a staff through the years that plans to stick around. That is a plus for the high repeat business, those who like to recognize a familiar face when they return to NIF.

It is a young staff of 70 people and highly organized. Everybody knows their jobs and they do them cheerfully. I got the feeling that if anybody was rude or disrespectful to a guest that that employee would be shown the door.

Sorenson is an exercise physiologist, and there are nurses and emergency medical technicians on staff as well as a nutritionist who holds a doctorate in food technology.

FOOD

The chefs at NIF subscribe to the five commandments for healthy eating: Don't eat fats or oils; Don't eat sugar; Don't eat salt; Don't eat cholesterol; Don't drink coffee or tea.

Despite all those Don'ts, NIF manages to produce pretty good meals. They are high in complex carbohydrates and vegetarian in nature. An example of a day's fare might be wheat pancakes with berry topping, yogurt, and cantalope for breakfast; tostadas and fruit for lunch; turkey burgers on pita bread, potato salad, and banana cake for dinner.

The three meals are low-fat but ample enough to make you feel full after dinner. NIF stresses that to lose weight, a guest must only eat what is offered. If a hunger pang just can't be tolerated, the kitchen will give you a bowl of rice or potatos to help you last until dinner.

SUMMARY

When you leave the doors of NIF, they are never closed. NIF wants everyone to take the ideas of aerobic fitness and healthy eating home with them so their weight loss can continue. And NIF encourages its guests to return to its program in southwest Utah whenever the need arises. Seventy percent of its business is repeat and referral – a lot of NIF graduates do return.

RESORT SPAS

Resort spas are flourishing in the West; it's a good time to take advantage of their good deals.

At a resort spa, as opposed to a destination spa, the spa is just a part of the amenities. You will often be able to choose spa activities a la carte — an exercise class here, a massage there, a facial after lunch. In this kind of setup, you can arrange your free time to suit yourself, whether it be lounging by the pool with a good book, shopping in a nearby town, or adding more exercise and therapy to your program. Resort spas are so well managed and fully outfitted that you'll feel as if spa-ing is your whole purpose for being there.

At resort spas, you'll be mixing with regular tourists, people who aren't in spa mode. This means you'll sometimes be obliged to wear street clothes to dinner rather than casual spa attire of sweats, leotards, swim suits, and jogging shorts. At many resorts, spa cuisine is limited to a few starred items on a regular menu.

One of the real assets of resort spas is their flexibility — if you're in town for a weekend, you can do a Sunday of spa-ing after a Saturday of meetings with the CEO. And a day at a spa is a lovely present to give yourself. With our extraordinarily busy lives, often all the time off we have for months on end is a weekend. Perfect for a little spa-ing. On the West Coast, within a few hours of your home is a spa that will take you in for a weekend, massage you, exercise you, feed you the right things and send you home ready to face another Monday.

CAMELBACK INN RESORT, GOLF CLUB & SPA

Of all the hotel/resorts that try to be destination spas, only Marriott's Camelback Inn Resort, Golf Club and Spa has all the right ingredients.

One of the granddaddys of Phoenix's many resorts, Camelback Inn added a spa in 1989, wanting to cash in on the fitness craze. But Camelback went the extra mile when it designed its spa program, unlike some resort spas that don't offer much more than a lap pool, beauty salon, and massage therapy.

The Spa at Camelback Inn has personal fitness programs, testing for body analysis, and nutrition counseling, plus massage, skin, and body treatments. And most of all, nearly all of its restaurants serve Spa cuisine. Even the gourmet restaurant, winner of numerous awards, hands out a Spa menu with its traditional menu. To me, this is an indication of Camelback Inn really trying to be a destination spa.

The managers and chefs I spoke with were unanimous in their determination to make this a destination spa. They want a guest to be able to leave The Spa and go to the Navajo Room or the Chaparral Room or even order room service and have Spa food. It is their goal to have healthy cuisine on every menu. The entree presentations are also upscale, with some of The Spa food unrecognizable as "that healthy stuff."

The Spa was opened in February 1989 with a unique aspect. It affiliated itself with The Institute for Aerobic Research in Dallas, Texas. The Spa uses the Institute's aerobic and wellness testing programs that were pioneered by Dr. Kenneth H. Cooper, one of America's first proponents of aerobic exercise and the founder and president of The Institute for Aerobic Research.

After testing clients with the Cooper method, you are provided with plenty of exercise and pampering. There are various fitness classes all day long and six different massage techniques: Swedish, Shiatsu, Sports, Aromatherapy, Reflexology, Thalasso Hydrotherapy.

The Spa also has its own restaurant, called Sprouts, for healthy eating, and its own staff dietician. But you don't need to dine at The Spa restaurant to eat healthy at this resort. I even ordered Spa cuisine from room service! It was salmon, and it was very, very excellent.

Camelback plans to add new treatments and further expand its Spa menus to as much as 30 percent to 35 percent for some restaurants and 25 percent for others.

Its managers think they underestimated the acceptance of the facility and are busier than they expected. However, The Spa is laid out in such a way that there can be 100 guests at The Spa and you don't realize it. On busy days 250-300 people can be at The Spa and it will remain a relaxing environment. I even met Erma Bombeck one day and we discussed the title of this book!

It should be no surprise that the Camelback Inn would do a program the right way. The hotel portion of the resort has received the Mobil five-star award for 22 consecutive years and holds such other awards as the AAA five-diamond award, the Gold Key Award, and the Pinnacle Award.

The Camelback Inn originally opened December 15, 1936 in Scottsdale, Arizona with 75 rooms. Room rates were $10-$16 for a single or $18-$25 for a double deluxe. Marriott Corporation acquired it in 1969, expanded it, and poured more money into making the resort what it is today.

THE LOOK OF THINGS

Hacienda-inspired, The Spa fits into Camelback Inn's southwestern feel. At its entrance, a helpful concierge directs guests where they want to go. On either side of the concierge are the men's and women's quarters with lockers, showers, 105-degree hot and 75-degree cold plunge pools, indoor and outdoor massage rooms, relaxation rooms, saunas, and steam baths.

In the middle is Sprouts restaurant, overlooking the 25-meter lap pool, a coed Jacuzzi, and two tanning patios.

The 25,000-square-foot spa also sports a fitness and exercise center, Phoenix's famous With Love, B'Anne beauty salon, a spa boutique, and a complete Wellness Center. The Center provides fitness assessments, nutritional counseling, computerized body composition analysis, executive wellness, and physical testing.

The 125-acre resort is nestled in the foothills of Mummy Mountain with views of the desert and overlooking the famous Camelback Mountain.

Camelback Inn has a 36-hole championship golf course just minutes away as well as three outdoor swimming pools and 10 tennis courts, half of which are lighted. There are 423 pueblo-styled "casitas" rooms, 23 deluxe suites, and seven suites with private swimming pools.

The rooms all have private patios, kitchenettes, service bars, desks, sitting areas, remote control TV, make-up mirrors, hair dryers, and in-room safes.

The resort also offers eight restaurants and lounges including continental dining, poolside, spa, golf, buffet, and a dancing lounge.

HOW TO GET THERE

The Camelback Inn Resort, Golf Club & Spa is minutes from downtown Scottsdale and only 12 miles from Phoenix's Sky Harbor Airport in Paradise Valley. There is commercial shuttle service available from the airport to resort as well as airport limousine service.

If you are renting a car and driving from Sky Harbor Airport, take the exit to Hohokam Expressway (44th St.). Go north on 44th Street, turn left on Tatum Blvd. and right on Lincoln Drive. The Inn is on the left at the first light. Travel time is about 20 minutes.

To make reservations at the resort, call toll free (800)-24-CAMEL or write Camelback Inn Resort, Golf Club & Spa, 5402 East Lincoln Drive, Scottsdale, AZ 85253. The resort telephone number is (602) 948-1700 and its FAX number is (602) 951-8469.

SURROUNDING AREA

The Phoenix area offers more than recreational resorts. Want some culture? Try the symphony or one of the many plays that are shown periodically.

In Camelback's daily newsletter, the Innsider Tomorrow, the concierge suggested the Scottsdale Symphony Orchestra one night I was there and the Dirty Dozen Brass Band on another night.

There are also many educational features in Phoenix/Scottsdale. The Desert Botanical Garden was showing off its saguaros blooming with creamy white flowers, while the Heard Museum featured displays of Southwest Indian arts and crafts.

Shopping is close by in old Scottsdale. Recreational activities outside the resort include horseback riding, mountain climbing, hiking, jeep tours, and hot air ballooning.

Camelback has desert jeep adventures which leave the resort at 7 a.m. and 6:30 p.m., and air tours of the Grand Canyon can be arranged daily.

WHAT'S INCLUDED IN THE PRICE

This is an expensive spa to visit because of the room rates and the food prices, but if you visit in the summer you can find some bargains.

The summers are getting stronger and stronger every year, but Phoenix resorts seem to continue to cut back their rates drastically. For example, a basic guest room at Camelback might be $225-250 in January, but $85 in the summer. The Spa's five-day packages are truly a bargain in the summer.

There are several types of one-day memberships called things like "The Beautifier," "The Retreat," and "The Energizer." The day packages include various massages, facials, and treatments. Some include lunch; others include fitness assessments.

Five-day packages provide calorie-controlled breakfasts and lunches, exercise classes, massages, facials, and other treatments. There are three-day programs that include Spa lunches as well as the other treatments.

A daily Spa membership for facilities is very reasonable and it includes a Spa wardrobe, private locker, use of facilities, and exercise classes.

An 18 percent service charge and a 6.5 percent sales tax are added to the cost of all The Spa packages, programs, and treatments. If you cancel less than three hours before a treatment, you will be billed.

Fitness services such as Fitcheck, Computerized Body Composition, Nutrition Consultation, and Personal Fitness One on One are extra. All of the spa services can be bought a la carte.

Reserve packages by calling 72 hours in advance to (602) 948-1700 X7740.

CLOTHING AND WEATHER

Phoenix and Scottsdale are widely known for their sunny, dry climate. In the winter, the days are warm, but the nights cool down. In the summer, expect very hot weather, but the nights will still cool down somewhat.

Camelback Inn Resort, Golf Club & Spa is a fancy resort and you should bring clothes which reflect that.

The Spa provides guests with private lockers and a Spa wardrobe of shorts, t-shirts, leotards, warm-up pants, bathrobes, slippers, and a variety of Spa amenities.

A TYPICAL DAY

Like other resort spas, you choose your own schedule at The Spa at Camelback Inn. At this spa, though, you need to fit that schedule in between the opening hour of 6:30 a.m. and closing hour of 7 p.m.

My day began at 8 a.m. with a test called PALS — Personalized Aerobics Lifestyle System. It is part of the fitness program Camelback received from The Institute of Aerobic Fitness in Dallas.

My blood pressure was tested, as well as my heart rate, body fat percentage, strength, flexibility, and cardiovascular fitness measurements. Then I had to take a test about my lifestyle that looked like a SAT exam for high school seniors. You remember, the No. 2 lead pencil and the computer dots to fill in for answers.

This PALS, which only takes an hour, outlines a person's current physiological status as it relates to wellness, fitness, exercise activity, nutrition, and personal well-being. The results are bound and sent to you, giving you a "blueprint" for adjustments you need to make.

I saw a nutritionst at 9 a.m. who told me to keep a three-day record of my diet and exercise for analysis and then at 12:15 p.m. I slid into a thalasso hydrotherapy tub. This is an underwater massage where pressured jet hoses pummel your body in a custom-designed tub.

A bindi hot oil treatment was in store for me at 2 p.m. This Ayurvedic treatment is an ancient way to restore vitality and youthfulness. If that wasn't enough to "restore" my body, at 3:15 p.m. I had an aromatherapy facial. The estheticians used natural essential oils and liposomes to rejuvenate my skin. My ego was rejuvenated after the shampoo and blow dry, pedicure and make-up application at the With Love, B'Anne Salon.

That was my day, but you can make yours whatever you want. Other treatments are the aloe body mask and seaweed body mask, several massage therapies, body treatments and skin care treatments.

Notice I didn't exercise. I chose to be pampered, but exercise classes are included in the daily guest fee and there are many to choose from. They are largely self-descriptive: Saguaro Stretch, Fat Burner Aerobics, Advanced Aerobics, Yoga, Body Sculpture, Water Aerobics, Sunrise Scenic Walk, Power walking, and Dance Aerobics.

Classes are taught throughout the day beginning at 6:30 a.m. and ending at 6:30 p.m. except Friday through Sunday when they end about noon.

EVENING PROGRAMS

The Spa closes at 7 p.m. and there are no evening Spa programs, although there is entertainment at the resort's lounges.

THE STAFF

The Spa at Camelback Inn is run by 70 professionals, including massage therapists, exercise instructors, skin care experts, and nutrition and wellness counselors.

People who work at the Camelback Inn do so because they enjoy working in a first-class resort. For example, the marketing director I talked to wanted the chance to work at Marriott's only five-star, five-diamond resort which also happened to be in a "fantastic place to live" where "the quality of life is outstanding."

If all the employees are as happy as he, Camelback Inn must be a well-run resort.

FOOD

You know what I liked about this place? When I ordered salmon, they asked me how I wanted it cooked. I like mine a little on the rare side and that's how I ordered it. Most places never ask a diner how they want their fish cooked.

That little touch is just one example of the empathy for fine dining that the chefs have at the Camelback Inn.

Another fine touch for those of us interested in the spa side of dining is their belief that spa food doesn't have to be bland and tasteless. You can have healthy items that are tasty and that don't even look like spa food. When I ordered room service salmon the cooks fooled me because I thought hollandaise sauce was served with it. Actually, that sauce was made from skim milk! I thought I had pretty refined tastebuds, but I couldn't tell this time.

The meals lack a lot of calories because lemon, vinegar, fresh herbs, and natural ingredients are used for taste.

There are eight restaurants in the resort complex, three of which are making a concentrated effort to include a large variety of spa cuisine on the menus.

Sprouts, in The Spa building itself, serves breakfast and lunch, high energy beverages, and healthful snacks. The Navajo Room has Spa-styled menus for breakfast, lunch, and dinner, while the Chaparral Room — given Mobil's highest award for its classification — serves a Spa menu with its traditional menu.

This dinner menu includes fruit with a poppyseed dressing; a Salade D' Agneau, which is lamb on greens with balsamic vinaigrette or a fish kabob with stir-fried vegetables, among other entrees. One of the fanciest Spa choices is the Chapon Fin Roti, which is roasted breast of capon stuffed with lowfat ricotta cheese and currants and served with a sweet plum sauce.

Each entree lists the calorie, fat, protein, carbohydrate, and cholesterol counts. A computer is used that counts the calories of each item. But Camelback's chefs warn that it's not the calories that are important; it is the fat content.

A lot of resorts are really lacking in the food department and don't have anything on the menu that is really spa cuisine. It is called light dining and includes cottage cheese, etc. but it is not really spa food. However, at Camelback Inn if they didn't call it a spa menu you wouldn't know — the food is that delicious!

SUMMARY

Camelback Inn Resort, Golf Club & Spa is a luxury destination resort with many more things going on than just a spa. But it is also a resort that takes its spa seriously, and I think, as The Spa matures, more and more people will visit Camelback for its spa first and its resort amenities second.

TUCSON NATIONAL RESORT AND SPA
The anticipation is almost as rewarding as the massage itself

TUCSON NATIONAL RESORT AND SPA

You want the spa treatments, but your mind is in a vacation mode. The Tucson National Resort and Spa is the best place to revel in the luxuries of spa facilities without committing yourself to an all-pervasive health and fitness mind-set.

This resort, located in the Tucson Valley outside of one of the Southwest's most interesting cities, is a former private country club. It was transformed from farmland into a first-rate private golf club resort more than 25 years ago. For 15 years, from 1965 through 1980, the Professional Golf Association's Tucson Open was played here on what has been called a "formidable" course. The private golf club was converted into a $60 million resort and programmed for regular players. The average time for an 18-hole round is four and a half hours. Despite the PGA pull-out in 1980, the 27 holes, with 10 lakes and numerous sand traps, are still held in awe, and Golf Digest holds its international schools here.

But creating a golfing paradise wasn't enough for Tucson National; it also wanted to attract conference business. So a full-service spa was added.

This is a pampering spa. Of course there are miles of trails around the golf courses to jog on and aerobic classes every morning, but the spa-goers come here for state-of-the-art treatments, with massage therapists who know how to knead deep into your tired muscles.

One can buy a single treatment a la carte or check into an entire spa package where one is led from luxury to luxury.

Because Tucson National Resort and Spa emanates more of a resort atmosphere, this is a perfect place to bring a spouse who's not interested in spas (and is crazy not to be interested). I know my husband could find plenty to do in this resort overlooked by the 9,100-foot peaks of the Santa Catalina mountains. When he tires of golf, there are six tennis courts, a pleasant swimming pool, and numerous sightseeing attractions close by.

While I'm busy with facials, massages, pedicures, and aerobic exercises, he could play golf or tennis. I'm sure he would be very happy.

At mealtimes, the spa cuisine is served in the restaurant for those on the spa program, but non-spa-going partners can order straight from the menu. The only problem is when you are eating a small salad and your companion has a delicious-smelling dish covered with sinful sauces.

This spa doesn't lock you away in some deserted valley to work only on getting fit and losing fat. There is some freedom involved here; but if you are like me, you'll choose to be pampered with spa treatments.

THE LOOK OF THINGS

Like most of the Southwest, Tucson National Resort and Spa chose to design its low buildings with tiled roofs, stucco, and desert pastels. The architecture is a mixture of Spanish, Mexican, and Native Indian influences and serenely blends into the desert landscaping.

The famous native saguaros are abundant throughout the resort, even on the golf course. These large cacti can only be found in the Sonoran Desert and have provided a backdrop for many a Hollywood western. They are interspersed throughout the resort with other cacti, potted plants, and native trees. Palms encircle the swimming pool.

The first thing I noticed about Tucson National is its expansiveness (650 acres). Every room either overlooks the golf course or the swimming pool. The accommodations, restaurants, and conference rooms were designed by the same architect who did the La Costa spa in California. Tucson National includes 170 deluxe villa suites, a 15,000-square-foot conference center, two ballrooms, a gourmet restaurant, an open-grill room, a temperature-controlled swimming pool, and golf, tennis, and spa facilities.

Each villa has its own private patio or balcony, wet bar, and refrigerator; some have kitchens and fireplaces. The villas are accented in wood and stone, earth tones, and desert pastels.

SURROUNDING AREA

For those truly in the vacation mode, there are several attractions around Tucson, but you'll need a rental car. Tucson National is 45 minutes from the city's international airport, and the Mexican border is 60 miles away. There are many things to do around Tucson, from shopping to stargazing to enjoying cultural attractions and local arts festivals. Tucson is vibrant with art and cultural events--it supports its own ballet, opera, symphony, and art museum.

If you just want to get away for a day trip before or after your spa experience, I recommend going to the twin cities of Nogalas. Take Interstate 19 to Mexico and you'll encounter the American version of Nogalas in Arizona before reaching Nogalas, Mexico. To hop over the border for a day, you'll only need proof of U.S. citizenship — a driver's license is sufficient.

In Nogalas, check out the bargains on liquor, leather, and clothes, and don't forget to bargain with the merchants to get a lower price — they expect it, and enjoy it, and so will you.

Either on your way to or from Nogalas, stop off at Tubac. This artists' community, off I-19, combines history with the arts. The historic Tubac Presidio was built centuries ago to protect nearby missions and settlements from hostile natives. Today, artists and craftsmen have settled around its walls to sell pottery, prints, jewelry, batiks, and paintings.

WHAT'S INCLUDED IN THE PRICE

Tucson National Resort and Spa offers both spa packages and a la carte prices. I would buy a spa package; otherwise, the little cash register in your head will always be ringing trying to figure out how much each treatment and activity costs. Besides, I believe the packages are better bargains.

Rates vary as much with the seasons as the temperatures do, with higher rates during the winter. Prices for a spa package are inexpensive to moderate depending on how many nights you stay. The packages require a two-night minimum, but extra nights can be tacked on if you want. Accommodations for doubles are considerably cheaper than singles.

The spa package includes accommodations, three meals daily, massage, facial, herbal wrap or suntan session, two exercise classes, use of gymnasium, hydrotherapy pools, inhalation room, sauna/steam cabinets for women, Russian bath for men, Swiss shower, unlimited tennis. Also, you can choose one of the following each day: salt glow, loofah, soap scrub, panthermal, Scotch shower, pedicure, paraffin foot dip, manicure, paraffin hand dip or makeup consultation, shampoo/set or blow-dry.

Spa packages do not include the 15 percent service charge and 5 percent sales tax.

The spa also offers a single day of spa treatments. I always wanted a place I could go for a whole day and tell them to take my body and fix it. For about $100, a person can have a massage, facial, herbal wrap, exercise class, spa luncheon, use of spa facilities, and a choice from beauty, health, and therapeutic treatments. This could be perfect for a friend who wants to go with you on your spa vacation but wants only one day of spa treatments. For the spouse who plays lots of golf, a golf package is available.

All of the treatments, from pedicures to massages, are offered at a la carte prices. All the exercise classes can be taken individually, as well as the spa treatments. The full-service salon has capabilities for styling, permanents, coloring, treatments, and full body waxing.

To make reservations at Tucson National Resort and Spa, call (800) 528-4856 outside of Arizona or (602) 297-2271 in Arizona, or write 2727 West Club Drive, Tucson, AZ 85741. A fax number is (602) 297-7544.

CLOTHING AND WEATHER

The Metropolitan Tucson Convention and Visitors Bureau boasts that the area has 360 days of sunshine. At 2,410 feet above sea level, the yearly temperature averages are 82 degrees maximum and 53 minimum. But summer can be extremely hot, with average temperatures in the 90s.

Wear light, comfortable clothes to Tucson National. Remember to bring the spa necessities — sweats, leotards, swimsuit, shorts, t-shirts, gym shoes and socks — but also bring resort clothing. A golf or tennis outfit isn't a bad idea in case you get tempted to try out the resort's facilities. Also, the dining room will be hosting conference groups, golf guests, and vacationers as well as spa guests, so you might feel more comfortable in casual clothes, not sweats.

Don't forget a warm coat; it can be very chilly at night.

A TYPICAL DAY

When I checked in at Tucson National, a program was already laid out for me. I really didn't even have to think, just float from one class to the next, from treatments to massages. But when booking in, you can define your schedule to your own tastes.

Bright and early, I went on 2.5 mile walks with my instructor at 7 a.m. to wake me up and ready my appetite for breakfast. Exercise classes are held throughout the day and your various treatments are scheduled around what exercise classes you want to take.

A 9 a.m. stretch and flex class offers a half hour of gentle stretching, while the 11 a.m. body sculpture is a "rubberband workout!" This half-hour class isolates and tones the major muscle groups and increases flexibility. Medium and low impact aerobics are taught, as well as a vigorous aqua-aerobics.

The staff likes to start individuals on a weight-training program through private instruction. The men's gym is equipped with a Universal multi-station machine, free weights, treadmill, stationary bikes, rowing machine, and benches. There is also a comparable women's gym.

Also in the exercise realm is the swimming pool, which is striped with lap lanes on half of it.

Spa treatments are usually scheduled for the afternoon, and I made sure I also had plenty of rest and relaxation penciled into my schedule as I'd caught a cold and was hoping a couple of naps would cure it.

I should have known that a spa can cure many ills—much better than naps. First thing the spa staff had me do was take a sauna, but a sauna with a difference. Eucalyptus and other herbs were sprayed in the sauna room. As part of the spa's regular treatments, this inhalation room is supposed to help open the sinuses and allow freer breathing. Take it from someone who had a cold, it works.

Stepping out of the sauna, I had a body facial where a sloughing creme (to scrub off dead skin), hot steamy towels and soft brushes are the magic ingredients to a wonderful massage. If this wasn't enough to break the back of that nasty cold, I took a panthermal next, just in case.

There are only a few of these machines in the United States and they resemble iron lungs. Sitting in one up to your neck, an invigorating heat treatment is applied for 20 minutes. This heat treatment is designed to break down the cellulite in your body, but it also makes you feel great. After the heat, a lotion of seaweed and algae extract is rubbed on your body and a lukewarm rinse cleanses your body.

The panthermal is just one of the treatments that makes the spa facilities at Tucson National Resort and Spa some of the best in the country. Others include hydrotherapy pools with both hot baths and cold plunges, tanning beds, a Finnish sauna set at 110 degrees, and a Swiss shower which pulsates your body for two minutes with 14 jets ranging from 80-100 degrees.

The Swiss shower is similar to the Scotch shower which is only available in the men's spa. The Scotch water massage uses 16 needle-spray jets and two high-pressure hoses to splash hot water on your body. It helps circulation and reduces arthritis and rheumatism pain.

Other treatments I fit into my spa experience were the herbal wrap, loofah, and salt glow. For the herbal wrap, I was wrapped in warm cotton sheeting that had been steeped in Oriental herbs to detoxify my body. The loofah is a dried plant that the staff used to rub down my body with dissolved peppermint soap. Talk about refreshing. Then the salt glow utilized three kinds of salt in a vigorous body rub-down to make me rosy and glowing.

EVENING PROGRAMS

There were no evening programs at this spa. Guests can enjoy a night in Tucson or relax by the lighted swimming pool after a leisurely dinner. Another way to spend at least a few minutes of the evening is to gaze up into the desert skies. The bright stars seem to touch the earth because they appear so close in the clear desert night.

THE STAFF

The staff is young and upbeat at Tucson National, always striving to add a special touch to your stay at the resort. The well-trained spa staff works your body over with professional ease. The resort's managing director, Charles Dyke, said, "Few properties in the country can offer the amenities of a world-class resort combined with the privacy of a country club setting. And we are dedicated to providing our guests an unequaled standard of service and comfort."

FOOD

On the first night I sat down to dinner in the restaurant, I was already targeted as a spa guest. While menus were freely handed out to those around me, I had no choices to make. And that was a good choice. The spa food was excellent and filled me up with a calorie count of only 350 that first night.

I had a cold pea salad with scallions and a mayonnaise-type sauce, a piece of steak done to perfection in a peppercorn sauce, rice with red and green peppers, fresh asparagus, herbal ice tea, and fresh fruit.

I left the restaurant very full, which is a plus for spa cuisine.

There is a large variety in the type of spa cuisine served here. Tucson National's chefs have chosen not to stay with a strict vegetarian diet or to ban red meat from its servings. For dinners, I had veal piccata, chicken breast, shrimp veracruz, lamb chops, along with fresh fruit desserts. Lunches were as large as dinners and included chicken enchiladas, beef steak, egg drop soup, lasagna, game hens, and orange roughy.

It is during breakfast that the spa-goer has to resist temptation. In the mornings, I was actually given a menu with the freedom to choose between fried eggs, french toast, ham, bacon, huevos rancheros, and so on. But no, I faithfully stuck to the low-calorie items and didn't really feel deprived.

Certain items on the breakfast menu include their caloric content and that was a marker for those seeking healthy food. I had Birchermuesli, a chilled blend of oatmeal, fruit, nuts, raisins, honey, and lowfat yogurt — 300 calories. It was wonderful.

Other items for the healthy minded were the West Indies omelette stuffed with crab meat at only 160 calories, and the oatmeal raisin pancake served with apple butter at only 245 calories.

Low calorie jams and jellies and no salt/no cholesterol margarine were also available.

SUMMARY

The country club atmosphere of Tucson National is quiet, sedate, sophisticated; I like this aspect of it very much. Almost as much as I like the panthermal treatment — or should I say "treat"?

LOEWS VENTANA CANYON

If you're seeking a little spa with a lot of luxury, this Tucson, Arizona resort could be just the place for you. Loews Ventana Canyon is a resort, and not a spa. It caters to conference groups and specializes in tennis and golf programs. Its luxury is ultimate; its service exceptional; its dining gourmet. Don't expect to lose weight here, or even maintain it, if you have as much difficulty passing up pecan pie and other goodies as I do. (Just a note, though — I did pass up that piece of pie.)

However, if you are an experienced spa-goer, or one with a lot of determination and iron-clad self-discipline, Loews Ventana Canyon offers spa amenities and activities that can keep you huffing, puffing, and in shape. The key to how much lies in each individual.

The resort includes a separate spa area called Lakeside Spa and Tennis Club. Although I got the feeling that the spa was designed for conference wives, it is a fully equipped facility. It has a heated lap pool and Jacuzzi, mirrored aerobics room with daily classes, massage therapy by appointment, dry sauna, steam room, Universal and free weight training equipment, 18-station fitness par course, bicycling, and another swimming pool with a cold splash.

You can shape up at Loews Ventana Canyon, but nobody is going to make you do it. It is a pleasant break from the regular spa routine of wake-ups at 5:30 a.m. with a fully-packed day until you drop dead at 9 p.m. Combining a sightseeing vacation at a luxury resort with a quasi-spa routine could be the new wave for America's health-conscious and travel-oriented public.

THE LOOK OF THINGS

Picture the Arizona desert with its sun-burnt red rock, its saguaro-studded vistas, and its mysterious canyons rising from the land. This is Loews Ventana Canyon.

The architects of this resort took a look at Ventana Canyon (named in Spanish for a window-shaped opening high in the

Catalina Mountains) and tried to blend its buildings into the Arizona landscape.

For example, the masonry block in the buildings is arranged in a vertical pleating to imitate the nearby saguaros for which the Sonora Desert is famous. Water is piped up to a spring that runs naturally in certain seasons, but with human assistance the spring provides year-round beauty for the resort.

The developer and architects were successful in their efforts to design a site that blends in with the desert; numerous industry awards have said so. To mention one — in 1985, the Arizona governor recognized Loews Ventana Canyon as an outstanding example of environmental responsibility. What might have swayed his mind was the developer's response to finding a 300-year-old saguaro cactus in the way of the proposed resort. Instead of moving the cactus, he moved the resort. If only all developers were so environmentally conscientious.

Located on 94 acres in northeast Tucson, the resort is the focal point of a 1,040-acre planned community. The 80-foot Canyon Waterfall flows from the mountains to a tiered waterfall and lake at the resort's entrance.

There are 366 rooms, 26 suites, an 18-hole golf course and 10 tennis courts. Rooms here have either a view of Tucson's skyline or of national forest. Decorated in desert tones with original lithographs of Arizona scenes, each room has three telephones, remote control television, refrigerator, wet bar, and a marble-encased bathroom sporting a spa-like tub for two.

All the amentities of a large hotel are offered here, including a lounge, disco, room service, and four restaurants, one of which offers a spectacular view of Tucson. It is an elegant resort and the $200,000 worth of original art scattered throughout restates its luxury.

HOW TO GET THERE

To make reservations at Loews Ventana Canyon, call LRI Loews Representation International at (800)-223-0888. For more information, you can write the resort at 7000 North Resort Drive,
Tucson, AZ 85715 or call it directly at (800)-234-5117 or (602)-299-2020. A fax number is (602)-299-6832.
When making airline reservations to Tucson, remember that the check-in time at this resort is 3 p.m.; the check-out time is noon.
Loews Ventana Canyon is 20 minutes from Tucson. To get to the resort from the Tucson International Airport, you can take a shuttle bus that carts people to various resorts in the area. This 24-hour bus is $14 each way. Look for Arizona Stagecoach Company when exiting the airport's baggage area. Or you may want to rent a car if you're planning on sightseeing in the area. When making reservations, ask the resort to mail you a map on how to get to Ventana Canyon.

SURROUNDING AREA

Loews Ventana Canyon is located in a canyon itself, but just minutes away is Sabino Canyon, a lush desert oasis that has cool ponds, waterfalls, a stream, and rock walls hundreds of feet high. There is a tram here that will take you into the canyon for a minimal price. Loews Ventana Canyon offers three free shuttles each way daily from the resort to Sabino Canyon three miles away. This is a good place to hike or even to take an early morning jog.
One good way to see a bit of Tucson is to hook up with Old West Excursions, 885-0085. This company offers seven sightseeing trips for full days and half days at an inexpensive price. I took a two-hour Old Pueblo tour of Tucson and learned a lot about the city's history—even a Civil War battle was fought here, where

1,500 yankee foot soldiers pushed a Confederate army back to Texas.

Other trips include Old Tucson where more than 150 Hollywood westerns have been filmed; the "living" Arizona-Sonora Desert Museum; "the towns too tough to die" — Tombstone and Bisbee; the Cave, Canyon and Cactus tour of Sabino Canyon, Saguaro National Monument, Colossal Cave and Webb Winery; Tucson to Tubac to Nogales, Mexico; and the summit of the Santa Catalina Mountains.

WHAT'S INCLUDED IN THE PRICE

There are golf, tennis, and spa packages available here in either a three-day/four-night set-up or a seven-day/eight-night option. There is also a "Celebration" package for two days beginning either on Friday or Saturday nights. These spa packages are a moderate price during the high season and inexpensive during low season, which is May to September. Tax and gratuities are included in the price of the package.

But you need to remember that meals are not included in the package costs. You can sign up for a meal package which includes either breakfast and dinner or all three meals. These meal packages are somewhat expensive, although they do include tax and gratuities.

Besides deluxe accommodations, the spa package gives you unlimited access to the spa facilities and assigns you a locker. There are unlimited aerobic classes, use of heated lap pool, use of bicycles, par course, jogging paths, and weight equipment.

Loews Ventana Canyon gives you one massage for every three days on a spa package, somewhat limited compared to a full-service spa.

CLOTHING AND WEATHER

Pack two bags for this 3,013-foot-elevation resort. In one, put all your exercise clothes — swimsuit, leotards, sweats, shorts, t-shirts, gym shoes, and socks. In the other, put resort apparel which can range from golfing attire to dress-up clothes for a fancy dinner. Bring comfortable and casual clothes in case you opt for a sightseeing tour. A jacket is advised because desert nights and early mornings can be chilly.

However, the days warm up nicely (in fact they are almost too hot in the summertime) and the sun supposedly shines 360 days of the year.

A TYPICAL DAY

A typical day at Loews Ventana Canyon can be whatever you want it to be. At this self-directed spa, you can fit in as much or as little activity as your body can handle. I'm going to tell you about different options available; it would be a good idea to talk to the spa staff when you get there, too.

The staff can give you a fitness appraisal to test flexibility, strength, and endurance, and they will help you establish personal fitness goals. The staff can also help you design an exercise program for the week. If you dare, measure your body fat at the beginning and end of your stay at Loews Ventana Canyon.

Yes, you can get up early at this resort and exercise. On Tuesdays and Thursdays, there is a morning power walk from 8-9 a.m. which covers the 2.5 mile par fitness course. I took this walk and was one of two people on it out of 400-some resort guests.

Exercise classes are held in the Lakeside Spa on a unique suspended wood floor; this helps to minimize impact. Schedules are 5-6 p.m. Monday through Friday and 9-10 a.m. Saturday for body fitness aerobics; 9-10 a.m. Wednesday and Friday for body contouring; and 1-2 p.m. Tuesday and Thursday for aqua fitness.

Aside from these set classes, your spa time is up to you. Plan out a schedule of activities remembering these options: lap swimming in a 50-foot pool; bicycling on 18-speed mountain bikes in the canyons or around the bike path that circles the resort (you can also join a guided bike tour); tennis and golf; weight lifting and toning with Lifecycles, Concept II Rowing Ergometer, Motorized Treadmills, Versa Climber, Schwinn AirDyne, Stairmaster 4000 and 12 separate Universal stations; and a par fitness course with 18 exercise stations.

Don't forget to schedule a massage, either a 50-minute or 80-minute one in your room or at the spa. All the massage therapists are trained at the National Desert Institute of Healing Arts.

Also, take advantage of the sauna and Jacuzzi for heat therapy. If you want facials, pedicures or manicures, the Great Waves Beauty Salon is located at the resort.

Other than exercise, I took one of the resort's daily sessions at 10 a.m. Each day, there is a different activity, free of charge, that lasts 30 minutes. On Mondays, a tour is given of the resort's art. Although the art isn't for sale, the tour guide can tell you where to find similar work at art studios and galleries around Tucson. Tuesdays is an environmental tour focusing on the Sonora Desert ecosystem. I learned about the prickly pear cactus (you can make ice cream from it) and the cholla cactus, as well as other vegetation on the resort grounds. Wednesday is a tour of the "back of the house" such as the kitchens, offices, etc; and on Thursday, golf pros give golfing tips. Friday, the resort's chefs share their favorite recipes (ask them for a spa recipe).

In addition, shopping shuttles are available each day to take you to Tucson's favorite shopping areas and malls.

EVENING PROGRAMS

There aren't any evening spa programs, but in this Southwestern city of arts, there will be some cultural event happening nearly every night. The four-year-old resort has already made a name for itself as a supporter of the arts and could possibly have a performance lined up at the resort. A dance mime troupe from New York was performing at Loews Ventana Canyon when I visited.

Each February, the Festival in the Sun features performers from all over the world. In addition, there are year-round opera, symphony, theater, and dance troupes based in Tucson. Call the Metropolitan Tucson Convention and Visitors Bureau at (602) 624-1817 for more information.

THE STAFF

The person you are most likely to deal with on a spa-minded vacation is Loews' director of the Lakeside Spa and Tennis Club. Bill McGrath leans more toward the tennis angle of the spa, having written the book, "Playing Your Best Tennis," and touring on goodwill tennis promotions. However, there is a full-time fitness director whose primary concern is the aerobics and exercise programs.

FOOD

Head chef Takashi Shirmizu is well-versed in spa cuisine. After training in Europe for several years, the Japanese chef found his way to Canada and then to the U.S., picking up different styles of cooking along the way. He learned spa cuisine at a Dallas, Texas spa where he had to prepare menus limited to 600 calories a day! He told me that feat was very difficult and practically eliminated all meat and pasta.

He said Loews Ventana Canyon offered spa cuisine for a year, but because not enough visitors opted for the spa package it was dropped from the menus.

So now it's up to a spa guest to find his or her own healthy choices off the menu. The best of the resort's four restaurants for this is the Flying V Bar and Grill. It has menu items starred that are "nutritionally sound dishes," generally low fat, low sodium, low cholesterol, and avoiding an excess of sugar.

These items include salads such as the resort fruit platter, salad Nicoise with tuna, tomato, olives and bell peppers in St. Andrews Vinaigrette, and combination salad with either tuna or chicken, fresh fruit, and low fat cottage cheese. There is one sandwich out of the 12 on the menu that is designed as a healthy choice — the grilled Pacific swordfish.

If you are also eating dinner here, I hope you like swordfish because it and the grilled turkey tenderloin are the only two starred menu items.

Stay away from the High Tea from 3-5 p.m. each day — it is a minefield of desserts. And the free hors d'oeuvres from 5-7 p.m. in the Cascade Lounge have not been made with a calorie count in mind.

There is not enough variety for healthful, low-fat food, but Loews Ventana Canyon's staff is accommodating and perhaps if you asked, a special diet plan could be made for you. The public relations director told me that Mary Ann Santander, the fitness director, could set up short- or long-term diet plans.

One other nice thing about food at Loews Ventana Canyon: Picnic baskets are available for hikes and sightseeing excursions.

SUMMARY

Loews Ventana Canyon is more resort oriented than spa oriented, but it offers all the spa activities you'll need. The food is the main problem; most of the offerings are not spa-conscious food! Watch yourself here, and you'll have a good time, lose weight and tone up.

CLAREMONT RESORT AND SPA

I doubt that one-tenth of one percent of the people who live in the San Francisco Bay Area know just how good the spa is at the Claremont Resort and Spa.

Located in Oakland only 20 minutes from downtown San Francisco, this spa is the ideal place for someone on the Bay Area's fast track to put mind and body back into shape. It has day packages where you check in early in the morning and go home late in the evening — a totally relaxing and rejuvenating day.

But for those who don't live in that metropolitan area (and even for those who do), the real fun of the Claremont Resort and Spa is the hotel itself.

The 75-year-old, elegant, Victorian hotel has been called a Bay Area landmark, and rightly so. It was originally built as an English-style castle for the wife of a Kansas man who struck it rich during California's Gold Rush days. It burned down in 1906, was rebuilt in its present form in 1915, and has been redone several times since.

The last renovation was completed just in time for the resort's 75th anniversary. During that renovation, more than $30 million was spent to upgrade the hotel, including the addition of a $6 million spa facility.

The spa opened in January 1989 and in that short time the spa has put its stuff together quite well. Even with my extensive visits to spas across the West, I was very impressed. As a resort spa, it has all the facilities and services, plus the extra amenities you need to make yourself presentable after a day of spa-ing.

Claremont Resort and Spa is the Bay Area's only resort, and adding a spa to this sprawling, enchanting hotel only makes it more special.

Famed architect Frank Lloyd Wright said of the Claremont, "...one of the few hotels in the world with warmth, character and charm." It appears that the hotel's new spa is on its way to living up to that compliment.

THE LOOK OF THINGS

Set on 22 acres overlooking San Francisco and San Francisco Bay, the Claremont Resort and Spa is an urban resort in the sense that it is close to city life. It is like a rural resort in that it offers just about anything a guest could desire, leaving little need to venture off the beautifully landscaped grounds.

Nestled in the Oakland/Berkeley hills, the Claremont looks more like a European castle or a private boys' school on the East Coast than a California resort.

There are 239 guest rooms in this huge, white stone building graced with romantic towers. The tennis courts and palm trees scattered around it add to the character and elegance of the Claremont. Twenty-eight meeting rooms make it practical for conferences.

Of course, what we're interested in is the spa, which is in a separate building from the hotel and is near the hotel's two heated lap pools and its outdoor whirlpool.

As well as facilities for the spa treatments, the Claremont spa has an exercise room that specializes in low-impact aerobics and features a "spring-fed" floor to prevent injuries, fully-equipped weight room, the lap pools and whirlpool, 10 tennis courts of which six are lighted, and a full-service beauty salon.

It also has four saunas, two steam rooms, computerized aerobic equipment, and a state-of-the-art fitness center. The 25-meter Olympic pool has six lanes and is heated to 79 degrees.

What more could you ask for, except for a beautiful body? And the spa staff will work on that too.

HOW TO GET THERE

The Claremont Resort and Spa is on Ashby and Domingo Avenues. in Oakland, California. To find the Claremont by car from San Francisco, take the Bay Bridge to Highway 24 East, exit at Claremont Avenue, turn left on Claremont and then right on Ashby.

Those arriving and departing by air can make transportation arrangements with the hotel's bell staff. There is complimentary transportation to and from Oakland International Airport between 7 a.m. and 10 p.m. The staff appreciates advance reservations.

Between the resort and the San Francisco International Airport, there are two city shuttles — Airport Connection and Bay Area Shuttle — that the bell staff will contact for you.

For hotel and spa reservations, write the Claremont Resort and Spa, Ashby and Domingo Avenues, Oakland, CA 94623-0363, or call (415)-843-3000.

SURROUNDING AREA

The Claremont Resort and Spa is smack in the middle of one of America's most famous metropolitan areas. San Francisco has a romantic appeal, a cosmopolitan air, an abundance of restaurants and shopping, and plenty of sightseeing. Oakland, not to be forgotten, caters to the convention business. It sports several great hotels and conference centers as well as restaurants and shopping opportunities.

The hotel staff can help guests get to nearby golf courses, horse races at Golden Gate Fields, the Oakland Museum, and the University of California Art Museum. There is also complimentary shuttle service to the BART subway system which can take guests into San Francisco to visit such sights as Fishermen's Wharf, Chinatown, Coit Tower, North Beach, and Lombard Street (the crookedest street in the world).

WHAT'S INCLUDED IN THE PRICE

The spa at the Claremont has put together such a variety of packages that just about anybody should be able to find what they're looking for. And if not, any service can be given a la carte.

There are no full-week spa packages, but one can put a couple of the 1- 2- or 3-day packages together. These are moderately expensive. They have limited spa treatments included with them, so costs could rise if more massages etc. are added. The overnight packages can come with or without meals and can include single, double occupancy, or double occupancy with only one spa participant.

Other packages include half-day, full-day, weekend, and special days such as The Refresher.

I'm enamoured of this package because I think it is such a good deal for someone who works or lives in the Bay Area. For $69 (prices are subject to change), The Refresher offers the use of all spa facilities as well as a massage, lunch, an aroma or a seaweed bath, and a small gift to boot. Such a deal.

Other day packages are somewhat more expensive but add more services. The ultimate day of pampering would be the package that offers a facial, massage, hair styling, make-up application, manicure, lunch, spa hike, herbal wrap, loofah or salt glo, an aroma or seaweed bath, and use of all facilities. You'd feel sublime after that.

There's also a package day that concentrates on services in the beauty salon—when you really want to look good and feel refreshed for a special occasion.

A 17.5 percent gratuity is added to all services.

Any treatment or service is also given a la carte.

To make spa services and treatment reservations, call (415)-843-3000 ext. 279. You must cancel at least four hours in advance to avoid being charged for the service, and spa packages must be cancelled 48 hours in advance.

CLOTHING AND WEATHER

Rand McNally rated Oakland as the No. 1 climate in the U.S. because of the gentle, Mediterranean-type weather: It never gets too cold or too hot. The average temperature in January is 48 degrees; in April, 56 degrees; in July, 63 degrees; and in October, 60 degrees.

Bring light-weight clothes in the summer, don't forget a jacket as it is usually cool and foggy; November through April it's a good idea to pack sweaters, a jacket, or coat because winter can be brisk and occasionally rainy.

Casual dress is accepted at Claremont, but something nicer for dinner is more appropriate. At the spa, towels and lockers are provided upon request and a robe is provided for spa use.

A TYPICAL DAY

As with most resort spas, a typical day is what you make of it. I had a massage, an aroma bath, and a pedicure. You can choose from four types of massages, several exercise classes, various spa treatments, and a variety of beauty/salon services.

The four types of massages are sports, Swedish, aromatherapy, and shiatsu, which is a massage that concentrates on pressure points to relieve tension.

Some of the treatments: an herbal wrap, where the body is wrapped in herb-infused linen sheets, followed by a hydrating honey-almond mixture that is massaged onto your body, a 12-nozzle Swiss shower, and a spritz of body spray; the salt glo is an exfoliating treatment using Epsom salts and a blend of oatmeal and cornmeal, followed by a Swiss shower and body spray.

The body spray, as well as all other skin care products used here, is Kerstin Skin Care, a very pure, natural skin care line.

A seaweed or aroma bath is an individual whirlpool bath with a choice of freeze-dried seaweed from the coast of Brittany, or an Aromatherapy essence.

Fitness classes start at 7 a.m. sharp with either low-impact aerobics or aerobics with weights, depending on the day. Other classes of stretching, toning, yoga, aqua aerobics, etc. are held until 11:30 a.m. when there is an option to take a spa hike. Exercise classes don't start again until 5:30 p.m. with Tai Chi, yoga, and aerobics.

The fitness center has available circuit aerobics, personalized fitness training, circuit weight workouts, fitness analysis, and water volleyball. The center is open from 6:30 a.m. to 10 p.m.

EVENING PROGRAMS

There are no specific evening programs at the spa, but the facilities stay open until 10 p.m. each night for individual use.

THE STAFF

The Claremont has the courteous staff you'd expect of a renowned hotel. At the spa, the staff runs things smoothly and is well organized. The massage therapists are all superbly qualified and trained.

FOOD

The Claremont serves a great selection of spa cuisine, as well as something called "Crossover Cuisine," a link between its famous progressive regional cooking and its desire to accommodate spa guests. The chefs do well with low calorie cooking.

The sea bass, shrimp cocktail and sorbet I had one night was wonderful, and low in calories, just 300 in fact.

At the three restaurants—the Pavilion, the Presto Cafe and the Bayview Cafe—there are two menus available, a spa menu and a regular one.

The spa menu is extensive (Appetizers, Entrees, Chef's Favorites, Vegetables, Desserts, and Beverages) and lists the calories and ingredients. The cuisine is low in cholesterol, fat, calories, and salt. Seasoning is accomplished with spices and herbs grown in a garden on the resort grounds. Protein portions are 2 oz. for lunch and 4 oz. for dinner.

On the regular menus, "Crossover Cuisine" is marked with a palm tree, and calories are listed. For the "Crossover Cuisine" the protein portions are 4 oz. for lunch and 5 oz. for dinner.

The spa staff also gives hints on which foods to eat and which foods to avoid for certain health conditions at the Pavilion's breakfast and lunch buffets.

The Claremont spa, unlike some spas, is not strict about the no-nos: alcohol, smoking, soda pop. In fact, a glass of wine with dinner is included with the spa packages. There are two bars at the hotel, too.

SUMMARY

I'm impressed with the Claremont Resort and Spa for its professionally run spa, its attention to spa cuisine, and its well-deserved reputation as an elegant urban resort.

LE MERIDIEN

Even though Le Meridien San Diego at Coronado isn't a destination spa, you can create a destination spa experience out of it. All the components are there — spa cuisine, fitness classes, fitness testing, pampering massages and facials, special packages — plus a staff that will set up any kind of spa program you desire.

If you want to sleep late, your appointments will start later. If you want extra fitness classes, those can be penciled in. On the opposite hand, more massages can be scheduled for those who want to be pampered.

The way Le Meridien can individualize every spa package makes the health club unique and gives it the flexibility to work with all sorts of people — from wives of corporate businessmen to honeymooning fitness nuts.

People come here on spa packages as part of a corporate business meeting or on an a la carte basis. The spa also opens its doors to San Diego residents who want to join it as a health club. The average ages are between 35 and 45, and about 70 percent of the guests are women.

Another unique aspect of Le Meridien is its use of Clarins massage techniques and skin care. This line of French skin care products has gained European fame, and Le Meridien is the first spa in the United States to implement its use in a spa program. Spa staff say that some people come to Le Meridien just for the skin care, especially the body rub. So proud is Le Meridien of its affiliation with Clarins that it also calls its spa the Clarins Institut de Beaute.

The affiliation with the French beauty products isn't surprising since Le Meridien has a French theme throughout the hotel complex. The San Diego hotel is one of more than 50 hotels in 30 countries around the world operated by the hotel chain. The Meridien hotels began in 1972.

I discovered why this hotel chain has made such a rapid expansion in less than 20 years. The impeccable service is varied and ample — from the way room service always comes on time to the maid turning down the bedding at night. This beautiful, fancy hotel also has no snob appeal at all, which appeals to me.

THE LOOK OF THINGS

All the spa guests—whatever program they design for their package—will enjoy the surroundings. Set in Coronado on the San Diego Bay, Le Meridien's 16 waterfront acres are absolutely lovely, and the views are magnificent.

The 300-room hotel is located next to a 20-acre park complete with walking paths, ponds, and grassy areas. It is also at the base of the Coronado Bay Bridge linking the hotel to downtown San Diego.

In addition to the hotel rooms, there are seven executive suites and a 28-unit villa complex with its own pool and whirlpool. The villas are named after French impressionistic artists Cezanne, Chagall, Degas, Dufy, Gauguin, Matisse, Monet, and Renoir and feature reproductions of these artists' works.

The main complex is a group of three-story buildings which connect to a central area of public space that includes meeting rooms, retail stores, and restaurants.

The hotel and villas are decorated in an elegant Country French look, designed to be bright and airy.

The rooms are magnificently big, over 500 square feet, in fact. Each is furnished with a sofa, sofa table, dining table and chairs, mini-bar, remote control color television, radio and alarm clock, and three telephone extensions including one in the bathroom. The bathroom itself is a cornucopia of goodies—bath scale, big fuzzy bath towels, shoeshine kit, sewing kit, hair dryer, Hermes or Lanvin toiletries, and Limoge bath accessories.

In the villas, there are comfortable Jacuzzi tubs and safes in the rooms.

Every room has a terrace to overlook the pretty grounds around the hotel. Lots of water. Three swimming pools are placed on the grounds, as well as lagoons, waterfalls, and ponds where the bright orange and red Japanese koi fish swim.

Le Meridien brought in geese, swans, and exotic ducks to live in ponds and in the walk-in aviary. Flamingos, ring teal, cape teal, and bar-headed geese all live the good life at the resort.

The complex also has lots of meeting space, a boutique arcade, currency exchange, and a business center complete with Fax service, secretarial services, copy machines, and computer hook-ups.

On the recreation side, there are six lighted tennis courts (with their own pro), the aforementioned pools (one is a 75-foot lap pool), two whirlpool spas, a gymnasium with Polaris equipment, free weights, and Lifecycles.

HOW TO GET THERE

There is a shuttle service from the San Diego International Airport for a minimal charge. Look for the courtesy phone in the baggage area. Taxis and limousine service are also available.

Le Meridien is located about 5 minutes from downtown and 15 minutes from the airport by way of Freeway 5 south and the Coronado Bay Bridge.

Check-in time is 3 p.m. and check-out time is noon. Reservations can be made by calling (619) 435-3000, ext. 6274, or by writing Le Meridien San Diego at Coronado, 2000 Second Street, Cornado , CA 92118. The FAX number is (619) 435-3032.

SURROUNDING AREA

San Diego is one of those cities that was meant for playing. A sunny, temperate climate and the Pacific Ocean combine for a wide variety of water sports. Here one can go sailing or yachting, scuba diving, jet skiing, deep sea fishing, even surfing.

For most of those activities, the concierge at Le Meridien can make the arrangements.

Across the street is an 18-hole championship golf course, and tennis courts are on the premises.

The hotel gives morning and evening bicycle tours, taking guests on a 45-minute guided ride along San Diego Bay to the Old Ferry Landing.

Beach-goers will appreciate the beach shuttle bus to Coronado Beach.

WHAT'S INCLUDED IN THE PRICE

I heard mostly good comments about the package prices, which are moderate and include accommodations and meals. Advance reservations are required, and local taxes and a 15 percent service charge are included in the various spa packages.

There are two,- three,- four, and five-day spa packages that include accommodations, meals, and a variety of services. The five-day, four-night package has 17 spa services included, as well as unlimited access to the spa and its fitness classes.

You can pay for any spa service a la carte, and there are several different options for a one-day package in the spa ranging from a fitness oriented day to a beauty and pampering day.

Hotel guests can use the health club, swimming pools, Jacuzzis, and saunas free of charge.

One aspect of the spa packages that I really like is meal coupons. Instead of limiting choices on what a spa guest eats, the spa gives out coupons worth so much money, about $19 for the dinner coupons.

Then you can go into the restaurants and choose your dinner. It should be off the spa cuisine menu, but you can apply the coupon toward a regular meal, too. It seems to work well and it allows flexibility.

The coupons are also good for room service as well.

CLOTHING AND WEATHER

For Le Meridien, you might want to bring something a little dressier. Most guests here dress for dinner, especially for the gourmet restaurant.

However, if you don't want to fuss there is room service which will bring you a spa menu.

Aside from dinner, casual attire is the norm; people here are on vacation. The only thing Le Meridien specifically asks is that no one enter the lobby or the restaurants in a bathing suit.

Bring swimsuits, walking and aerobic shoes, and exercise clothes. The spa provides terry robes and sandals. The swimming pools provide towels between 9 a.m. and 5 p.m., but you might want to bring a beach towel for the beaches and for early morning and late evening swimming.

Bring a coat or jacket, because the evenings can be cool even though San Diego has a temperate year-round climate. The amenities are fantastic here; don't bother with shampoo, etc.

A TYPICAL DAY

The spa staff will individualize everyone's "typical day" so each guest gets the right amount of fitness classes and pampering to make him or her happy.

To give you an idea, my schedule for a Monday included a facial, exfoliating body treatment, paraffin hand treatment, make-up application, and a low impact aerobics class.

There are a variety of exercise classes with names like Hip Slimmers, Belly Burners, Back Booster, Lanky Legs, Happy Feet, Waist Reducers, Tone and Trim, Stetch and Strengthen. I think you can get the gist of the classes by their names. A weight room is open from 6 a.m. to 10 p.m. with a staff person always in attendance to help with the equipment.

The spa staff is working toward making the spa's fitness program stronger with harder classes. Right now, the spa's strength is in its massages and Clarins beauty treatments.

The Clarins line of specialized massages and skin care products was established more than 30 years ago by Frenchman Jacques Courtin-Clarins. The products use camomile, cucumber, mint, and myrrh to soften and smooth skin and keep it from aging.

Clarins treatments at Le Meridien Spa include a deep cleansing facial, regenerating and firming facial, desensitizing facial, pick-me-up facial, as well as firming body treatment, contouring body treatment (for spongy cellulite skin), and exfoliating treatment for super soft skin.

Besides these Clarins treatments, the spa also has hydrotherapy, herbal wrap, Swedish massage, sports massage, and shiatsu. (Shiatsu is a traditional Japanese massage technique developed from accupressure treatments); the sports massage concentrates on muscle groups that have been overstressed, such as tennis elbow or runner's heels.

Everybody should get at least one massage — then they will be hooked for life. I know I am.

Beauty salon services like facials, pedicures, and manicures are available also, and a fulltime staff oversees daily recreation activities.

There is a one-hour free clinic for tennis each day, and during summers and holidays there is a daily activities program for children.

A typical day might begin with an early morning walk or jog followed by breakfast and a tennis clinic or water volleyball.

An aquacize class would be held mid-morning with time enough for an herbal wrap before lunch at noon.

In the afternoon, there would be some free time for a bike ride or sunbathing by the swimming pool before having a Swedish massage and a paraffin hand treatment and manicure. Try a facial just before dinner.

Most of the fitness classes, such as the Back Booster (abdominal exercises that improve posture and relieve tension and back pain) and the Derriere Contouring (for women only and for a better rear view), will be held at different times each day, perhaps in the morning one day and the afternoon the next.

The spa opens at 6 a.m. and closes at 9 p.m.. The tennis courts are open from 8 a.m. to 9 p.m., and the swimming pools from 6 a.m. to 9 p.m.

EVENING PROGRAMS

There are no set evening programs at the spa, but it offers special classes and seminars at different times of the year. I was told by the spa staff that they are working to bring in more of these classes. They want to emphasize things people wouldn't normally do at home but would be interested in if given the chance.

Those things include reflexology, palm reading, Tai Chi, belly dancing, and hypnotherapy classes to lose weight, stop smoking, reduce stress, and improve concentration.

Backgammon and chess challenges also use the spa as their venue during the evenings.

THE STAFF

Service, service, service. That is my impression of the Le Meridien staff. They bend over backwards to give you individualized attention in this 300-room hotel. Breakfast when ordered from room service always comes on time and with a newspaper on the side. Other room service are just as quick.

The massage therapist I had was excellent. She gave me a long, slow, intense massage that wasn't rushed.

The managing director of Le Meridien is a native of Italy with experience in Le Meridien hotels in Europe and the Caribbean. He obviously knows what he's doing because this hotel's employees are wonderfully accommodating from the top down.

FOOD

Le Meridien's executive chef is Roland Muller, who hails from the Alsace region of France next to the Rhine River. He is not into spa cuisine specifically but is interested in creating dishes that are low in fat and calories and that taste good. He is also very pleasant, cute — and married.

I would suggest having breakfast in your room and perhaps having your lunch delivered to the spa so you don't have to change clothes or fix up to go eat. Dinner can again be room service if you like or the hotel's L'Escale restaurant which serves spa cuisine, seats 120 people indoors and 88 people outdoors with views of the San Diego Bay, the city skyline, and the main pool. L'Escale serves breakfast, lunch, and dinner in a bright, casual atmosphere and specializes in both California and French cuisines with an emphasis on fresh seafood.

The theme is very French, but special Japanese amenities are available as well. For one room service breakfast, I ordered the Japanese breakfast of appetizers, rice, Miso soup, and steamed vegetables which took a $12 coupon. For another room service meal, I had poached fish with a nice white sauce, salad with Roquefort dressing, and V8 juice. I cleaned the plate.

I pretty much stuck to the spa menu which offered some kind of fish with practically every dish. The fish was so tender I asked chef Roland how he prepares it. He said his secret is to not overcook the fish but to serve it on the rare side.

SUMMARY

I really enjoyed Le Meridien. It was small enough and intimate enough so that I couldn't get lost, and the personalized attention I received was excellent. I was a victim of spa brain most of the time, which was great!

LE MERIDIEN
A yoga class beside the black swan's pool

MARRIOTT'S DESERT SPRINGS RESORT AND SPA

I loved the little touches at Marriott's Desert Springs Resort and Spa: the way you could order tomorrow's breakfast today on the video breakfast menu, or the way the TV guide in my room had a bookmark placed in that night's television schedule.

I also loved the spa at this resort located 13 miles outside of Palm Springs, California. Although it wasn't a destination spa, it did a great job of keeping me busy with fitness classes and relaxing beauty treatments. It is also nice that I didn't have to go rummaging through a menu looking for a healthy dish. A special spa menu is available for spa guests and what's more, the spa food is excellent.

Marriott's Desert Springs Resort was opened in February 1987 at a cost of $250 million. It is primarily geared toward large convention business, sporting 51,300 square feet of meeting space. In fact, 75 percent of the business is from conferences.

The spa here is just one more amenity to attract large conference groups, and spa packages are specifically arranged for these groups.

However, the spa is operated in such a way that I would imagine more and more individuals will be interested in coming simply for a luxury spa vacation at the Desert Springs Resort. The spa regime will keep you fit; the hotel's ambiance will keep you happy and relaxed.

The hummingbird was chosen as a symbol for the Desert Springs Resort because of its energy, color, and positive attitude. After staying at the resort, I think it is an appropriate symbol. The overall picture here just made me feel so good.

THE LOOK OF THINGS

First impressions of Marriott's Desert Springs Resort and Spa are formed by the 100-foot-high atrium lobby that has two waterfalls, an indoor lake, and greenery hanging off the many balconies. Black swans in the lobby lake; it looks like fantasy land.

My room overlooked the lobby and it was just beautiful, with those little touches that make Desert Springs Resort a magical place to stay. Each room or suite includes a refrigerator, mini-bar, large private bath with separate shower and tub, and a spacious balcony overlooking the gardens. A special section in the hotel is reserved for spa guests where smoking is not allowed.

The 892-room resort situated on 400 acres is elegant in all areas. A boat will take guests to various restaurants around the resort or on a tour of the 23 acres of water—lakes, waterfalls, rivers, ponds. This desert resort even includes a beach.

The Santa Rosa mountains rise above the desert floor, adding scenic vistas to the two 18-hole golf courses and the 16-court lawn and tennis club.

The spa building is separate from the hotel and is set, light and airy, among lakes, swimming pools (just for spa guests) and green lawns. The 27,000-square-foot spa is jam-packed with all the spa treats — an outdoor water exercise pool, private sundeck, whirlpool, plunge pools, 22-station fitness gym, luxurious locker rooms, relaxation lounges, Finnish saunas, Turkish steam rooms, inhalation room, health-oriented snack bar, exercise lawn, jogging and walking paths, body treatment center, individual whirlpool baths, fitness apparel shop and Jose Eber's full-service beauty salon. It's a Disneyland for health addicts.

HOW TO GET THERE

The Marriott is located in the Palm Springs resort area, which is a nice place for the hotel corporation's flagship on the West Coast. Limousine or taxi service will take you from the Palm Springs Airport to the resort for a modest fee. However, the spa director told me that guests on a spa package can call the spa to arrange complimentary transportation.

Ontario International Airport is one hour's drive away, and the Bermuda Dunes Airport for private planes is nearby.

The resort city is 100 miles from Los Angeles, Newport Beach, and San Diego.

For reservations call toll-free (800) 255-0848 or from California call (619) 341-2211. Or write Marriott's Desert Springs Resort and Spa at 74855 Country Club Drive, Palm Desert, CA 92260.

SURROUNDING AREA

There are only 60 golf courses and 300 tennis courts to keep a person occupied in Palm Springs. But if golf and tennis aren't your bag, try the many shopping centers. The Marriott offers free shuttle service Thursday through Sunday to the newly renovated Desert Fashion Plaza. The shuttle also takes shoppers to the Palm Desert Town Center and to the Marriot's sister resort, the Rancho Las Palmas.

The Southern California desert in this area is dotted with small resort towns, each with its own share of golf courses, shops, and restaurants. Palm Springs, Rancho Mirage, Palm Desert, La Quinta, Indian Wells, Cathedral City, Coachella, Desert Hot Springs, Bermuda Dunes, and Indio are the desert communities that you might want to check out. These are the places where movie stars play, and if you keep your eyes open, you might just see Bob Hope or some of his cronies.

WHAT'S INCLUDED IN THE PRICE

The Marriott's Desert Springs resort can accommodate a spa guest in several ways. You can stay in the resort and pay for spa services a la carte or you can opt for a half-day, full-day, four-day or seven-day package. A full-day package includes thalassotherapy, terratherapy (a mud mask), facial, superspace relaxer (a dry flotation environment), spa lunch, shampoo, make-up, day use of spa facilities. Other full-day packages add golf, tennis, or a personal fitness session. Prices are on the expensive side, but darn well worth it.

For a la carte spa-goers, there is a day fee that includes complimentary mineral water, use of all facilities, body and beauty amenities, and a spa wardrobe. Add a 17 percent service charge to any treatments you might take.

Unless you cancel a treatment three hours in advance, you will be billed for the treatement.

The four-day and seven-day spa packages include accommodations, three meals a day, medical screening, nutritional, fitness and individual program consultations, massages, facials, treatments, and unlimited tennis. The seven-day program allows additional treatments and massage therapy.

CLOTHING AND WEATHER

This resort is located in the center of Southern California's world famous desert retreat. Because of its dry air, sunny days, and balmy nights, Palm Springs has attracted Hollywood stars for decades. It is now also an attraction to retiring folk — those with plenty of money.

The most comfortable time to visit is in the winter when the days are in the 70s and 80s. In the summer, temperatures reach into the 90s and 100s, but it is a dry heat and bearable. Temperatures routinely drop 30 degrees at night, summer or winter, because this is the desert.

When I was there in May, it was mostly sunny with gusty winds, highs in the upper 80s and lows in the mid-50s. A nice touch at this resort is the way it gives you tommorrow's weather forecast so you can plan your day.

This is a resort that caters to conferences, not just spa guests, so you will want to bring dressier clothes than for a resort that is only a spa. Dinner clothes are needed for night; golf and tennis wear might be needed during the day.

But when you are on the spa package, you come down to the spa first thing in the morning and you stay until you change for dinner. You don't need to bring much with you to the spa because everything is there: blow dryer, leotards, combs, brushes, shaving cream and razors, etc. The spa provides a wardrobe for its guests that includes a terry robe, slippers, warm-up suit, leotard, t-shirt, and gym shorts. Each spa guest needs to bring his or her own shoes, socks, and bathing suit.

A TYPICAL DAY

If you are on the spa package, the spa staff will work out an individualized schedule for you. To make that schedule really work for your specific needs, it's a good idea to have a fitness assessment which includes body composition tests and fitness consultations.

I began one day with a nutritional consultation, followed by the white water workout (a form of aquacise) and Easy Does It aerobics. Toward the end of the day, I went for relaxation: a Superspace, Stretch Away Stress class, and a Bindi Herbal body treatment.

A Superspace is a small cubicle-type area with a float mattress. Inside, one can listen to music, watch relaxation videos or cybervision weight control videos while somehow getting a back rub from the float mattress.

The Stretch Away Stress class is a program designed to stretch key muscle groups and unwind the tension built up in them.

A Bindi Herbal body treatment is an Ayurvedic treatment (a 5,000-year-old healing science of India) that uses special oils, creams, and massages.

The next day I took the 7 a.m. sunrise walk and did four exercise classes afterward—weight room training, Wonder Bands, Flex First, and the white water workout. The afternoon was reserved for an aromatherapy massage, a pedicure, and a manicure.

Those were two typical days for me, but each person can come up with their own. There are exercise classes on the hour and each is rated for beginners, intermediates and advanced fitness levels. Walks, and Tai Chi are early morning classes open to the entire hotel, not just spa users.

The different treatments available include the water treatment thalassotherapy, terratherapy (which uses Italian mud masks), herbal wraps, loofah body buffs, Swedish massage, and Shiatsu (an acupressure massage). A Turkish steam bath with moist heat at 120 degrees or a Finnish sauna with dry heat at 175 degrees are perfect toppers to one of these treatments.

Each day I was given a sheet that told me my personal schedule as well as a general one that gave the weather forecast and several ideas about things to do around the resort, such as golf, tennis, Ping Pong, or boat tours.

The spa is open from 6:30 a.m. to 7:30 p.m. for those 18 years and over.

THE STAFF

It's difficult not to leave the spa feeling clean and healthy because every employee in the spa aims to make you walk out happy and rejuvenated. The spa director said, "We're trying to create a feeling for the guests of being relaxed and not distracted." Employees might do that by giving a mini-shoulder rub while a guest is waiting for something.

The spa hires trained massage therapists, as well as licensed technicians. It has also brought in a Swedish skin care expert, a registered dietician, and hair stylist Jose Eber, who is known for his movie star clientele.

FOOD

This isn't a destination spa, but if you're on the spa package there is no reason why you can't eat spa food during each meal. An elegant, 225-seat restaurant, called Lakeview, serves a special spa menu.

By substituting fresh herbs, fruits, and vegetables for high caloric foods, the Lakeview chefs can keep a spa guest at 900-1,000 calories a day. For example, for breakfast and lunch one day I had only 450 calories. Dinners at Lakeview might include mushroom ravioli for 239 calories or grilled salmon for 314 calories.

The head chef told me that once the resort began promoting its spa menu, it found that more and more people were interested in it. The attitude toward healthier eating has tempered the recipes for the other restaurants in the resort. Meats are broiled and heavy sauces are eliminated.

I ate at the Sea Grille ordering lobster and steamed vegetables, but I was careful to ask for the spa salad dressing for my salad. At this restaurant, eight varieties of fresh fish are flown in every day from Los Angeles. There are 16 fish and seafood selections prepared five different ways with five different sauces. That leaves you with 400 choices — as a spa guest you'll pick the healthiest choice, right?

There are 10 restaurants, lounges, and snack bars at Desert Springs, from Japanese to the traditional country club fare of steaks and burgers. The restaurants are all good, but to be safe calorie-wise it is best to stick with the Lakeview restaurant.

The national Marriott corporation is duly impressed with the Desert Springs' spa recipes and is planning to distribute them to other Marriotts around the country.

SUMMARY

I loved Desert Springs as a resort and as a spa. The attention to details and the friendly staff made this one of my favorite spa vacations. Even though this is a resort and not a destination spa, they do a jam-up job.

LA COSTA

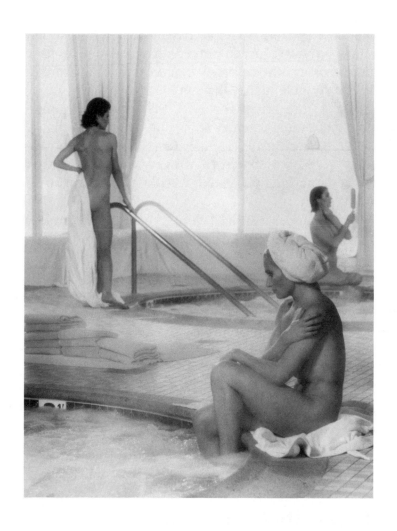

La Costa in Carlsbad, California is mentioned by "Lifestyles of the Rich and Famous" as one of the 10 best spas in the world, but only the rich and famous would be able to tell you that.

This four-star, four-diamond resort, now owned by a Japanese company, caters to the wealthy, and its spa reflects that.

Even when paying the expensive rate for accommodations, a guest must pay extra just to enter the spa, as well as for all spa services, however, the resort is beautiful and the stars of Hollywood, sports, and finance have made it their own.

Staying in the hotel, you have the services of babysitters, doctors, dry cleaning, laundry and valet, currency exchange, post office, safe deposit boxes, security, and anything else you might need. It's a destination resort in every meaning of the word; there's really nothing you need outside of its boundaries for a vacation.

La Costa underwent a $100 million renovation and expansion in 1986 and now has two 18-hole championship golf courses, a 23-court racquet club, eight restaurants, and a spa.

As part of the spa is the La Costa Lifestyle Clinic with its nutrition center, exercise center and Life Fitness and Longevity Center. This center will personalize a health plan for you during a seven-night, in-depth program dealing with nutrition, weight control, stress management, and communication in personal and work relationships. A full-time medical doctor specializing in preventive medicine, lifestyle counselor, nutritionist, and exercise physiologist lead the classes and lectures included in the Longevity Center.

Minimum age at the spa is 18.

THE LOOK OF THINGS

There are 478 rooms, suites, and homes at La Costa, as well as the golf courses, tennis courts, swimming pools, and conference rooms that make this a destination resort.

Situated on 400 acres between the Pacific Ocean and the foothills, La Costa's buildings are shades of pink and terracotta designed in the Spanish/Mediterranean style.

Aside from housing the accommodations and conference facilities, the buildings also hold a 180-seat theater, nine boutiques for shopping, and eight restaurants (six in the Clubhouse, one in the racquet club, and one in La Costa Plaza).

The golf courses dominate the spread-out grounds with their lush green fairways and manicured greens. An aquatic complex includes swimming pools and a snack bar.

The racquet club has choices of clay, grass, or hard courts, and a jogging trail meanders through the grounds. If these don't offer enough exercise for you, there is the spa and health center.

The spa has separate facilities for men and women, including locker rooms, saunas, rock steam baths, Swiss showers, Roman pools, whirlpools, and a solarium. A men's spa pool and a women's spa pool are totally separate from each other.

The weight room employs Eagle weights, Lifecycles, and computerized treadmills in its offerings for a fitness regime.

La Costa Salon was voted "Salon of the Year" by Modern Salon Magazine, and its make-up artists use La Costa Cosmetics.

I found the rooms very pretty with comfortable feather pillows and mattresses. They were decorated in light pastels with patios overlooking the grounds.

HOW TO GET THERE

La Costa is 90 minutes south of Los Angeles and 30 minutes north of San Diego off Interstate 5. Limousine service is available from La Costa to both the Los Angeles and San Diego airports as well as to area points of interest. A minibus service at both airports is available if it is arranged at least 24 hours in advance.

Check-in time is at 4 p.m.; check-out time is 2 p.m. for spa guests and noon for other guests.

For reservations call La Costa at (800) 854-5000.

SURROUNDING AREA

La Costa will offer special sightseeing trips to the San Diego Zoo or SeaWorld or the La Jolla/Prospect Street shopping area.

Rental bikes are available if guests want to visit the surrounding area of Costa Brava country on their own.

CLOTHING AND WEATHER

This is Southern California — sunny, warm days all year long. La Costa is a fashionable resort and there is a dress code. Robes, swimsuits, beach sandals, and athletic attire must be worn only in the proper areas. Shorts are not allowed after 7 p.m. in the clubhouse or in the restaurants.

Bring dressy clothes. This is a fancy place with fancy people.

WHAT'S INCLUDED IN THE PRICE

A stay at La Costa will be expensive, especially if you plan to use the spa on an a la carte basis. Just having an accommodation doesn't mean you go to the spa free. A fee is required to enter the spa which then allows you use of the whirlpools, Roman pools, rock steam rooms, sauna rooms, inhalation rooms, Swiss showers, exercise pools, steam cabinets, exercise gyms, and jogging track. Lockers, sweatsuit, toga, and slippers are handed out.

This daily fee is slightly cheaper if you are paying for another spa service, such as a massage.

The spa plan is a seven-night, eight-day package with accommodations, all meals, personalized consultations, daily spa admission, daily massage, facial, herbal wrap, tanning session and exercise classes, skin analysis and review, hair styling, other massage treatments, and unlimited golf and tennis. It is expensive.

The four-night spa plan includes accommodations and meals and many of the spa services.

A 15 percent service charge and sales tax will be added to the bill. La Costa takes just about all major credit cards.

A TYPICAL DAY

The first stop for spa package guests is to check in at the medical office for an evaluation. Spa schedules are given to each guest after an individual tour of the facility.

Exercise classes are coed and start at 8:20 a.m. and include total workout, water volleyball, rebounder (aerobics on a mini-trampoline), aquatics, stretch and relax. There are special classes for women, including gym exercise classes, a spa walk at 8 a.m., low impact aerobics, and yoga.

Lectures are given weekdays at 10:20 a.m. on nutritional concerns. Some topics might be "Focus on Fiber," "Fat Facts," "New-trition in the Marketplace."

There are also two make-up classes a day and special classes on exercise and skin care at various times.

The La Costa spa will do medical and fitness evaluations; spa services include skin analysis, facials, massages, herbal wraps, and loofah scrubs.

The spa is open from 7 a.m. to 9 p.m. and offers tours at 9:15 a.m. and 2:15 p.m.

EVENING PROGRAMS

The in-house movie theater shows first-run movies for a charge, and there are three lounges for entertainment. On the spa side of things, evening lectures are held twice a week on controlling fat and creating fitness, and a spa cooking demonstration is given once a week.

THE STAFF

As well as the multitude of help needed to run a large resort, the spa also has a permanant staff physician, a resident nutritionist, dietitian, and exercise physiologist.

FOOD

The chef of the Spa Dining Room believes that you don't have to suffer to lose weight or eat nutritionally correct.

He is more concerned about overall nutrition than counting calories and goes to great lengths to ensure that the spa cuisine is not only low in calories but healthy.

The Spa Restaurant serves a five course meal for less than 300 calories. That's soup, salad, appetizer, entree, and dessert, all for fewer calories than a fast-food specialty hamburger.

Presentation is very important in the Spa Restaurant. It's along the lines of nouvelle cuisine with a very gourmet presentation. The Chef wants to make it an event to eat at the Spa Dining Room and even has a large selection of nonalcoholic beers and wines.

But if spa food is not what you're after, there are seven other restaurants which specialize in Italian, Chinese, Mexican, gourmet continental, and seafood. A regular, everyday restaurant is available too, as well as a steakhouse.

SUMMARY

La Costa is beautiful, but expensive. It's not a place to receive individual treatment, to really learn about a lifestyle change in eating and exercising habits (unless you are on the Life Fitness & Longevity Program where your entire week is devoted to learning a healthy lifestyle). It is a place to mingle with the wealthy, which may or may not be a high priority for you. It wasn't for me.

SONOMA MISSION INN

Luxury—whether a la carte or on a spa package—is best served at Sonoma Mission Inn. This hotel and spa offers exercise with class, spa cuisine that can only be called gourmet, personalized attention from the spa's staff of 100 (that's not including the hotel staff), and body treatments to pamper you.

People may leave their hearts in San Francisco, but they'll leave their bodies anytime at Sonoma Mission Inn 50 miles outside the city.

This is a resort retreat for many San Franciscans tired of the city, but it is also a full-blown spa for those wanting a week or just a day or two of pampering and fitness. It's a good place to leave stress behind and just totally relax.

At Sonoma Mission Inn, all you can think about is yourself— which is wonderful because there's no guilt involved; it's what your supposed to do while you're there. So many times in business or in our personal lives we're constantly thinking about the other people around us. Every now and then we need a place to come and be selfish without feeling guilty.

A five-day spa package at Sonoma Mission Inn is an elegant vacation. The staff will push you to a healthier lifestyle only as much as you want them to. You can jump into tough fitness classes all day long or laze by the swimming pool until your massage is scheduled. I did a little of both.

Although the spa was originated because of the natural mineral waters found in the ground, its pools are not naturally heated anymore. The Inn does bottle its own pure mineral water to sell to its customers.

The philosophy of the Inn's spa is to help people achieve a balance in their lives whether it is to eat more nutritiously or eliminate stress. The staff hopes that visitors will be able to take a renewed vigor home with them. They gave me an underwater hydrostatic weighing to accurately determine the amount of fat in my body. I was also given a fitness test where my heart rate was taken along with my blood pressure. But it didn't stop at the testing.

Sonoma Mission Inn then devised a personal "exercise prescription" for me. The advisor told me what my percentage of body fat should be and how much weight I needed to lose (in two phases). She also gave me exercises to do and encouraged me to keep up my daily walks. I won't tell you what my body fat percentage is, but I'll let you know for women it should be 20-24 percent and for men 15-16 percent.

This kind of personalized pampering attention is evident throughout the Sonoma Mission Inn, from providing every toiletry imaginable in the spa to the full-time concierge who will arrange any kind of activity you desire.

One other aspect of Sonoma Mission Inn that makes this a luxury spa is its food. Chef Charles Saunders, formerly of the famous Maxaluna restaurant in Boca Raton, Florida, has put new meaning into spa cuisine. It is still the healthy food we need, but he has added the gourmet touch we crave.

THE LOOK OF THINGS

This inn, first developed as a spa in the mid-1800s, was rejuvenated in 1980 as a luxury resort that has since earned the Mobil Travel Guide four-star award and the Triple A four-diamond award.

As the Boyes Hot Springs Hotel, it was a retreat for wealthy San Franciscans from 1883 to 1923 but fell into disrepair until the European-style spa was built in 1981. The new owners then renovated the main building, which is an architecturally accurate replica of a California mission, and expanded the number of rooms from 99 to 170.

Today, when arriving at the Sonoma Mission Inn, you see a pink stucco building complete with arcade and bell towers set among eight landscaped acres of eucalyptus trees.

There are two parts to Sonoma Mission Inn — the 60-year-old main building and a pair of new wings. The accommodations in these buildings have woodburning fireplaces and minibars. Our room had two televisions — one in the sitting area, another in the bedroom - and was furnished with an elegant country decor.

A restaurant at the Inn, called The Grille, has begun to win much acclaim since chef Saunders began overseeing its wine country cuisine two years ago. It is an elegant restaurant dressed in pastels, with a wine list that features more than 200 Sonoma and Napa wines.

Another restaurant on the corner of the grounds called the Big 3 Cafe is more informal. Next to it is a store selling cookbooks, magazines, gifts, and logo merchandise, as well as gourmet food products from Sonoma County.

The spa building, open from 7 a.m. to 10 p.m., includes an aerobic studio, sauna and steam rooms, indoor and outdoor whirlpools, outdoor exercise pool, two gyms with weight lifting equipment (Keiser Cam II and Inertia Variable Resistance system), exercise bikes, and locker rooms with showers.

The spa's interior is clean with tiled floors and stucco walls. It has a boutique that sells spa apparel, t-shirts, and their own line of products that are used in spa treatments.

The spa exercise pool is heated to 83-86 degrees year-round; the Olympic-sized pool is heated April through November. There are also two lighted tennis courts.

HOW TO GET THERE

Sonoma Mission Inn is 50 miles northeast of San Francisco on Highway 12 in the Boyes Hot Springs area of Sonoma County. If arriving by airplane at San Francisco International Airport, you will have to rent a car to get to the Inn. Call ahead to get directions and a brochure showing a map.

For reservations, call the toll-free number in California, (800) 862-4945 or outside California (800) 358-9022 or (800) 358-9027. You can write Sonoma Mission Inn at P.O. Box 1447, Sonoma, CA 95476.

Check-in time at Sonoma Mission Inn is 4 p.m., but if you arrive earlier, you can use the facilities until your room is ready. There is a 72-hour cancellation policy for accommodations.

SURROUNDING AREA

Sonoma Mission Inn is in the heart of California's Wine Country. It is in the Sonoma Valley, Napa Valley just a short drive away. But why drive to Napa when you can visit more than 100 wineries in Sonoma County alone? Many nearby wineries have tours as well as wine tastings, and the concierge at Sonoma Mission Inn can arrange a day of touring the wine country for you.

Aside from visiting the wineries, there is a myriad of activites to do in Sonoma County, from hot air ballooning to horseback riding to picnicking. Several golf courses are close to the Inn, and the Sonoma Golf Club, less than a mile from the Inn, re-opened in October, 1990 after undergoing a $6 million renovation.

The historic town of Sonoma is only two miles away from Sonoma Mission Inn. This is a fun town for shopping, with its boutiques and food specialities. In the town itself is a cheese-maker located in an old stone brewery who specializes in a two-year-old jack cheese that is tempting to take home in bulk. Sonoma also offers a lot of events throughout the summer such as Shakespeare productions, concerts, jazz festivals, and food and wine festivals.

For the nature buff, hiking is abundant in Jack London State Historic Park or in the Mayacamas Mountains. The country setting of rolling green hills and long rows of vineyards contributes to Sonoma County's peaceful atmosphere.

WHAT'S INCLUDED IN THE PRICE

Many stay at Sonoma Mission Inn and buy their spa treat-ments and fitness programs a la carte, but I recommend a spa package, which in this luxury resort can be termed expensive.

The five-night deluxe package includes accommodations, three spa cuisine meals a day, one aromatherapy massage and two full body massages, choice of two body scrubs, two herbal wraps or two seaweed hydro massages, choice of two facials or a facial and a make-up application, a manicure or pedicure, hair and scalp treatment, all fitness classes, five morning hikes, fitness evaluation, choice of nutritional consultation, hydrostatic weighing or one-on-one fitness training, spa tote bag, t-shirt, visor, cookbook, and in-room movies.

The one-, two-, and three-night packages are similar but offer fewer treatments.

All the packages include a tax and service charge in lieu of gratuity. Advance reservations are required for all packages.

If you decide to go a la carte, be aware that the spa treatments can be expensive alone and then a 17 percent service charge is added to the total. Any guest of Sonoma Mission Inn is entitled to use the steam room, sauna, whirlpools, exercise equipment, heated spa pool, changing rooms with showers, and tennis courts.

Club memberships are available for those who live near the Sonoma Mission Inn.

CLOTHING AND WEATHER

During my stay in February, it was sunny with temperatures around 65-70 degrees. Sonoma County does have its seasons (such as grape-harvesting season), but the weather is balmy year-round. Mornings and evenings are a tad chilly, however, so bring a windbreaker or jacket for early hikes and evening tete-a-tetes by the swimming pool.

This is not a "sloppy" spa. At some spas you can run around in sweats or even a bathrobe for most of the day, but not Sonoma Mission Inn. I even felt obliged to dress for lunch one day and my husband wore a jacket to dinner. Don't forget that as well as a spa, this is a hotel with an upper-income clientele.

Besides nicer clothes for dining, bring the usual spa attire – leotards, shorts, t-shirts, bathing suits, gym shoes and socks, clothes to go walking and hiking in, and lightweight hiking shoes. The spa provides towels and full-length robes for day use.

It is a co-ed spa so you can't get away with leaving your swimsuit at home. My husband forgot his and had to buy one in the boutique.

You can forget all the necessary toiletries because they are all provided – shampoo, creme rinse, razors, shaving creme, deodorant, hair spray, body soap – just about anything.

A TYPICAL DAY

Each morning starts with a delightful hike led by one of the staff members. They load us up in a van and drive us to a different part of Sonoma County for about a 2.5 mile walk. They call them hikes, but they are really more like walks, except that they do get a little bit more difficult every day. The last day's hike in the Jack London State Historic Park is more like hiking, instead of walking.

After the walks, a yoga class is offered every morning for those who like to start their day in a relaxed frame of mind.

Exercise classes run from 6:45 a.m. to 6 p.m. all day long and you can choose just how much and how hard you feel like exercising. The classes are ranked for beginning, intermediate, and advanced levels. A tough aerobic class is held for those who want to burn calories and increase fat loss, a low impact aerobic class focuses on toning. Other exercise classes include water works, body sculpting, tennis pointers, stretch and relax class, and an endurance (75 minute) low impact aerobic class.

It's also a good idea to take advantage of the class (offered daily) that teaches you how to use the weight and aerobic equipment properly.

Body treatments, that you must schedule in advance, include different kinds of massages and an herbal wrap. During an herbal wrap, your body is swathed in steaming linens soaked in herbs. This eliminates toxins through perspiration.

There are two kinds of herbal blends used in Sonoma Mission Inn's herbal wraps. To give you an idea, here are the ingredients to one of the blends: 1 part comfrey root to regenerate aging tissue; 1 part peppermint leaves for a cooling and antiseptic effect; 1 part old-fashioned red rosebuds to cleanse and act as an astringent; 1 part French lavender to stimulate sore muscles; 1/2 part orange blossoms which has a yang quality and is soothing on the emotions; 1/2 part yarrow as an astringent; and 2 parts chamomile to soothe aches and pains and help in relaxation. How would you like to be the one mixing up that potion?

I would recommend the revitalizer therapy — a two-hour session that combines several treatments. It was just great.

The Shiatsu massage, which uses Japanese finger pressure to stimulate energy pathways, is also a good bet at Sonoma Mission Inn.

You can schedule the seaweed hydro massage, a body scrub, or aromatherapy massage, among others. Beauty treatments from manicures to a European back treatment are also available.

Another thing to fit into your days at the spa is the personalized session with spa staff. I had my body fat measured, a fitness test, and a nutrition session. All were informative and important for me to understand how to take my body and fix it.

EVENING PROGRAMS

There are no evening programs, but the spa facilities are open until 10 p.m. for a pre-bedtime whirlpool or sauna. If you are interested in some lectures, the spa offers them during the day. On Mondays at 2 p.m. a nutrition lecture is given, on Tuesdays at 2 p.m. a stress management lecture, and at 3 p.m. an exercise prescription class.

THE STAFF

The spa staff of more than 100 includes experts in aerobics, fitness, tennis, beauty, massage, yoga, and nutrition. The woman who led our early morning hikes knows more than the best places in Sonoma County for walking, she also holds a degree in physical education.

The staff was young, upbeat, knowledgeable, and very health-conscious. This is a spa that allows each person to make his or her own schedule, but the staff will give individualized help at any time so you can get the full benefit of your stay here.

The hotel has 170 rooms and more than 400 employees — a pretty good ratio of three employees for every room.

FOOD

I spent some time with Sonoma Mission Inn's highly touted chef, and was impressed with his attitude toward spa cuisine.

He doesn't look at the Inn's spa cuisine as a type of food unto itself; rather, it is an outgrowth of his basic philosophy of using fresh, local products. He calls it Sonoma cuisine.

With spa cuisine, he'll control the portion sizes, the salt intake and make sure it's a balanced meal. But the types of vegetables, meats, and food products he uses are the same as what's in the regular food Sonoma Mission Inn serves.

I found this intriguing, and maybe it's why I loved the food here so much. Let me give you an example of an appetizer and an entree off the spa menu: the appetizer is angel hair pasta, field mushrooms, roasted garlic, tomatoes and basil; and the entree is Bodega Bay sturgeon steamed in corn husks with masa harina and fine diced marinated vegetables.

On the spa menu, the calories were listed as well as the prices. Can you believe that a lemon chiffon dessert with strawberry sauce was only 85 calories?

The chef said his spa cuisine shocks a lot of people who think healthy food just can't taste good. In reality, spa cuisine can be Italian, Oriental, Mexican, or any of the foods you like to eat, but prepared in a healthier way.

He gave the example of beef — a no-no to many spas — by saying that a 3 oz. slice with the fat trimmed off isn't that unhealthy. Also, salsa, chutneys, marmalades, and compotes are often made at Sonoma Mission Inn, but they are made with less sugar and more fresh fruit (which is naturally sweeter anyway).

Most impressive was not just his gourmet touch to spa food, but that a certified nutritionist approves all of the spa meals. There is no item that is served on the spa menu (or starred as a healthy entree on the regular menus) that hasn't been given her approval.

SUMMARY

Because California's northern wine country is one of my favorite areas on earth, I enjoy anything connected with it. This made my trip to Sonoma Mission Inn doubly pleasing. But also, luxury is luxury: I'm a sucker for it, and Sonoma Mission Inn has it. Although it will lighten your wallet, you'll return home feeling like a million bucks.

THE HYATT REGENCY
WAIKOLOA

It's been called the "Disneyland" of resorts by many people, and rightly so. The Hyatt Regency Waikoloa, with its free-form swimming pools, canal boats, dolphin swim-alongs, flamingos, parrots, and staged luaus, is a resort beyond any other. It is a luxury entertainment experience.

The Hyatt Regency Waikoloa sprawls along the tropical coastline of the Big Island of Hawaii serving its guests with three hotel towers, two golf courses, eight tennis courts, eight restaurants, and a system of lagoons, swimming pools, and canals. It is a mammoth resort, but one that still has nooks and crannies where a person can sway in the breeze on a hammock or find a secluded spot of sand for sunbathing.

The Hyatt Regency Waikoloa was opened in December 1988 after $360 million was poured into developing 62 acres of Hawaiian beachfront. The resort caters to conferences and groups but is happy to accommodate anyone who can afford its pricey rooms and restaurants.

At $6 million — and costing just a fraction of the entire resort — is the ANARA spa. During the Hyatt's research about Waikoloa, its executives discovered that the number of spas in the United States grew from 30 in 1983 to 150 in 1988. In 1989, 1.3 million Americans visited health spas seeking to better their physique and their mental outlook.

So the ANARA spa was included in the Hyatt Regency Waikoloa as the answer to more and more fitness and health-conscious travelers and business executives. It is considered the Hyatt corporation's "prototype spa."

ANARA stands for A New Age Restorative Approach which means that its treatments lean toward the holistic; you'll hear a lot of New Age music wafting through the spa building. The spa focuses on five aspects of health — fitness, spa treatments, nutrition counseling, beauty counseling, health and meditation counseling.

It also aims to help people eliminate and control stress in many different ways. One unique way is the fitness mini-classes that break up conference meetings by giving those in attendance a 15- minute exercise "alertness" break.

However, if you are going to the Hyatt Regency Waikoloa for its spa alone, plan on being distracted by the resort's other amenities. This is a resort where you pay as you go and that includes spa treatments and meals. There is no specific spa regimen and therefore you may, and at this Disneyland resort, probably will, get waylaid by other attractions.

Attractions like dolphins. This is the resort that allows its guests to swim with its dolphins. They are kept in a lagoon filled with saltwater that is replaced every two hours. Guests can swim with the eight Atlantic bottlenose dolphins for a mere $55 a half hour. Part of that fee goes to marine education and conservation with the Waikoloa Marine Life Fund.

The swim with the dolphin program is so popular that the Hyatt uses a lottery to decide which guests will swim with the gentle marine mammals. Guests receive a dolphin lottery card for each day they stay at the resort and then hope they are lucky. Unfortunately, I wasn't so lucky and I missed out on a frolic in the water with Flipper.

But I frolicked plenty on the waterslides, enjoyed a facial, a massage, and the luxury of this resort where every wish is catered to and where the expansiveness overwhelms you.

In spite of its modern magnificence, one little piece of Hawaiian luxury incorporated into the resort is older than Captain Cook's discovery of Hawaii. The lomi lomi massage has been practicied by Hawaiian natives for centuries, passed on from generation to generation. Masters of lomi lomi massage see it as a spiritual act that can transfer good energy from one person to another. For the average client, it just feels good. I had one and loved the long strokes that started at the top of my shoulders and ended at my toes.

A massage therapist uses hands and forearms to give a lomi lomi massage. The technique feels like four hands are massaging your body. The Hawaiian natives who work in the spa have the lomi lomi massage down to a spiritual art.

THE LOOK OF THINGS

On an expanse of barren lava field, the lush palm trees, grass, and flora at the Hyatt exemplify the resort's attention to detail and its commitment to luxury at any cost. Each of the 1,640 transplanted coconut trees cost $1,000 apiece. Its 1,241 rooms, eight restaurants, 12 lounges, and 36 holes of golf indicate the resort's breadth.

Water is everywhere at this resort. The Hyatt Regency Waikoloa is built around the Anaehoomalu Bay with a lagoon lapping right up to the $2 million grand staircase of the pink flagstone lobby. Several free-form swimming pools are scattered throughout the grounds, including one that is nearly an acre in size. A river pool with a current will carry you from pool to pool. At one pool, there is a hidden grotto bar (but if you are really on a spa vacation, maybe it's better if you don't find it).

Three main towers house the rooms of which 75 percent have ocean views. Decorated in pastels, the rooms each have decks overlooking the ocean.

Recreationally, there are two golf courses, eight tennis courts, racquetball and squash courts, and of course, the spa.

Centrally located next to the tennis courts and not far from the main swimming pool, the ANARA spa has 25,000 square feet in which its staff can pummel, exercise, counsel, and make you over.

The ANARA spa has separate facilities for men and women that would be complete spas for some resorts. Each gender's facilities include a Turkish steam bath, Finnish sauna, outdoor Jacuzzi, showers, locker rooms, spa wardrobe, and amenities. There are also seven private massage rooms, four facial rooms, two loofah rooms, four herbal wrap rooms, and two private whirlpools each for men and women.

The spa also manages to fit in a full-service beauty salon, an aerobic gym, a weight room, and an indoor/outdoor Jacuzzi surrounded by tropical foilage and a mountain view.

HOW TO GET THERE

The Hyatt Regency Waikoloa is 25 minutes from the Kona Airport on the Kona Coast of Hawaii's Big Island. I planned to take its shuttle bus, but it broke down and I took a taxi instead. The shuttle bus is cheaper than a taxi, however. Once you check into the resort, the next mode of transportation is a canal boat or tram to get to your room. It's too far to walk to your room on this property.

To make reservations for the resort, call (800)-228-9000 or write One Waikoloa Beach Resort, Big Island of Hawaii 96743. The resort's fax number is (808) 885-7474 and its Hawaiian number is (808) 885-1234.

SURROUNDING AREA

The Big Island, as its name implies, is the largest of the Hawaiian islands with 4,000 square miles. It is 93 miles long and 76 miles wide at its largest point. People from all over the world gather at this southernmost point of the United States to fish for the famous Pacific blue marlin or to compete in the Ironman Triathlon.

Formed by a volcano, the Big Island is still home to active volcanoes. Most have read about Kilauea, which is destroying homes with its red-hot lava. The Volcanoes National Park offers the best way to learn about Hawaii's thermal activity. The two highest mountains in Hawaii are on this island, Mauna Kea and Mauna Loa, at 13,796 and 13,677 respectively.

You may be interested in sightseeing around the island but don't want to be your own tour guide. Don't worry. The Hyatt has you covered with its fantasy program that takes guests on the best possible tours — at the highest prices too.

The resort plans the adventures you want to take and adds its own special touch to make it seem like a fantasy. For example, one of it most popular is the Lauhala Point Picnic Helicopter Fantasy. Guests are taken on a sightseeing tour of the island, passing over fiery Kilauea Volcano, the beautiful Kohala mountains, and lush valleys with cascading waterfalls. Then a private picnic is served on a 3,000-foot ocean cliff at Lauhala Point, accessible only by helicopter.

Other fantasies include a gourmet champagne dinner for two aboard a 45-foot cutter during a Hawaiian sunset, ranching and riding with Hawaiian cowboys on the Kahua Ranch, hiking remote valleys and beaches with a guide, or taking customized bird-watching trips.

WHAT'S INCLUDED IN THE PRICE

The ANARA spa is an a la carte facility where your accommodations and meals are charged separately from your spa activities. The accommodations are expensive and range in various levels of luxury suites right up to the presidential suites that cost more per day than many Third World families' average annual income.

There is no charge for children 15 and under. Check-out time is noon; check-in time is 3 p.m. Reservations need a minimum of two nights' room rates within 14 days as a deposit.

At the ANARA spa, it's probably best to buy a five- or 10-day pass to the spa if you're planning to stay a few days. The facility fees include use of the Turkish steam room, Finnish saunas, outdoor whirlpool, relaxation lounges, weight room, locker rooms, towels, toiletries, and spa wardrobe.

That wardrobe consists of a bathrobe, slippers, shorts, and t-shirt.

After the facility fee, all the treatments are an a la carte expense, but there are several different packages to fit different spa desires.

For example, the "Day at Anara" is an all-inclusive day-long package that includes fitness classes, massages, facials, and salon services. Mini packages focus on salon services, spa services, "after sun" services, and "after sport" services among others.

All spa services have a 15 percent service charge added on as well as the state's 4 percent sales tax. Those under 18 are not allowed in the spa. There is a four-hour advance cancellation policy.

There are a few spa classes that are complimentary for all Hyatt guests. Those include tai chi classes, stress management reduction classes, yoga, meditation, power walks, and water workouts.

CLOTHING AND WEATHER

The resort lies on the leeward side of the island along the Kona Sunshine Coast. This area is protected from Hawaii's wet trade winds by the island's large mountains. This makes the Waikoloa area of the Hyatt Regency sunny all year round.

The dress is Hawaiian casual, but at the Hyatt Regency the casual moves toward a little more formal in the evening. Ladies are expected to get dressed up at night; men need to wear jackets.

To go to the spa, don't worry about your looks. There is even a cafe next to the spa where it is appropriate to eat breakfast or lunch any old way.

A TYPICAL DAY

As in most a la carte spas, a typical day is whatever you make it. There are specific times for the fitness classes, but other than that the scheduling of salon and spa treatments is up to you. Whatever schedule you choose, the spa's director is hoping that you will pick up the peacefulness of Hawaii's scenic mountains and beaches. She aims to make this a "paradise spa" where people from the hustle and bustle of cities like New York and Los Angeles can find serenity.

One way she does this is to encourage those guests coming in with jet lag to take an herbal wrap. After being massaged with seaweed and mineral-rich plants and then wrapped in a warm blanket, those suffering jet lag are going to feel great for the next 48 hours.

The fitness schedule begins each day with a 50-minute sunrise walk. Powerwalks are held in the mornings and the evenings. I went on one of these, a brisk walk by the ocean and across lava beds.

Also held in early morning and again at mid-morning are classes in tai chi and yoga. Hawaii is where East meets West, and a practical application of Oriental philosophy is taken for granted in this state where there are large numbers of Chinese and Japanese. Taking its cue from this Hawaiian lifestyle, the ANARA spa tries to keep alive the Eastern influence through these two classes.

Throughout the day are stress reduction classes, low impact and high impact aerobic workouts, stretching and toning classes using rubber bands and weights, and water workouts. There are also weight rooms with Stairmasters, treadmills, stationary bicycles and biocycles if you want to work on your own. However, you could do fitness classes continuously if you wanted.

I didn't. I chose to have a facial and a lomi lomi massage. The facial was incredible; I could feel myself drifting off as she did my face. Then my hands were given a massage and wrapped into warm, electrically-heated mittens. Mmm.

Spa treatments include massage, Shiatsu, aromatherapy massage, thaalassobath, reflexology, underwater massage, and herbal wraps. A loofah scrub uses warm almond oil with a fine sea salt applied to your skin; afterward take an aromabath with its essential oils from herbs, flowers, and trees.

EVENING PROGRAMS

There are no regularly scheduled spa programs at night, but the spa staff is working on developing some. Currently, the spa offers lectures in nutrition, fitness, and make-up demonstrations to groups. Also a massage therapist will take a willing volunteer and explain to an audience how she performs a massage.

Occasionally, an artists' champagne reception will be held to recognize a new display at one of the art galleries.

THE STAFF

Imagine: The Hyatt Regency Waikoloa washes about 205 pounds of dirty linen a day and serves 5,000 meals a day. This is just a small part of this huge resort and accounts for just some of its many employees — about 2,000 in all. They travel from restaurant to restaurant and to each hotel tower by a long underground tunnel.

I found the spa staff to be very courteous and accommodating. Many of the massage therapists were native Hawaiians well-trained in the lomi lomi massage.

FOOD

There are eight restaurants at the Hyatt resort, but only one of them specializes in spa cuisine. The Kona Provision Company is an excellent place to eat lunch because it does have spa food on the menu with the calories listed alongside the menu items. The Orchid Cafe next to the health spa concentrates on fresh foods and ingredients, offering a little bit of spa cuisine.

However, the chef says the resort will gradually put spa cuisine onto all of its restaurant's menus, so everyone can have an alternative at each venue.

He is also innovatively incorporating a taste of Hawaii into all of his restaurants, beginning with French Hawaiian cuisine. What is that? It is using Hawaiian fruits, vegetables, herbs, and spices prepared in the traditional French way.

Each of the restaurants specializes in a different aspect whether it is food or scenery. There are Polynesian, Italian, and Japanese restaurants. There are restaurants in tea gardens, with bay views, and ones accompanied by a Polynesian show.

The Water's Edge offers continental cuisine with a spectacular view of the ocean, plus dancing to the sounds of the Big Band era.

SUMMARY

A money-is-no-object genius designed this fantasy resort, said to be the number-one-booked resort in the world. It is luxurious fun, definitely an a la carte spa, so enjoy. This resort's attractions make the Hyatt Regency Waikoloa a one-of-a-kind experience.

THE CLIFF LODGE AT SNOWBIRD

Mention Snowbird and images come to mind of skiing in deep, dry powder on steep, challenging runs. The Utah ski area has earned a national reputation for its snow — 500 inches a year and its skiing terrain — 3,100 vertical feet.

But Snowbird is not all skiing, nor is it only a winter resort. Aside from ample activites during any of the four seasons, it also offers the highest-altitude spa in the United States. At 8,200 feet, the fresh, clean, invigorating atmosphere of mountain life contributes to a refreshing experience at The Cliff Lodge.

Not only does alpine air somehow seem healthier, the scenery alone is enough to promote a feeling of well-being. While sitting in the spa's outdoor rooftop Jacuzzi with the water jets massaging me, the mountains across the valley looking surreal — more like a mural on a wall than actual behemoths of granite and snow. I felt privileged indeed.

Massages, hydrotherapy, and herbal wraps are all lusciously given by experienced therapists, and if the skiing, hiking, or golfing aren't enough for you, aerobic classes are available.

Snowbird is first of all a destination resort; and it is a very good one. As a spa, however, it has all the pieces and parts, but not the package. Only three percent of Cliff Lodge's guests sign up for a spa package. The rest of the spa's business comes from tired skiers, hikers with sore muscles, or spouses who don't like to ski.

The Cliff Spa was added in 1986 to Snowbird's 15-year-old hotel and ski resort complex. Conference facilities and 370 more rooms were also constructed at the same time. Originally, the spa was planned as a destination spa with 3-, 5-, 7-, and 10-day packages. But after its first two years, spa managers realized that The Cliff Spa was not attracting destination spa-goers, although it was very popular as an a la carte facility.

Skiers, especially the ones who may only get two weeks of vacation and exercise a year love the spa. They trash themselves on the ski hill and then go into the spa pleading "fix me."

Aside from "fixing" skiers with massages, the spa offers several body treatments, skin care, salon services, aerobic classes, exercise equipment, heated outdoor swimming pool, whirlpool, saunas, and a spa cafe.

Pampering is this spa's specialty, while the exercise classes and the spa cuisine are available but not sought after. Its year-round, heated swimming pool and large outdoor whirlpool seem to be the most popular aspect of Cliff Spa. When the ski lifts shut down at 4 p.m., the 104-degree hot tub is the place to be. Holding up to 40 people, it can get very crowded and very noisy with the apres ski crowd.

Beyond the spa, Snowbird's main attraction is the Wasatch Mountains. The resort complex is nestled in the center of Little Cottonwood Canyon, and the activities available here take their cue from the canyon's walls. Skiing lasts until July, and in the off season hiking, mountain biking, golfing, tennis, cultural performances, and nature programs abound. But there really is no off season at Snowbird.

Resort owner Richard Bass is marketing that idea to conference groups, corporations, and the lucrative Japanese tourist trade. He has begun special programs for groups such as the Super-Stars Olympic Games; designed a mentally and physically challenging Snowbird Executive Experience for business groups; and erected ski area signs in Japanese as well as English.

The spa services available to these different interest groups and skiers are the icing on the destination resort's cake. If you want the sweet taste of pampering during your next recreation-oriented vacation, this could be the place for you.

THE LOOK OF THINGS

When driving into Little Cottonwood Canyon, the 11,000-foot peaks of the Wasatch Mountains surround you and emphasize Snowbird's largest feature — its ski hill. Covering 2,100 acres, Snowbird is served by seven ski lifts and a tramway. The area averages 200 ski days a year with a remarkable variety of terrain making it a fun place for skiers of all levels.

At the base of the mountain is The Cliff Lodge, a full-service hotel with 532 rooms, four restaurants and the 27,000-square-foot spa. This multi-story hotel is charmingly alpine. A large lobby is braced with reinforced concrete girders for a mountain appeal. The rooms are large and luxurious, with huge bathrooms. Best of all, every window offers a spectacular view of the mountains and skiers schussing down the hill.

The spa is located on the ninth and 10th floors of The Cliff Lodge. On the ninth floor is a reception area and 12 cubicles for massages and herbal wraps, as well as hydrotherapy cubicles. Stunning views of the canyon will entertain those having beauty treatments and hair styling in this floor's beauty salon. The men's and women's locker rooms, each with their own sauna, are also here.

Aerobic, weight and stretching rooms are located on the 10th floor with the spa cafe and the popular year-round heated outdoor swimming pool. This pool and the whirlpool are on the rooftop, encased in glass walls for wind protection.

There are also three condominum lodges for accommodations. The Iron Blosam Lodge, The Inn, and The Lodge at Snowbird all have saunas, outdoor pools, and whirlpools.

More restaurants, shops, a bank, a post office, and other boutiques can be found at the Snowbird Center, which is also a good place to grab a sandwich, sit on the sunny deck and watch the snow skiers.

An Activities Center will set you up with any mountain sport imaginable and even offers quick transportation to golf courses by helicopter. Five tennis courts are at the tennis facility. Snowbird also has a state-licensed daycare facility, laundry facilities, ski rentals, in-room babysitting, and ski schools.

HOW TO GET THERE

Snowbird is a destination resort, which means it is easily accessible from an international airport, and rental cars are not needed. The resort is only 29 miles from Salt Lake City International Airport and 25 miles from downtown Salt Lake City. There are taxis and shuttle buses from the airport to Snowbird. You can fly into Salt Lake City in the morning and be skiing in the afternoon.

Car rentals are available but aren't necessary. All the amenities, accommodations, and activities around the resort are within walking distance.

Transportation information can be obtained by calling (800)-255-1841 from out-of-state or 255-1841 from Utah.

SURROUNDING AREA

Operating in the Wasatch and Uinta national forests, Snowbird is surrounded by mountains, forests, cliffs, and meadows. The obvious winter attraction is skiing, but the area is full of things to do in spring, summer, and fall.

Old mining roads criss-cross the forests, just waiting for adventuresome mountain bicyclists to discover meadows of wildflowers and scenic viewpoints. Mountain bikes can be rented at the Activities Center, which also has free guided hikes if you want to see the mountain meadows without wheels.

A mountaineering school on the third floor of The Cliff Lodge arranges rock climbing lessons and tours, as well as snow and ice climbing lessons. The mountaineering staff also leads rock climbs and overnight camping trips in the nearby Lone Pine Wilderness Area.

Those not into scaling cliffs might find that a trip up Hidden Peak on the tramway is a great way to see the countryside, and the walk down is a pleasant hike.

Seminars such as mountain photography, stargazing, hawk watching, arts and crafts, dance and music are scheduled throughout the warmer months. A concert weekend featuring the Utah Symphony and a Bluegrass weekend are held each year, as well as the annual Oktoberfest.

The Activity Center can give you the dates for these weekends and set you up for just about anything you want to do whether it's horseback riding, river float trips, fly fishing excursions, scenic helicopter flights, or golfing. The Activity Center also sponsors a Kid's Night Out with movies, entertainment, and dinner. This allows parents to check out some of the many restaurants at Snowbird or to go into Salt Lake City for one of its attractions.

Salt Lake City is famous for its Mormon Tabernacle which is in the center of downtown and the site for activities such as the Temple Square Concert Series. Utah's universities, like Brigham Young and University of Utah, have many muscial events in Salt Lake City. Theater is performed by the Pioneer Theater Company and the Salt Lake Acting Company.

And for NBA fans, the Utah Jazz play on their home court in Salt Lake City.

This metropolitan area is a clean, well-kept city, with friendly people.

WEATHER AND CLOTHING

This is "Rocky Mountain high" and the weather reflects the mountains' changing moods. Whether in summer or winter, be prepared for anything. I visited in the spring when the average temperature at the base of the mountain was 25-degrees, but the high altitude sun warmed the air and brought me outside to bask in its rays.

Besides heavy clothing and skiwear in the winter, don't forget to pack a t-shirt and sunblock for that absolutely sunny day that will appear. In the summer, don't forget a heavy coat for a chilly night. Mountain residents know to dress in multiple layers, and that's a tip visitors should take to heart.

The spa recommends that you bring two sets of leotards, tights or shorts, t-shirts, aerobic shoes and socks, swimsuit, walking or jogging shoes, bath robe or cover-up, and a pair of thongs.

I recommend that you bring more than just spa clothes. Since Snowbird is a destination resort you will want to feel dressed up to go out to eat at night. Women should bring a slack outfit.

WHAT'S INCLUDED IN THE PRICE

Accommodation prices vary greatly depending on whether you book a hotel room, a suite, or one of the many condominium options. All the rooms require a deposit within 10 days of the reservation and the full payment within 30 days. There are cancellation fees and minimum stay requirements, especially during the peak season. Children under 13 stay free. For reservations call (800) 453-3000.

The Cliff Spa operates on an a la carte basis and use of all the spa's facilities is included with any of the spa services or treatments. Full-day and half-day treatment packages are available too. If you are visiting during a peak week (like Christmas), the spa suggests making treatment reservations two weeks in advance by calling (801) 742-2222.

If you are staying at The Cliff Lodge, all of the spa facilities are free. If you're staying in the Snowbird complex at one of the condominiums, the spa facilities cost $5 a visit to use. The fee is $10 for those without Snowbird accommodations.

A TYPICAL DAY

First of all, a typical day is anything you typically like to do at a spa and destination resort. There are no set schedules; you make your own.

Secondly, you will be doing all of these things at an elevation of 8,200 feet. Take advantage of the high altitude's clean air and fresh breezes, but don't overdo it at first. You could end up in bed with altitude sickness.

One day I skied in the morning, taking advantage of Snowbird's host/hostess service. A Snowbird employee takes a group of skiers on a complimentary 90-minute tour of the mountain, pointing out different runs, lifts, and areas in each group's ability level. However, I think our guide overestimated my group's ability level because I slid halfway down the mountain on an intermediate run. Nah, it had to be an expert run.

After that experience, I was ready for sitting on the sunny deck and soaking in the hot tub.

The next day I luxuriated in the spa's treatments with an herbal wrap, facial, and massage with essential oils. In the afternoon, I tried a scalp treatment where the therapist used seaweed and other sea products on my head. It was wonderful.

The spa is open from 7 a.m. to 10 p.m., with the beauty salon open from 10 a.m. to 6 p.m. However, the peak time to use the spa facilities are after a day of skiing, or hiking, or golfing. Once 3 p.m. rolls around, this spa is full.

Some of the treatments include an herbal wrap and a parafango. For the herbal wrap, cotton linens are soaked in 160-degree hot herbal tea and placed on the bottom of a massage table. The client is then wrapped in hot linens, and two herb-soaked towels are placed on top of him or her. The temperature is about 110 degrees when someone is fully wrapped. This detoxifying treatment is capped by a loofah shower and massage.

A parafango will relieve muscle pain, ease soreness, and increase circulation at specific points in the body. Fango is Italian for mud which is the texture of this mixture of paraffin wax and volcanic ash. The volcanic ash helps the mixture retain its heat, causing the mixture to stay a consistent temperature for about 30 minutes. The parafango is heated and molded to certain portions of your body, such as the back and shoulders.

Other treatments include aromatherapy, hydromassage, and the salt glow, as well as a wide variety of hair, skin, and nail treatments.

Aerobic classes are offered, and the gymnasium room is currently adding $30,000 worth of equipment to the Keiser K300 pneumatic resistance exercise equipment already in place. The new exercise machines include Stairmasters, aerobicycles, cardiovascular equipment, and a Nordic ski exerciser.

The spa is not everyone's main bill of fare at Snowbird, but it is an essential part of many people's day. One day in the elevator I heard a fatigued young man who vowed to take a massage no matter what the cost. Judging from the busy activity at the spa, he wasn't the only one.

EVENING PROGRAMS

There are no evening programs sponsored by the spa and the nightlife is lacking, which surprised me because everywhere I looked were young, energetic, single people. There are about a dozen restaurants to sample at dinnertime, and in the summer, a mountain barbecue is held at the top of the tramway on the 11,000-foot Hidden Peak.

THE STAFF

The staff is composed of a young group of workers who try hard but aren't really in a spa mentality. I asked for decaffeinated coffee once and got caffeinated coffee instead. How do I know? I walked the floors that night. However, the spa's massage therapists, therapists, and salon staff are all professional, accommodating, and willing to help. The massages and treatments are all done very well by the staff.

FOOD

The Spa Cafe on the top floor of The Cliff Lodge serves spa cuisine, but I sampled some of the great food at Snowbird's other restaurants also.

The lunch buffet in The Atrium had a delicious choice of soup, salad, sandwiches, and fresh fruit. In the grand lobby of The

Cliff Lodge, The Atrium provides an excellent view through an 11-story wall of windows.

One of the best steak and lobster dinners I've ever had was served to me at the Steak Pit in the Snowbird Center. The lobster tail was immense, a whopping 32 ounces of tender meat. I started the dinner delighted with the shrimp cocktail, but was ecstatic with the main course.

Snowbird has 15 restaurants and lounges, including a Mexican cantina and a number of delis and sandwich places. For a small fee, you can join the "Club at Snowbird" which allows you to drink at seven restaurants and lounges in the complex. These range from French restaurants to Italian to contemporary American cuisine.

Many of these restaurants will occasionally have a spa special as a healthy alternative to other meals.

SUMMARY

Although The Cliff Lodge at Snowbird is not a destination spa, it has all the ingredients of one, so if you set your own pace and take advantage of the offerings, you'll enjoy a spa experience anyway. And, oh, those views!

SPA RECIPES

BREAKFASTS

Yolkless Omelette with Steamed Spinach and Wild Mushrooms
(Sonoma Mission Inn)

3   egg whites
1   oz. spinach, steamed
2   oz. mushrooms, steamed
      fresh fruit for garnish

Using teflon pan, combine egg whites with steamed spinach and steamed mushrooms. Garnish with fresh fruit.

Serves 1
1 serving = 100 calories

Blue Corn Pancakes
(Sonoma Mission Inn)

3/4   c. blue corn pancake mix
1   egg
1 1/2 tsp. vegetable oil
3/4   c. nonfat milk

Mix ingredients together. Pour onto hot nonstick griddle (or use nonstick spray), shaping 3" pancakes. Serve with sliced fresh apricots and sugar-free apple butter.

Serves 4
1 serving = 280 calories

S.M.I. Granola
(Sonoma Mission Inn)

1	large container rolled oats (42 oz.)
1 1/2	lbs. sliced almonds
2	c. raw sunflower seeds
2	c. sesame seeds
1	c. filberts
1/2	c. poppy seeds
1	c. wheat germ
2	Tbsp. cinnamon
1	c. vegetable oil
1	c. honey
1	Tbsp. orange flavor
1	Tbsp. almond flavor
1	Tbsp. vanilla extract

Mix dry ingredients together. Add liquids and mix thoroughly. Spread mixture evenly on a flat cookie sheet. Bake at 350° F until toasty in color. Store in an airtight container.

Makes 3 pounds
1/4 cup serving = 133 calories

248

Blueberry Buckwheat Pancakes
(Rocky Mountain Wellness Spa)

1 1/2	c. oat flour
1/2	c. whole oats
1/4	c. buckwheat flour
2	tsp. baking powder
2	c. soy milk
1	egg
2	tsp. vanilla
1	banana
1/3	box blueberries

Put all dry ingredients in blender. Add milk, egg, vanilla and banana. Pour into bowl and stir in blueberries. Let stand for a couple of minutes if batter is thin.

Serves 3
4 pancakes = 298 calories

With permission from Sheri Stephens

Syrup
(Rocky Mountain Wellness Spa)

1	c. apple-pear juice
1/2	c. pure maple syrup
1/2	tsp. cinnamon
2	Tbsp. arrowroot

Combine all ingredients except arrowroot and bring to a boil. Thicken with arrowroot. When cool, this can be used as a spread on breads and muffins.

Yields 1 1/2 cup

With permission from Sheri Stephens

Granola
(Rocky Mountain Wellness Spa)

1	c. whole oats (not quick cooking)
1/3	c. slivered almonds
1/4	c. walnuts, chopped
1/4	c. cashews
2	Tbsp. sunflower seeds
2	Tbsp. sesame seeds
1	tsp. cinnamon
1	Tbsp. honey
1	Tbsp. cold pressed safflower oil
	raisins, dates, figs, dried apricots

Toss all ingredients except fruit. Spread evenly on Teflon baking sheet and bake in 350° F oven for 20 minutes. Stir often and keep an eye on it the last 5 minutes of browning. After baking add fruit. Variation: For Trail Mix, add more dried fruit and carob chips.

Yields 2 cups
2 Tbsp. = 66 calories

With permission from Sheri Stephens

California Frittata
(Camelback Inn Resort, Golf Club & Spa)

1/4	oz. broccoli
1/4	oz. snow peas, julienned
1/4	oz. carrots, julienned
1/4	oz. red bell pepper, chopped
1/4	oz. green bell pepper, chopped
1/4	oz. mushrooms, sliced
1/4	oz. safflower oil
5	oz. Egg Beaters
1	oz. soy cheddar cheese
	wheat browns*
	fruit garnish

California Frittata (Cont.)

tortillas

Saute vegetables in oil. Cook Egg Beaters into an omelette. Place vegetables on top of omelette. Sprinkle cheese over top. Serve with wheat browns, fruit garnish and tortillas.

Serves 1
1 omelette = 355 calories

* *see glossary*

Torte
(Camelback Inn Resort, Golf Club & Spa)

2	c. onion, 1/4" dice
1	Tbsp. garlic, minced
1	c. red pepper, 1/4" dice
6	c. mushrooms, sliced
1/8	c. safflower oil
10	oz. fresh spinach, chopped
1 1/2	c. lowfat cottage cheese
2 1/2	c. fresh Parmesan cheese, grated
1	c. lowfat yogurt
8	oz. Egg Beaters
1 3/4	c. seasoned bread crumbs
1/4	c. parsley, chopped

Saute the onions, garlic, peppers and mushrooms in oil until tender. Add spinach and saute until spinach wilts. Drain mixture and cool. In a large bowl, combine the remaining ingredients. Pour mixture into a lightly greased spring form pan. Bake at 350° F until firm and top has browned. Chill overnight. Cut into 6 portions.

Serves 6
1 serving = 330 calories

Muesli
(The Hills)

3	c. rolled oats
1 1/2	c. wheat germ, fresh
1/2	c. bran
1/4	c. soy flakes
1/4	c. hazelnuts, ground
1/4	c. walnuts, chopped
1	tsp. fructose (optional)
1/4	c. raisins
1/4	c. dried apricots, chopped
	skim milk
	plain yogurt
	fruit or berries

Combine all ingredients. Place in a covered jar and store in a cool, dry place. Use 1/4 cup skim milk and 1/4 cup plain yogurt for each serving. Serve with fruit or fresh berries.

Yields 7 cups
1/3 cup serving = 450 calories

Whole Wheat Pancakes
(The Hills)

1 1/2   c. whole wheat flour
1 1/2   tsp. baking powder
1/4   tsp. sea salt (optional)
1/4   c. egg whites
1 1/4   c. skim milk
         vegetable spray
         lowfat yogurt for garnish

Combine flour, baking powder and salt in mixing bowl. Mix together egg whites and milk in separate bowl. Stir into flour mixture until just moistened (batter will be lumpy). Spray large nonstick skillet with vegetable spray. Heat over moderate heat. Spoon the batter into hot skillet to make 4" pancakes. Cook over low heat until bubbles form on surface. Turn; cook other side until bottom is golden brown. Garnish with 1 tablespoon lowfat yogurt.

Serves 8
1 serving = 93 calories

BEVERAGES

Revitalizer
(Cal-a-Vie)

1	46 oz. can vegetable cocktail juice
2 1/2	c. water
2	stalks celery, coarsely chopped
1	large carrot, coarsely chopped
1	bunch parsley
2	bay leaves
1/2-1	tsp. crushed chile flakes
2	tsp. dried whole rosemary
1/2	fennel seed
1	Tbsp. dried basil leaf or 4 fresh sprigs of basil
2	c. vegetables (mushrooms, tomatoes, onions, red pepper, green pepper), cut up

Put all ingredients into a 2 quart soup pot. Bring just to a boil, then simmer for 40-60 minutes. Strain broth into a pitcher and discard vegetables. Serve hot or cold.

Makes 10 8 oz. servings
1 serving = 35 calories

Smoothies
(Meadowlark)

1	c. fresh fruit
1	banana, broken into small chunks
1	tsp. vanilla extract
1/2	c. lowfat yogurt (optional)
1/2	c. juice; apple, pineapple, etc.
5	ice cubes

Blend all ingredients in a blender on chop speed to crush and smooth the ice cubes. Turn the blender on high speed to form the consistency of a smooth milk shake.

Serves 4
1 serving = 87 calories

Apple and Yogurt Cocktail
(Le Meridien)

2 1/2   lbs. apples (to yield 1 1/2 lb. apple pulp)
2   c. lemon juice
1   qt. plain yogurt
        dash cinnamon
        mint leaves for garnish

Peel, seed and slice apples. Put in mixer with lemon juice. Mix until smooth. Add yogurt and cinnamon and mix for a few seconds. Pour in glasses and decorate with mint leaves.

Serves 10
1 serving = 105 calories

Broth
(The Plantation Spa)

1   leek
1   onion
3   carrots
3   lb. potatoes (Other vegetables you might use are:
        cabbage, celery and broccoli stalks)
1   gallon water
        big bunch parsley

Clean all vegetables, leaving the skin on the potatoes. Slice in small pieces, add water and let cook for 1 hour. If on a fast, use only the broth and if not fasting, put some of the broth with the vegetables into a blender to make a thick soup, adding some of the whole vegetables. For more flavor, add fresh garlic and herbs. Garnish with fresh parsley. This broth is very alkaline and one of the best drinks to get your day started. You may make a large quantity and freeze it in small plastic bottles. Take it out of the freezer the night before you will use it and heat until tepid before drinking.

Yields approximately 6 cups
1 cup = 67 calories

Crossover Tropical Smoothie
(The Claremont)

1/4   c. mango, peeled and seeded
1/4   c. papaya, peeled and seeded
1/4   c. pineapple, peeled
1/2   c. fresh squeezed orange juice
1   tsp. unsweetened coconut for garnish

Place fruit evenly on a sheet pan. Cover with plastic wrap and freeze until solid. Remove fruit and place in blender with orange juice. Puree until smooth. Pour into glass and garnish with coconut. Serve immediately.

Serves 1
10 oz. serving = 93 calories

BREAD

S.M.I. Bread Sticks

(Sonoma Mission Inn)

9	c. bread flour
4	tsp. sugar
1 1/2	tsp. salt
1	c. fresh herbs (such as basil, rosemary, chives), finely chopped
1/2	c. olive oil
3	oz. yeast
2 1/2	c. water

Mix flour, sugar, salt, herbs and olive oil together. Dissolve the yeast in warm water and add to flour mixture. Mix with electric beater until dough is formed. Let dough sit for 10 minutes. Pinch off golf ball sized pieces of dough and roll into stick shapes. Place bread sticks on a cookie sheet that has been lined with parchment paper and bake in a 350° F oven until toasted brown, approximately 20 minutes. Optional: For a glazed appearance, brush tops of bread sticks with egg whites before baking.

Yields 50 bread sticks
1 bread stick = 60 calories

S.M.I. Whole Wheat Rolls

(Sonoma Mission Inn)

1/2	c. hot milk
1/2	c. molasses
1	tsp. salt
3	Tbsp. margarine
2	oz. yeast
3/4	c. warm water
1	egg
2 3/4	c. bread flour
2	c. whole wheat flour
1/2	c. bran

S.M.I. Whole Wheat Rolls (Cont.)

1/2   c. sesame seeds

Heat milk until hot but not boiling. Add molasses, salt and margarine to hot milk and stir until melted. Let cool. Dissolve yeast in warm water. Add to milk mixture. Beat egg and add to above mixture. Mix dry ingredients together and add to wet ingredients. Mix thoroughly for 5 minutes with an electric mixer or knead by hand for 10 minutes. Let rise until doubled in size. Form into rolls and let rise again. Rolls may be frozen at this point in an airtight container. Brush tops of rolls with egg white. Bake at 350° F for 12 - 15 minutes or until golden brown.

Yields 24 rolls
1 roll = 70 calories

Rancho La Puerta Bran Muffins
(Rancho La Puerta)

2 1/2   lbs. bananas, peeled and diced
2/3   c. milk
3/4   c. yogurt
1/4   c. honey
2 1/2   c. apple juice
4   eggs, beaten
4   egg whites, beaten
3 1/2   c. bran
2 1/2   Tbsp. baking soda
3 1/2   c. whole wheat flour

Preheat oven to 350° F. Mix the bananas, milk, yogurt, honey, and apple juice together. Add the eggs and egg whites. Gently mix in the bran, baking soda and whole wheat flour. Pour the mixture into muffin tins. Bake for 35 minutes.

Yields 36 muffins
1 muffin = 120 calories

Tecate Bread
(Rancho La Puerta)

1/2	oz. dry active yeast (2 packets)
4	c. lukewarm water
1/4	c. corn oil
1/4	c. honey
10	c. whole wheat flour
1	c. (heaping) Miller's bran, unprocessed
1	tsp. sea salt
2	tsp. poppy seeds

In a large bowl, dissolve the yeast in the lukewarm water. Stir in oil and honey, then slowly add the flour, bran, salt and poppy seeds. Blend this together with your hands. Knead dough until it is no longer sticking to your hands. It should feel elastic and heavy. (Add more flour if necessary.) Lightly coat the dough with oil, top and bottom. Place in a bowl, covered with a towel, in a warm, draft-free place and let rise until doubled in size (about 1-2 hours). Punch down dough and place on a lightly greased board. Knead for 1 minute. Divide into 3 equal parts and throw the dough against the board 3 times. Generously oil 3 8 1/2"x4 1/2"x2 1/2" loaf pans (preferably clay loaf pans) and line the bottoms with wax or parchment paper. With lightly oiled hands, shape the dough into loaves and press lightly into the pans. Run knife tip down the center of each loaf, cover again with a towel and let rise for 30 minutes. Preheat the oven to 350° F. Bake for 1 hour and 15 minutes until well browned. Unmold by running a knife around the edges of the loaf. Wrap in towels and plastic bags until cool. Rewrap in plastic and refrigerate or freeze. Tastes best if toasted before serving.

Makes 3 loaves with 16 slices each
1 slice = 104 calories

Carrot Yogurt Bran Muffins
(Cal-a-Vie)

2 1/2	c. whole wheat pastry flour
1/2	c. bran
1/2	c. bran cereal (All Bran)
1/3	c. sesame seeds
1	tsp. allspice
2	tsp. cinnamon
1/2	tsp. ground cloves
1	tsp. baking soda
1	tsp. baking powder
2	Tbsp. safflower oil
4	Tbsp. honey
1	ripe banana, mashed (appoximately 2/3 c.)
2/3	c. plain lowfat yogurt
1/2	c. fresh orange juice
1/2	c. currants or raisins, soaked and drained
1	Tbsp. lemon peel, grated
1 1/2	c. carrots, grated
1	egg

Mix well the flour, bran, bran cereal, sesame seeds, allspice, cinnamon, ground cloves, baking soda and baking powder. Make a well in the center and add the rest of the ingredients. Mix with a spatula. Oil or spray with PAM 18 regular muffin molds or 24 small ones. Bake in a preheated 350° F oven for 25-30 minutes. Bake 20 minutes for smaller muffins. Note: The muffin mix can be made the night before, covered and stored in the refrigerator to be baked fresh when desired.

Makes 18 large or 36 small muffins
1 large muffin = 120 calories; 1 small muffin = 60 calories

Linny's High Fiber Seed Bread
(Cal-a-Vie)

2	Tbsp. yeast
3	c. warm water
1	c. molasses
1/2	c. oil
2	c. oat bran
2	c. wheat bran
9	c. whole wheat flour
1	c. poppy seeds
1	c. sesame seeds
1	c. sunflower seeds
1 1/2	tsp. salt
1	c. cracked wheat, soaked in 2 cups boiling water and cooled
1 1/2-2 c. flour for kneading	

In a mixing bowl, combine yeast and water and let dissolve. Add molasses and oil and let yeast proof. Mix in the bran, whole wheat flour, poppy seeds, sesame seeds, sunflower seeds and salt. When the soaked cracked wheat has cooled, add wheat and water to the bread mixture. Mix well on medium speed or by hand and form into a ball. Remove dough to a lightly oiled bowl and let rise until doubled in volume, about 1 hour. On a floured board, punch the dough down and knead well. Divide the dough in 4 well oiled 9" bread pans. Let rise again to double the volume. Bake in preheated oven at 350° F for 35-40 minutes. Let cool on rack.

Makes 4 loaves with 24 slices each
1 slice = 85 calories

Cal-a-Vie Wheat and Molasses Bread
(Cal-a-Vie)

2	Tbsp. dry yeast
5	c. lukewarm water
2	tsp. iodized sea salt
1/2	c. safflower oil
1	c. blackstrap molasses
4	Tbsp. honey
1	c. cornmeal
2	c. bran
1/2	c. nonfat dry milk
10-11	c. whole wheat bread flour

In a mixing bowl, combine yeast, water, salt, safflower oil, molasses and honey. Let yeast proof. With paddle of electric mixer gradually add all other ingredients and mix well for several minutes. Cover with towel and let rise in warm spot to double the volume. Generously dust the table with flour and punch down dough. Divide the dough in 4 equal parts and knead to form 4 loaves. Coat 4 9" long loaf pans with safflower oil and place loaves in pans. Let rise again to double the volume and bake in a preheated 350° F oven for 50 minutes to 1 hour. Let cool on a rack before serving.

Makes 4 loaves with 18 slices each
1 slice = 75 calories

Sun-Dried Tomato Baguette
(Cal-a-Vie)

1	Tbsp. dry yeast
1	c. warm water
3/4	c. unbleached flour
3/4	c. oat flour
3/4	c. whole wheat flour
1	tsp. salt
2	Tbsp. oil

Sun-Dried Tomato Baguette (Cont.)

8	sun-dried tomatoes, soaked in warm water and chopped
1	Tbsp. shallot, chopped and sauteed
1	Tbsp. fresh basil, chopped
1/2	tsp. red chile flakes
	cornmeal
1	egg white, beaten lightly with 1 tsp. water

Dissolve yeast in water and let proof. Add flours, salt and oil and mix. Knead dough on floured board for 5 minutes until smooth and elastic. Put in an oiled bowl, cover and let rise until doubled. Knead in remaining ingredients. Form into baguette and place on a cookie sheet that has been lightly oiled and sprinkled with cornmeal. Let rise until doubled. Brush on egg white. Bake at 400° F for 25 minutes. Variation: Broccoli-Rosemary Baguette - substitute 1/3 c. chopped, blanched* broccoli, 1 Tbsp. minced, sauteed shallot and 1/2 Tbsp. chopped fresh rosemary for tomatoes, chopped shallot and basil.

Yields 1 loaf
1 slice = 85 calories; 77 calories for Broccoli-Rosemary Baguette

*see glossary

Oat Bran Muffins
(Rocky Mountain Wellness Spa)

1	egg white
1	whole egg
1 1/2	Tbsp. molasses
1 3/4	c. apple juice or pear nectar
2 1/4	c. oat bran
1	Tbsp. baking powder
1	tsp. apple pie spice "cinnamon mix"

Filling

(banana-nut, peach-blueberry, diced apple-raisin, orange-strawberry, pineapple-macadamia nut)

265

Oat Bran Muffins (Cont.)

Blend liquid ingredients and add to dry. Stir in filling. This batter does not rise so you can fill pans most of the way. Cook in 375° F oven for 20-30 minutes. Keeps in refrigerator for up to a week or freezes. Use crumbled up muffins for a crust for desserts.

Yields 12 muffins
1 muffin = 153 calories

With permission from Sheri Stephens

Banana Nut Bread
(Cal-a-Vie)

1/4	c. canola oil or butter
1/2	c. honey
2	whole eggs or 4 egg whites
1 1/2	c. very ripe bananas, mashed
1 1/2	c. whole wheat pastry flour
1/2	tsp. baking soda
1/2	tsp. salt (optional)
1/2	c. nuts, sliced

Cream the butter with a wooden spoon. Add honey and beat until creamy and light. Add eggs, one at a time, then thoroughly mix in the bananas. Sift together flour, soda and salt and blend thoroughly into banana mixture. Finally, fold in nuts. Spray an 8 1/2 x 4 1/2 x 2 1/2 inch loaf tin with PAM and pour in the batter. Bake in a preheated 350° F oven 1 hour or until a knife inserted in the center comes out clean.

Yields 1 loaf, 18 slices
1 slice = 136 calories

Apple Nut Muffins
(The Palms)

	nonstick vegetable cooking spray
1/2	c. buttermilk
1/4	c. water
1	egg
3	Tbsp. honey
1/2	c. whole wheat flour
2/3	c. wheat bran
3	Tbsp. oat bran
1/2	tsp. baking soda
1/2	tsp. baking powder
1/2	tsp. ground cinnamon
1	c. apple, unpeeled, coarsely chopped
1/3	c. carrot, finely grated
3	Tbsp. walnuts, chopped

Preheat oven to 350° F. Spray 12 2 1/2" muffin pan cups with nonstick vegetable spray. Stir together buttermilk, water, egg and honey in 2 cup glass measure. Combine flour, wheat and oat brans, baking soda, baking powder and cinnamon in large bowl. Add buttermilk mixture to dry ingredients along with apple, carrot and walnuts. Stir with wooden spoon to combine. Spoon batter into prepared muffin pan cups. Bake for 15 minutes or until muffins begin to pull away from sides of pan. Remove muffins from cups and cool on wire rack. Serve warm.

Makes 12 muffins
1 muffin = 75 calories

Banana Nut Muffins
(Meadowlark)

1	c. rice flour
1	c. barley flour
1/2	tsp. sea salt
1	Tbsp. cinnamon
1	tsp. allspice
1/2	c. butter
1/2	c. honey
2	eggs, beaten
3/4	c. lowfat milk or nut milk
1 1/2	c. bananas, mashed
1/2	c. walnuts, chopped

Mix dry ingredients. Cream butter and honey, then add eggs and milk. Combine with bananas and walnuts. Add dry ingredients. Be careful not to overmix. Pour into oiled muffin tins. Bake at 400° F for 20-30 minutes.

Makes 12 muffins
1 muffin = 245 calories

Whole Wheat Bread
(The Hills)

2	Tbsp. active dry yeast
4	c. lukewarm water
1	Tbsp. unpasteurized honey
1	tsp. sea salt
8	c. whole wheat flour

In a large bowl, dissolve yeast in 1/2 cup of lukewarm water. Stir in honey. Let sit until yeast mixture is bubbly. Add remaining water and salt. Stir in 4 cups of flour. Beat the batter until it is "stretchy". Add remaining flour, one cup at a time, stirring well after each addition. Knead dough for about 10-15 minutes. Put dough into bowl, cover with a damp towel and let rise for 1 hour.

Whole Wheat Bread (Cont.)

Punch dough down after it has risen and allow to rise a second time in the bowl with a damp towel over it for about 1 hour. When dough has risen a second time, punch down, divide in half and place into nonstick bread pan. Bake for 45 minutes at 350° F.

Yields 1 loaf, 20 slices
1 slice = 80 calories

SOUPS

Vegetable Stock for Soup
(Rancho La Puerta)

3   lbs. vegetables (leftovers are fine; do not peel, cut into small pieces)

1   gallon water

Saute all of the vegetables over low heat until tender, in a saucepan that has been sprayed with PAM. Add the vegetables to the water in a large pot. Cook slowly until reduced to approximately 1/2 gallon. This process usually takes 1 1/4 hours. Strain the vegetables out of the stock and discard. This vegetable stock is used as the base for all of the soups served at Rancho La Puerta.

Makes 8 cups
1 cup = approx. 25 calories

Barley and Vegetable Soup
(Cal-a-Vie)

1   Tbsp. safflower oil
2   cloves garlic, minced
1   leek, white part only, cut into 1" slices
10   c. light chicken broth
1 1/2   c. raw barley
1   carrot, peeled and cut into 1" chunks
1   russet potato, cut into 1" chunks
2   celery ribs, chopped
2   c. broccoli florets
1   red bell pepper, cut into 1" chunks
1   jalapeno pepper, seeded and chopped
1   Tbsp. dry or 2 Tbsp. fresh mixed herbs
1/2   tsp. ground black pepper
    dash of cayenne
1/2   c. chives or basil, minced

Barley and Vegetable Soup (Cont.)

Heat the safflower oil over medium heat and stir in the garlic and leeks. Stir until leeks are soft, about 1-2 minutes. Bring stock to a boil. Add barley and bring to a boil again. Simmer for 1 hour or until tender. Add the sauteed leeks and the remaining vegetables with the herbs and seasonings. Let simmer for 30 minutes. Serve piping hot with a garnish of fresh chives and basil.

Serves 12
1 serving = 125 calories

Spinach Soup
(Tucson National Resort)

6   c. chicken broth
2   c. fresh spinach, chopped
1   Tbsp. vegetable seasoning
1   pinch nutmeg (optional)

Combine ingredients, bring to boil and simmer 20 minutes. For added flavor, puree 1/2 cup additional spinach and add to mixture.

Serves 8
1 serving = 20 calories

Egg Drop Soup
(Tucson National Resort)

6   c. chicken stock
2   eggs, well beaten
       green onion tops for garnish, chopped
       sodium reduced soy sauce (optional)

Bring the chicken stock to a boil. Add the beaten eggs, stirring constantly. Continue stirring until the eggs are cooked and stringy. Garnish each serving with a sprinkle of the chopped green onion tops and add a drop or two of soy sauce if desired.

Serves 8
1 serving = 20 calories

Leek Soup
(Tucson National Resort)

2   Tbsp. arrowroot
5   c. chicken broth
1   c. fresh leeks, sliced 1" long
1   clove garlic, crushed
1/2 tsp. black pepper
2   Tbsp. vegetable seasoning

Dissolve arrowroot in small amount of cold chicken broth. Add remaining ingredients. Bring to a boil and simmer 20 minutes. Serve hot.

Serves 6
1 serving = 20 calories

Bouillabaisse
(Tucson National Resort)

2   large onions, diced
2   leeks, white part only, thinly sliced
2   garlic cloves, finely chopped
4   tomatoes, peeled and diced
1/4 c. parsley, finely chopped
1/2 c. celery, finely chopped
1   bay leaf
1/4 tsp. fennel, crushed, using a mortar and pestle
1/4 tsp. thyme, crushed, using a mortar and pestle
1/4 tsp. saffron
1/8 tsp. black pepper, freshly ground
4   c. fish or chicken stock
2   c. dry white wine
1   lb. firm white fish (snapper, sea bass, etc.)
1   lb. shellfish (shrimp, crab, lobster, scallops, etc.)

Bouillabaisse (Cont.)

Combine the onions, leeks and garlic and cook, covered, over very low heat until soft, stirring frequently to prevent scorching. Add the tomatoes, parsley, celery, bay leaf, fennel, thyme, saffron and pepper. Mix well. Add the stock and wine and bring to a boil. Reduce heat. Add the seafood and simmer, covered, for 7 or 8 minutes or until the fish turns white. Divide equally into 8 bowls.

Serves 8
1 serving = 170 calories

Basic Blender Broccoli Soup
(Tucson National Resort)

2	c. chicken stock
2	c. broccoli, coarsely chopped
2	Tbsp. onion, finely minced
1/2	tsp. curry powder (optional)

In a saucepan, combine the chicken stock, broccoli, onion and curry powder and bring to a boil. Remove from heat and let cool. Pour into a blender or food processor and puree until smooth. This soup can be reheated and served warm, or chilled in the refrigerator and served cold. Note: If you want a hearty, main dish cream of broccoli soup, add 1/3 cup nonfat dry milk at the puree stage. The dry milk adds a lot of protein to this soup and only 6 calories per serving.

Serves 6
1 serving = 14 calories

Consommé Au Sherry
(Tucson National Resort)

1	qt. chicken stock
4	oz. sherry
1	clove garlic, crushed
2	Tbsp. dried or fresh chopped parsley

Consomme Au Sherry (Cont.)

Combine all ingredients in a 2 quart saucepan. Bring to boil and simmer 15-20 minutes. Serve hot.

Serves 6
1 serving = 20 calories

Red Lentil Soup
(Rocky Mountain Wellness Spa)

5	c. vegetable stock
1 1/2	c. red lentils
4	Tbsp. fresh cilantro
1/2	tsp. cumin
1	tsp. paprika
3	Tbsp. fresh oregano
1/8	tsp. cayenne
1 1/2	tsp. curry powder
6	cloves garlic, chopped
1	carrot, diced
1/2	c. red pepper, diced
1	celery stalk with leaves, diced
1/2	yellow onion, diced
1/4	red onion, diced
6	green tomatillos, chopped

Mix together first 8 ingredients and cook 30 minutes. Add garlic, carrot, red pepper, celery and yellow onion and cook 15 minutes more. Add red onion and tomatillos and cook an additional 5 minutes.

Serves 4
1 serving = 209 calories

With permission from Sheri Stephens

Minestrone Soup
(Canyon Ranch)

2	c. Vegetable Stock (see recipe under Soups)
3/4	c. beer
1	small carrot, peeled and sliced
1/2	medium onion, chopped
1	celery rib, without leaves, chopped
1/2	c. cabbage, chopped
1	16 oz. can tomatoes, undrained
1/4	tsp. salt (omit if using salted stock)
1/8	tsp. black pepper, freshly ground
3/4	tsp. dried leaf rosemary, crushed using a mortar and pestle
3/4	tsp. chili powder
1	garlic clove, finely chopped
1	c. canned kidney beans, drained and rinsed
1/2	c. green beans, cut into 1" pieces
1/2	c. very thin dry spaghetti, broken into 1" pieces
2	oz. Parmesan cheese, freshly grated

In a large pot, combine first 12 ingredients. Bring to a boil, then reduce heat and simmer, covered, for 30 minutes. Return to a boil. Add the kidney beans and green beans and cook for 5-10 minutes more. Add the spaghetti and continue cooking until al dente*, 5-6 minutes. Sprinkle 1 tablespoon Parmesan cheese over each portion before serving.

Serves 8
1 cup serving = 150 calories

* see glossary

Carrot Soup
(Canyon Ranch)

3	c. carrots, scraped and sliced
1 1/2	c. onions, chopped
1/2	c. leeks, chopped
1/2	c. celery, chopped
4	c. Vegetable Stock (see recipe under Soups)
3/4	c. nonfat milk
1/4	tsp. salt
	pinch white pepper
1/4	tsp. nutmeg
	sprig of fresh tarragon for garnish

Combine the carrots, onions, leeks and celery in a saucepan with the Vegetable Stock. Bring to a boil, cover pan and reduce heat. Cook 15-20 minutes or until carrots are tender. Puree the mixture adding the milk, salt, pepper and nutmeg. Adjust thickness with more stock if necessary. Garnish with a sprig of fresh tarragon. Can be served hot or cold.

Serves 8
3/4 cup serving = 63 calories

Texas Onion Soup
(Marriott's Desert Springs Resort and Spa)

1/4	Tbsp. virgin olive oil
2	Tbsp. honey
6	lbs. spanish onions, sliced 1/8" thick
2	Tbsp. chili powder or 1 whole pasilla chile
1	gallon lean veal stock
3	c. zinfandel or full bodied red wine
1	c. celery juice
1	tsp. liquid smoke
1	bouquet garni*
1	Tbsp. Mrs. Dash mixed with no salt Vegit seasoning

Texas Onion Soup (Cont.)

2	jalapenos, seeded and diced
1/3	c. cilantro, chopped
1	Tbsp. cumin, ground
12	juniper berries, crushed
5	cloves garlic, minced
3	tsp. corn flour
6	oz. low salt, lowfat Jack cheese, grated
12	corn tortillas

In a saucepan heat the oil then brush a sheet pan with half of it. Add the honey to the remaining oil and reserve. Lay the onions evenly on the sheet pan. Brush with remaining oil and honey mixture. Sprinkle with chili powder and bake at 500° F until brown; reserve in a large pot. Bring stock, wine, celery juice, liquid smoke, bouquet garni, seasoning, jalapenos, cilantro, cumin, juniper berries and garlic to a slow simmer and reduce* for 15 minutes. Add onions, dissolve corn flour. Sprinkle with cheese and serve with corn tortillas.

Serves 12
1 serving = 164 calories

* see glossary

Vegetable Stock
(Canyon Ranch)

1	small head cabbage, chopped
4	onions, chopped
6	carrots, scraped and chopped
1	small bunch celery without leaves, chopped
1	small bunch parsley, chopped
3	bay leaves
2	tsp. dried leaf marjoram, crushed, using a mortar and pestle
1	tsp. salt
	cold water

Vegetable Stock (Cont.)

Combine all ingredients in a large pot. Add cold water just to cover. Bring to a boil. Reduce heat, cover and simmer for 1 hour. Strain stock and refrigerate or store in the freezer in individual containers.

Yields 3 quarts
1 serving = 17 calories

Mexican Vegetable Soup
(Bermuda Resort)

1	c. fat-free beef broth or soup base
1/3	c. carrots, chopped
3	Tbsp. onion, chopped
1/3	c. cauliflower, chopped
1/3	c. broccoli, chopped
1/3	c. mushrooms, quartered
1/2	small bell pepper, chopped
1/3	c. zucchini, sliced
1/3	c. crookneck squash, sliced
1/3	c. kidney beans, cooked or use canned, rinsed well
1/3	c. pinto beans, cooked or use canned, rinsed well
1	tsp. jalapeno pepper, chopped and rinsed
6	oz. canned stewed tomatoes

Heat broth or stock to boiling; cook over moderate heat. Add carrots, onions, cauliflower and broccoli and cook 5 minutes. Add mushrooms, bell pepper, zucchini and squash and cook 5 more minutes. Add beans, jalapeno peppers and tomatoes and cook 5 minutes longer. Let soup refrigerate overnight. Add herbs if desired. Serve cold or heat before serving.

Serves 6
1 serving = 60 calories

Lentil Soup
(The Hills)

1	c. lentils
1	stalk celery, chopped
1	medium carrot, chopped
1/3	c. onion, chopped
1	clove garlic, minced
3	c. water
1/4	c. lemon juice
1/4	tsp. sea salt
1/4	tsp. granular kelp

Simmer lentils, celery, carrot, onion and garlic in water 1 1/2 hours until tender. Add remaining ingredients and cook another 5 minutes.

Serves 6
1 serving = 211 calories

SALADS

Coral Spa Slaw
(Tucson National Resort)

6   medium carrots, grated
2   medium oranges, peeled and cut into bite-size pieces
6   leaves romaine lettuce, washed and dried

Combine the grated carrots and orange pieces in a medium bowl. Place a lettuce leaf on each salad plate and top with approximately 1/2 cup of the slaw. Note: When you cut up the orange, do it over the grated carrot. The juice from the orange will act as a dressing as well as supply vitamin C.

Serves 6
1/2 cup serving = 46 calories

Cold Pea Salad
(Tucson National Resort)

1   c. sour cream
1   c. chives or green onion tops, finely chopped
1/2   tsp. seasoned salt
3   c. peas, cooked and cooled to room temperature

Combine the sour cream, chives or green onion tops and seasoned salt. Fold the sour cream mixture into the cooled peas. Cover and refrigerate for 2 days before serving.

Serves 12
1/4 cup serving = 55 calories

Minted Cucumber Salad
(Tucson National Resort)

3   large cucumbers, peeled and sliced very thin
        salt
1/2   c. fresh lemon juice
1   Tbsp. fructose
1/4   c. fresh mint, finely chopped
        mint sprigs for garnish

Spread the cucumber slices out in a large glass baking dish and sprinkle evenly with salt. Cover and allow to stand for at least 2 hours. Drain the cucumbers and rinse thoroughly. Combine the lemon juice and fructose and mix thoroughly. Combine all ingredients, mix well and chill before serving. Garnish with mint.

Serves 8
3/4 cup serving = 30 calories

Marinated Artichoke Hearts
(Tucson National Resort)

1   c. canned artichoke hearts, drained
1 1/8 tsp. vegetable oil
2   Tbsp. red wine vinegar
1/4   tsp. salt
1/4   tsp. dried oregano
1/4   tsp. dry mustard
        sweetener equivalent to 1 tsp. sugar
        pepper to taste

Combine all ingredients in a medium bowl. Cover and refrigerate several hours or overnight, stirring occasionally. Serve cold.

Serves 1
1 serving = 58 calories

Spinach Mushroom Salad
(Tucson National Resort)

3   c. fresh spinach, washed and deveined
8   large fresh mushrooms, sliced
     diet Italian dressing

Pull spinach apart into bite-size pieces and portion into 4 bowls. Place mushrooms over spinach. Chill well. Serve with diet dressing.

Serves 4
1 serving = 20 calories

Marinated Mushrooms
(Tucson National Resort)

2   c. fresh mushrooms, thinly sliced
1/2   c. wine vinegar
     dash black pepper
     juice of 1 lemon
     pimiento strip
1   Tbsp. parsley, chopped
1   head leaf lettuce

Combine ingredients except lettuce and chill overnight. Portion into 4 dishes lined with leaf lettuce. Serve well chilled.

Serves 4
1/2 cup serving = 20 calories

Gazpacho
(Tucson National Resort)

1/2   c. cucumbers, peeled and diced
3/4   c. red and green bell peppers, peeled and diced
3/4   c. onions, diced
1   c. tomatoes, peeled and diced
2 1/2   c. tomato juice
1/2   tsp. garlic powder

Gazpacho (Cont.)

1/4   tsp. black pepper, freshly ground
1/4   tsp. Worcestershire sauce
2   Tbsp. lemon juice, freshly squeezed
      chives or green onion tops, chopped, for garnish
2   lemons, cut into 4 wedges each, for garnish

Combine all ingredients except the chives or green onion tops and the lemon wedges and mix thoroughly. Prepare a day in advance and chill. Serve in chilled bowls and garnish with the chopped chives or green onion tops and lemon wedges. Note: This recipe may also be used as a soup or as a sauce (salsa) on salads, vegetables and entrees. It can also be used as a dip.

Serves 8
1/2 cup serving = 30 calories

Tarragon Walnut Chicken Salad
(Cal-a-Vie)

3/4   c. chicken breast, cooked and shredded
1 1/2   c. cooked wild rice
3/4   c. red seedless grapes, cut in half
      Tarragon Dressing (recipe follows)
1/4   c. toasted walnuts, chopped

Combine shredded chicken, cooked wild rice and halved grapes in a bowl and toss. Add dressing and toss. Add walnuts and serve on a bed of fresh lettuce.

Serves 6
1 serving = 195 calories

Tarragon Dressing
(Cal-a-Vie)

1   shallot, chopped
2   cloves garlic, minced
1/4   c. white wine vinegar
1/4   c. white grape juice, water or white wine
2   Tbsp. canola oil
1   Tbsp. peanut oil
       fresh pepper to taste, cracked
2   Tbsp. fresh tarragon, chopped

In blender, puree shallot, garlic, vinegar and grape juice. While blender is running, slowly add oils, then pepper. Turn off blender to add tarragon.

Baby Bok Choy, Marinated Tofu, Daikon, Sesame Oil and Rice Wine Vinegar
(Sonoma Mission Inn)

3   oz. baby bok choy
2   tsp. sesame oil
1   tsp. rice wine vinegar
1/2   tsp. light soy sauce
1/4   tsp. wasabi*
1   oz. daikon*, shredded
1   oz. carrot, shredded
1 1/2 oz. tofu

Place washed bok choy on perimeter of plate. Combine sesame oil, rice wine vinegar, light soy sauce and wasabi in bowl. Toss daikon and carrot in dressing mixture. Mound daikon and carrot in the center of the plate. Cut tofu into triangles. Place tofu around plate.

Serves 1
1 Serving = 175 calories

* see glossary

Hearts of Romaine, Thai Lemon Yogurt Dressing
(Sonoma Mission Inn)

	hearts of romaine
	hearts of romaine
1/2	tsp. mayonnaise
1	Tbsp. yogurt
1/4	tsp. ginger, minced
1/4	tsp. garlic, minced
1/8	tsp. cilantro, minced
1/2	tsp. scallions, minced
	white pepper to taste
1	tsp. light soy sauce

Clean and cut romaine into thirds or quarters lenghtwise. Combine all remaining ingredients for dressing and pour over romaine.

Serves 1
1 serving = 50 calories

Spinach Salad with Sherry Vinegar
(Sonoma Mission Inn)

	leaf spinach
	leaf spinach
1	oz. sherry vinegar
1/4	apple, diced
1	oz. celery, diced
2	oz. daikon*, diced
1	tsp. red onion, diced
4	raspberries, for garnish

Trim and clean spinach. Toss with sherry vinegar, apple, celery, daikon and red onion. Place on plate and garnish with raspberries.

Serves 1
1 serving = 35 calories

* see glossary

288

Slices of Vine Ripened Tomatoes & European Cucumbers, Basil & Cabernet Vinegar
(Sonoma Mission Inn)

4   oz. tomato, sliced
2   oz. European cucumber, sliced
     salad greens
1   oz. cabernet vinegar
4   basil leaves

Lay tomato and cucumber around exterior of plate. Place a small amount of greens on plate. Pour Cabernet vinegar over greens and garnish with basil leaves.

Serves 1
1 serving = 40 calories

Tofu Eggless Salad
(Canyon Ranch)

1   lb. firm tofu, drained
1   c. celery, finely chopped
1   tsp. turmeric
4   Tbsp. low-calorie mayonnaise
1/2   c. scallions, minced
1/4   tsp. salt (optional)
1/2   tsp. reduced sodium soy sauce
2   Tbsp. mustard
1/4   tsp. black pepper
3/4   c. cauliflower, steamed crisp
1/8   tsp. cayenne
6   lettuce leaves
3   medium whole wheat pitas

Tofu Eggless Salad (Cont.)

Mash tofu until smooth. Mix ingredients together. Cut each pita in half. Put a lettuce leaf and 1/2 cup tofu mixture in pita pocket.

Serves 6
1/2 cup serving = 255 calories

The Palms Super Salad
(The Palms)

1/2	c. onion, chopped
1	clove garlic, finely chopped
1/2	tsp. vegetable oil
1	c. whole canned tomatoes, undrained and chopped
1/2	tsp. chili powder
1/8	tsp. leaf oregano, crumbled
1/8	tsp. leaf thyme, crumbled
1/2	c. kidney beans (not canned), cooked
1/2	c. lentils (not canned), cooked
1/2	c. brown rice, cooked
2	Tbsp. cilantro or parsley, chopped
4	c. lettuce, shredded
1 1/3	c. carrots, grated
1 1/3	c. fresh tomatoes, chopped
1 1/3	c. alfalfa sprouts
16	avocado, thin slices
8	Tbsp. Sour Cream (see recipe under Dressings/Dips)

Saute onion and garlic in hot oil in medium size nonstick saucepan until softened, 3 minutes. Add canned tomatoes, chili powder, oregano and thyme. Simmer over medium-low heat for about 10 minutes or until most of the liquid evaporates. Watch carefully and stir occasionally. Stir in kidney beans, lentils and rice just to heat through. Add cilantro. Prepare 4 individual plates. For each serving place 1 cup shredded lettuce on each plate. Top each with 2 scoops (1/4 cup) bean mixture.

The Palms Super Salad (Cont.)

Garnish each with 1/3 cup grated carrots, 1/3 cup chopped tomato, 1/3 cup sprouts and 4 slices avocado. Top the bean mixture with 2 tablespoons Sour Cream.

Serves 4
1 serving = 260 calories

Spa Waldorf Salad
(Marriott's Desert Springs Resort and Spa)

3	endive leaves
1	oz. shallots
2	tsp. garlic
2	tsp. arrowroot
1	tsp. basil leaves, chopped
1/2	tsp. cumin seeds
1/4	tsp. cayenne pepper
1 1/2	tsp. corn oil
1	tsp. orange peel
20	oz. fresh orange juice
1-2	oz. salad greens
1/2	c. honey
1	c. plain yogurt
1	Tbsp. orange zest*
3	oz. apple, diced
1 1/2	oz. walnuts, chopped

In soup bowl, place endive leaves in spoke arrangement, 12, 7, 5 o'clock. For Citrus Dressing: Combine next 9 ingredients in blender and blend until smooth. Toss spring greens in Citrus Dressing and place in center of bowl. For Honey Yogurt Dressing: Mix honey, yogurt and orange zest. Toss diced apples and 1/2 ounce walnuts in Honey Yogurt Dressing and place on top of salad mixture. Garnish top with remaining walnuts.

Serves 1
1 serving = 55 calories

* *see glossary*

Potato Salad
(The Plantation Spa)

6	small red potatoes, cut into small cubes
1	c. cottage cheese
1	c. natural yogurt
1/2	clove of pressed garlic
	dash of Spike* to taste
1	tsp. fresh dill, chopped
1	tsp. fresh parsley, chopped
1	Tbsp. apple cider vinegar

Steam potatoes until soft and let cool. Mix cottage cheese and yogurt with garlic, Spike, herbs and vinegar. Combine the potatoes and cottage cheese mixture. Adjust seasoning to taste.

Serves 6
1/2 cup serving = 95 calories

* see glossary

Caesar Salad
(The Plantation Spa)

1	large head Romaine lettuce
1/4	c. olive oil
1	clove garlic
1/4	c. lemon juice
1/4	block silken tofu
1	handful herbed croutons (optional)
1/3	c. Parmesan cheese, grated
1/4	c. capers, rinsed

Rinse and dry lettuce. Cut into medium sized pieces and place in bowl. For dressing, combine next 4 ingredients in blender and blend for 30 seconds. Add croutons, Parmesan cheese and capers to lettuce and pour dressing over. Toss and serve as an entree with whole grain bread.

Serves 6
1 serving = 160 calories

Greek Salad
(Spa Cafe*, Cliff Lodge at Snowbird)

8	medium tomatoes, diced
2	cucumbers, seeded and cut into bite-sized pieces
1	medium red onion, diced
2	green bell peppers, julienned
1	c. Kalamata olives
2	Tbsp. red wine vinegar
2	Tbsp. olive oil
	salt and pepper to taste

Mix vegetables and olives together. Pour vinegar and oil over ingredients and toss lightly. Season with salt and pepper.

Serves 4
1 serving = 760 calories

*For Members of the Club at Snowbird, a Private Club.

Galisteo Fiesta Salad with Black Bean Jicama Salsa
(Vista Clara)

1	carrot, grated
1	zucchini, grated
1	summer squash, grated
1	bunch scallions, diced
1	red onion, diced
3	tomatoes, seeded and diced
1	each red, yellow, green pepper, julienned, then diced
1	cucumber, seeded, peeled and diced to 1/4"
1	medium jicama, peeled and cubed to 1/4"
2	bunches cilantro
3	Tbsp. canola oil
	juice from 1 lime
3	Tbsp. balsamic vinegar
	dash medium hot chili sauce

Galisteo Fiesta Salad with Black Bean Jicima Salsa (Cont.)

3   cloves garlic, minced
1   Tbsp. cayenne
2   Tbsp. ground cumin

For Black Beans:

2   c. black beans, washed
3   mild green chilies
2   medium cloves garlic
2   tomatoes, seeded and diced
2   Tbsp. ground cumin
1   Tbsp. cayenne
1/2   c. fresh cilantro
       tomato for garnish

Combine first 13 ingredients for Jicama Salsa. Add chili sauce, garlic, cayenne and cumin. If Jicama mixture needs more liquid, consider using juice of 1 tomato, additional lime juice or more vinegar. It is best to avoid using more oil. To prepare beans, place beans in a pot and cover with water. Bring to a fast boil, then cover and allow to simmer on medium to low heat. To prepare green chilies, place on a sheet pan in a preheated 425° F oven about 2 inches from heat until skins begin to blacken. Turn until the chilies are dark on all sides. Remove from oven and wrap tightly in a plastic bag. Allow to steam until cool enough to touch. Peel off blackened skins, remove seeds and dice. Add remaining prepared ingredients to the beans except for cilantro and tomatoes. Keep adding water to the beans to allow for another 2 1/2-3 hours cooking time. This can be done gradually, as the water level falls below the beans. Beans should remain covered with water until tender. Cool completely before adding to the Jicama Salsa. Serve at room temperature over a fresh garden mixture of greens. Garnish with cilantro and tomato wedges.

Serves 6
1 serving = 370 calories

Tomato Salad
(The Hills)

4	large tomatoes
1	oz. skim mozzarella, cut into slices
3	sprigs marjoram
2	c. shredded spinach
1	Tbsp. olive oil
	dash of sea salt (optional)

Cut 2 slices from the center of each tomato (keep remaining tomato for another use). Use a small cookie cutter to cut a design in the cheese slices. Place a piece of cheese on each of the tomato slices. Top each with a sprig of marjoram. Arrange the tomato slices on a bed of spinach on a serving dish. Spoon a little olive oil over each serving. Season to taste. Serve with rice cakes.

Serves 4
1 serving = 84 calories

DRESSINGS & DIPS

Hot Ginger Sauce or Dressing
(Cal-a-Vie)

4	Tbsp. fresh ginger, coarsely chopped
2	Tbsp. red wine vinegar
1	Tbsp. rice vinegar
1	Tbsp. mirin (sweet sake)
1	Tbsp. honey
1	Tbsp. low salt soy sauce
2	tsp. dried basil
1/2	tsp. oriental red pepper (or regular chile flakes)
1	Tbsp. water
1/2	c. peanut oil

Put all ingredients in blender except peanut oil. Gradually pour oil in blender until smooth. Excellent with broiled seafood, chicken or spinach salad.

Yields 1 1/4 cups
1 Tbsp. = 70 calories

No Oil Dressing
(Cal-a-Vie)

2	Tbsp. concentrated apple juice
2 1/2	Tbsp. apple cider vinegar
1	Tbsp. water
1	large shallot, cut into pieces
2	tsp. Dijon mustard
1	tsp. dried tarragon
6-8	sprigs parsley
	ground black pepper to taste

Blend all above ingredients together in a blender on high. Serve over vegetable salads, chicken or shrimp.

Yields 1/2 cup
1 Tbsp. = 15 calories

Pommery Mustard Dressing
(Cal-a-Vie)

1   egg white
1   shallot
2   Tbsp. apple cider vinegar
2   Tbsp. whole grain pommery mustard
1/4   tsp. black pepper, freshly ground
1/2   c. plain lowfat yogurt
1/4   c. sesame oil or safflower oil

Mix all ingredients in a blender except oil. Slowly pour in oil in a fine stream until thick and creamy.

Yields 1 cup
1 Tbsp. = 40 calories

Oriental Creamy Dip
(Rocky Mountain Wellness Spa)

10   oz. soft tofu (1 small box)
2   Tbsp. red miso*
1 1/2 tsp. peanut butter
1   Tbsp. tahini*
1   tsp. sesame chile oil
6   cloves garlic, minced
2   Tbsp. fresh ginger
2   dashes cayenne
1   Tbsp. white vinegar
2   Tbsp. lemon juice
3   Tbsp. soy sauce

Blend all ingredients together in blender or food processor.

Yields 1 cup
1 Tbsp. = 53 calories

With permission from Sheri Stephens
* see glossary

Creamy Curry
(Rocky Mountain Wellness Spa)

2	c. nonfat yogurt
2	Tbsp. curry powder
2	Tbsp. honey
2	Tbsp. Dijon mustard

Blend all ingredients together in blender or food processor.

Yields 1 1/4 cups
1 Tbsp. = 24 calories

With permission from Sheri Stephens

Oriental Vinaigrette
(Rocky Mountain Wellness Spa)

2	Tbsp. soy sauce
	drop of chile oil
1/4	c. safflower oil
4	Tbsp. cider vinegar
4	Tbsp. water
2	tsp. fresh ginger, minced
2	tsp. fresh garlic, minced
2	Tbsp. fresh scallions, minced
1	Tbsp. toasted sesame seeds

Blend together all ingredients in blender or food processor.

Yields 1 cup
1 Tbsp. = 35 calories

With permission from Sheri Stephens

Garlic-Dijon Vinaigrette
(Rocky Mountain Wellness Spa)

1	c. safflower oil
1/2	c. water
1/2	c. white vinegar
2	Tbsp. Dijon mustard
8	cloves garlic, minced
	dash cayenne

Blend together all ingredients in blender or food processor.

Variations to Garlic-Dijon Vinaigrette:

Mexican - add fresh cilantro, salsa, cumin and chili powder.

Italian - add Basil Pesto (see recipe under Sauces) or lots of chopped fresh oregano, chives, parsley, etc.

Oriental - use thickened Stir Fry Sauce (see recipe under Sauces).

Tomato-Dill - add fresh dill and tomato, carrot juice and Tomato Basil Sauce (see recipe under Sauces).

"Spa" Ranch - use thick drained yogurt cheese* and blend in olive oil, lemon juice and thin with soy milk. Season with chopped fresh herbs and cayenne or white pepper.

Yields 2 1/4 cups
1 Tbsp. = 45 calories

With permission from Sheri Stephens
* see glossary

Hummus
(Rocky Mountain Wellness Spa)

1	c. chickpeas (garbanzo beans)
1/2	c. soft tofu
1	Tbsp. garlic
2	Tbsp. olive oil
1/8	tsp. sesame chile oil
1	Tbsp. tahini*
2	Tbsp. lemon juice
1 1/2	tsp. curry powder
	parsley, minced
	green onion, chopped

Blend all ingredients except parsley and green onion. When smooth, stir in minced parsley and green onion.

Yields 2 cups
1 Tbsp. = 145 calories

With permission from Sheri Stephens
* see glossary

Lemon Thyme Dressing
(Cal-a-Vie)

1	tsp. lemon zest*
1	Tbsp. lemon juice
1	large shallot, coarsely chopped
1	egg white
1/4	tsp. black pepper, freshly ground
1	Tbsp. fresh lemon thyme leaves
3	Tbsp. rice vinegar
1/2	c. safflower or sesame oil

301

Lemon Thyme Dressing (Cont.)

Put all ingredients except oil into blender and blend for 30 seconds. Add oil gradually while continuing to blend. Should dressing be too thick, add 1 tablespoon hot water. Note: For a lower calorie dressing, use 1/3 cup oil instead of 1/2 cup and add 3 tablespoons white wine or vegetable broth to initial ingredients.

Yields 1 cup
1 Tbsp. = 62 calories; 44.5 calories for low calorie version

* see glossary

Light Soy & Rice Wine Vinegar Dressing
(Sonoma Mission Inn)

1/2	oz. light soy sauce
1	oz. rice wine vinegar
1/4	tsp. pickled ginger
1/4	tsp. garlic, chopped
1	Tbsp. scallions, sliced

Combine all ingredients and mix well.

Serves 1
1 serving = 60 calories

Tarragon Vinaigrette Dressing
(Canyon Ranch)

1/2	c. red wine vinegar
1	Tbsp. dried tarragon, crushed
1/4	tsp. black pepper
1/2	tsp. salt
1	Tbsp. fructose
1/2	tsp. garlic, minced
2	tsp. Worcestershire sauce
1	Tbsp. Dijon mustard
	juice of 1/2 lemon (approximately 1 Tbsp.)
1	c. water

Tarragon Vinaigrette Dressing (Cont.)

Combine all ingredients except water and stir well. Add water, mix again and refrigerate. The dressing is better if it sits overnight.

Yields 2 cups
2 Tbsp. = 5 calories

Gazpacho Vinaigrette
(Sonoma Mission Inn)

8	oz. fresh tomato juice
2	oz. red pepper, finely diced
2	oz. yellow pepper, finely diced
3	oz. red onion, finely diced
2	oz. cucumber, finely diced
	pinch each of chives, parsley, basil and chervil
1	tsp. garlic
2	oz. red wine vinegar
4	oz. fish stock
16	oz. tomatoes

Combine all ingredients and mix well.

Yields 1 quart
1 Tbsp. = 10 calories

Sour Cream
(The Palms)

8	oz. lowfat plain yogurt
3	Tbsp. onion, chopped
1/2	tsp. garlic paste (from a tube)

Stir together yogurt, onion and garlic paste in small bowl. Refrigerate, covered, until ready to use. Great for topping potatoes, vegetables, meats and salads.

Makes 1 cup
1 Tbsp. = 10 calories

Parsley Dressing
(Meadowlark)

1 1/4	c. safflower or sesame oil
1 1/4	c. fresh parsley, chopped
1	Tbsp. Bronner's protein powder (optional)
1/2	tsp. kelp
1/4	tsp. garlic powder
1	Tbsp. tamari*
3	Tbsp. apple cider vinegar or lemon juice
3/4	c. water (optional)

Combine all ingredients in blender.

Yields 3 1/2 cups
1 Tbsp. = 45 calories

* see glossary

Yogurt Dressing
(Meadowlark)

1	c. lowfat yogurt
1/2	onion, chopped
1/4	c. celery leaves
1/2	clove garlic, minced
1/4	c. parsley, chopped
1/2	tsp. salt
1	tsp. honey
	dash dill weed

Blend together all ingredients.

Yields 2 cups
1 Tbsp. = 4 calories

Cheesy Salad Dressing
(Meadowlark)

1/4   c. sunflower seeds
1/4   c. mayonnaise or soft tofu
2   tsp. Worcestershire sauce
1/4   c. lowfat white cheddar or roquefort, grated

Place sunflower seeds in a food processor and chop. Add remaining ingredients and blend.

Makes 3/4 cup
1 Tbsp. = 70 calories

Raspberry Dressing
(Le Méridien)

    fresh or frozen raspberries
1   c. raspberry vinegar
2   c. sunflower oil
    salt and pepper to taste

Using a high speed blender or food processor, puree raspberries to yield 1 cup. Mix raspberry puree with vinegar. In blender, slowly add the oil to the raspberry mixture until it thickens and turns pink. Season.

Makes 1 quart
1/4 cup = 250 calories

SAUCES & CONDIMENTS

Chutney
(Sonoma Mission Inn)

1/2   c. sugar
1/2   c. white wine vinegar
1/2   c. mixed dried fruit
1/4   c. dried apricots
1/4   c. dried cherries
1/4   c. raisins
1/8   c. toasted walnuts, chopped

Combine sugar and vinegar in a heavy-bottom saucepan. Bring to a boil over medium heat and let cook until a thick syrup is formed. Mix all fruit together and add syrup. Mix in nuts. Season to taste with additional vinegar. Let sit overnight in an airtight container in refrigerator.

Makes 1 3/4 cups
1 Tbsp. = 40 calories

Spicy Yellow and Red Tomato Salsa
(Sonoma Mission Inn)

1   yellow beefsteak tomato
1   red beefsteak tomato
2   Tbsp. European cucumber, peeled and seeded
1   Anaheim chile, seeded
1   Tbsp. Italian parsley, chopped
    splash white wine vinegar to taste
    salt and pepper to taste

Peel and seed tomatoes. Roughly chop tomatoes and cucumbers into 1/4" squares. Finely dice chile and Italian parsley. Mix together and add white wine vinegar and salt and pepper. Let flavors blend for at least 1 hour.

Makes 1 cup
1 Tbsp. = 10 calories

Stir Fry Sauce
(Rocky Mountain Wellness Spa)

1	c. light soy sauce
1/4	c. pineapple juice
1/4	c. water
3	cloves garlic, chopped
1	Tbsp. curry powder
1	Tbsp. fresh ginger, minced
1	Tbsp. peanut butter
1	Tbsp. tahini*
1	Tbsp. red miso* paste
	cayenne to taste
2-3	Tbsp. arrowroot

Combine all ingredients except arrowroot in saucepan and bring to a boil. Thicken with arrowroot. Keeps in a jar in refrigerator for weeks. Use in stir fry, soups, dips and salad dressings.

Makes 2 cups
1 Tbsp. = 53 calories

With permission from Sheri Stephens
* see glossary

Basil Pesto
(Rocky Mountain Wellness Spa)

1	c. fresh basil
1/4	c. fresh spinach
1/4	c. pine nuts
1/4	c. olive oil
10	cloves garlic

Puree all ingredients in blender. Thin with warm water. Keeps for weeks in a jar. Use in sauces, salad dressings and soups.

Makes 4 cups
1 Tbsp. = 117 calories

With permission from Sheri Stephens

Tomato Basil Sauce
(Rocky Mountain Wellness Spa)

20	plum tomatoes, blanched*, peeled and seeded
1/2	c. carrot juice
1/4	c. olive oil
1/2	c. fresh basil
10	cloves garlic
4	shallots, minced
1/4	c. fresh oregano
	cayenne to taste

Puree all ingredients in blender. Cook slowly for 45 minutes. Can be thickened with a little no salt tomato paste.

Makes 4 cups
1 Tbsp. = 98 calories

With permission from Sheri Stephens
* see glossary

Salsa
(Canyon Ranch)

4	c. tomatoes, diced
1 1/2	c. onions, diced
1/4	c. cilantro leaves, finely chopped
2	tsp. jalapeno peppers, finely chopped
1	tsp. garlic, minced
1 1/2	tsp. ground cumin
1 1/2	tsp. oregano
1/4	tsp. salt
2	Tbsp. lemon juice
2	Tbsp. lime juice

Combine all ingredients. Cover and chill at least 2 hours before serving.

Makes 4 cups
1 Tbsp. = 17 calories

Szechuan Peanut Sauce
(Canyon Ranch)

6	Tbsp. unhomogenized peanut butter
1/2	c. plain nonfat yogurt
1 1/2	tsp. fructose or 2 tsp. sugar
1	tsp. low sodium soy sauce
1/4	tsp. dark sesame oil
1/2	tsp. garlic, finely chopped
1/4	tsp. red pepper flakes, crushed, or to taste
2	Tbsp. rice wine vinegar

Combine all ingredients in a blender and blend until smooth. Refrigerate in a tightly covered container. Sauce will keep a week.

Makes 1 cup
1/4 cup serving = 144 calories

Lemon Sauce
(The Palms)

1	egg
1 1/3	c. lowfat cottage cheese
1/4	c. fresh lemon juice
1	Tbsp. chives, chopped
2	tsp. red wine vinegar
2	tsp. parsley, chopped
1	small clove garlic, pressed or crushed
	pinch dry mustard
1	Tbsp. safflower or corn oil

Combine first eight ingredients in container of food processor or electric blender. Cover and blend until smooth. Scrape down sides of bowl several times with rubber spatula. With machine still running, add oil until well blended. Use over steamed vegetables and broiled meats and fish.

Makes 2 cups
1 Tbsp. = 14 calories

Mango Chili Chutney
(Camelback Inn Resort, Golf Club & Spa)

4	oz. onion, diced
2	serrano peppers, minced
2	Tbsp. fresh mint, minced
1/4	oz. safflower oil
8	oz. mango, diced into 1/4" pieces

Saute onions, peppers and mint in oil until tender. Add mango and cook 2 minutes. Cool.

Yield 14 oz.
2 oz. serving = 84 calories

Ratatouille
(Marriott's Desert Springs Resort and Spa)

1	Tbsp. extra virgin olive oil
3/4	c. onion, diced
3/4	c. red bell pepper, diced
3/4	c. yellow bell pepper, diced
1 1/2	c. eggplant, diced
1 1/2	c. zucchini, diced
1	bay leaf
1	Tbsp. fresh basil
2	cloves garlic, minced
1	Tbsp. Vegit seasoning
1/2	Tbsp. Mrs. Dash seasoning
1	c. fresh tomato sauce
2	c. roma tomatoes, seeded, diced

In a nonstick pan, add oil, onion, peppers, eggplant, zucchini, spices and tomato sauce. Simmer for 10 minutes. Add fresh tomatoes. Simmer an additional 5 minutes.

Serves 4
1 serving = 144 calories

Guacamole
(Meadowlark)

1	avocado
1	tomato, chopped
1	onion, chopped
1	clove garlic, minced
1	tsp. lemon juice
1	Tbsp. yogurt or whipped tofu
	salt to taste

Scoop avocado meat out of shell and into bowl. Add tomatoes, onion, garlic, lemon juice, yogurt or tofu and salt. Serve immediately. (This is never as good the second day.)

Yields 1 cup
1 Tbsp. = 28 calories

Mushroom Sauce
(Meadowlark)

1/4	c. oil
1/4	c. barley or other flour
2	c. boiling water
1	tsp. onion powder
1	tsp. garlic powder
1/2	tsp. tamari*
1/4	tsp. thyme
1/4	tsp. dill weed
1	lb. mushrooms, washed and sliced

Heat oil and flour together until flour begins to brown. Meanwhile, boil water. Add boiling water to oil and flour mixture a little at a time, while stirring with a whisk. Watch out for steam. Add onion powder, garlic powder, tamari, thyme and dill weed. Add mushrooms. Bring to simmer. Keep hot until ready to use.

Yields 3 cups
1 Tbsp. = 16 calories

* see glossary

Cheese Sauce
(National Institute of Fitness)

2	c. skim milk
2	Tbsp. butter extract
2 1/2	Tbsp. cornstarch
1	tsp. Jensen's Instant Gravy
1/2	c. lowfat skim milk mozzarella, grated
1/8	tsp. white pepper

Combine all ingredients. Bring to a simmer, stirring constantly. Remove from heat when thickened. For fettuccine: Add 1/4 teaspoon garlic powder and 1 tablespoon Parmesan cheese.

Yields 2 3/4 cups
1/4 cup = 98 calories

Broccomole
(National Institute of Fitness)

3	c. broccoli, well cooked
3/4	c. lowfat sour cream
1	Tbsp. lime juice
1	tsp. Jensen's Instant Gravy
	pepper to taste

Place in blender and blend until of creamy consistency. Refrigerate.

Yields 3 3/4 cups
1/2 cup = 36 calories

313

White Sauce
(National Institute of Fitness)

2   c. skim milk
2   Tbsp. butter extract
2 1/2 Tbsp. cornstarch
1   tsp. Jensen's Instant Gravy
       ground pepper to taste

Combine all ingredients. Bring to a simmer, stirring constantly. Remove from heat as soon as thickened.

Yield 2 1/4 cups
1/2 cup = 60 calories

Turkey Chili Sauce
(National Institute of Fitness)

1/2   c. onions, minced
3/4   lb. ground turkey
4   c. tomato puree
1   heaping Tbsp. Jensen's Broth Seasoning
1 1/2 tsp. cumin
2   tsp. chili powder
1   small clove garlic, crushed

Saute onions and ground turkey in saucepan. Add the tomato puree and simmer for 10 minutes. Stir in remaining ingredients.

Yields 6 cups
3 Tbsp. = 25 calories

314

Catsup
(National Institute of Fitness)

2	c. tomato puree
1/2	tsp. celery seed
1 1/2	tsp. Jensen's Instant Gravy
2	tsp. barley malt sweetener
1 1/2	Tbsp. cider vinegar
1/4	tsp. dry mustard
1	tsp. barbeque spices*
1/4	tsp. cinnamon
1/4	tsp. white pepper

Combine all ingredients in a jar and shake well.

Yields 2 1/2 cups
1/4 cup = 8 calories

* see glossary

Spa Cafe & Deli Gazpacho
(Spa Cafe*, Cliff Lodge at Snowbird)

1/2	c. olive oil
1	c. red wine vinegar
1	c. apple cider vinegar
1	Tbsp. dill
1	Tbsp. basil
1/4	lb. onions, chopped
1/8	lb. Anaheim chile peppers, chopped
1/3	lb. tomatoes, chopped
1/4	lb. cucumbers, peeled, seeded, sliced
35	oz. V-8 juice
1/8	c. tamari soy sauce
1	Tbsp. Worcestershire sauce
	avocado slices for garnish

Spa Cafe & Deli Gazpacho (Cont.)

Mix together oil, vinegars, dill and basil. Pour over all vegetables, except cucumbers, and place in refrigerator for 2 days to marinate. Add cucumbers, vegetable juice, soy sauce and Worcestershire sauce before serving. Garnish with avocado slices. Can be used as soup or sauce.

Makes 16 8 oz. servings
1 serving = 104 calories

For Members of the Club at Snowbird, a Private Club.

Crossover Roasted Red Pepper Sauce
(The Claremont)

2	red bell peppers
1	small bulb garlic
1	tsp. olive oil
1	tsp. lemon juice
1	tsp. sherry vinegar

Roast peppers under broiler until blackened on all sides. Place in paper bag to steam. Brush garlic bulb with olive oil and wrap in foil. Bake at 350° F for 30 minutes. Remove foil and cool. Peel peppers carefully, removing core and seeds. Squeeze garlic cloves into blender. Add peppers, lemon juice and vinegar. Puree until smooth.

Serves 2
1 serving = 46 calories

Italian Tomato Sauce
(Maui Challenge)

12	large or Roma tomatoes, washed
1	onion, chopped
2	stalks celery, chopped
1/4	lb. mushrooms, sliced
2	Tbsp. olive oil
4	cloves garlic, minced
2	c. water

Italian Tomato Sauce (Cont.)

1	6 oz. can tomato paste
4	tsp. honey
2	bay leaves
2	Tbsp. Italian seasoning
3	tsp. oregano
4-5	parsley sprigs, chopped
1	tsp. marjoram
1	green pepper, chopped
2	Tbsp. fresh basil, chopped

Place tomatoes in a large stockpot and pour cold water over them until totally immersed. Bring to a rolling boil and let boil for 1-2 minutes. Remove from heat. Let stand for 5 minutes. Drain off water and let tomatoes cool long enough to handle. Peel skins off and squeeze the seeds from the tomatoes through a sieve or strainer so as to reserve liquid. Discard seeds. Coarsely chop pulp and combine with reserved liquid. In a saucepan, saute onions, celery and mushrooms in olive oil for 5 minutes; add garlic and saute an additional 2-3 minutes. Add tomato pulp, water, tomato paste, honey and seasonings, except basil, and simmer for 1 hour. Add green pepper and basil and simmer 10 more minutes.

Yields 6 cups
1/2 cup serving = 70 calories

Pecos Pesto
(Vista Clara)

1	c. fresh basil
1	c. fresh cilantro
1/4	c. garlic (10 medium cloves)
1/4	c. canola oil
1/4	c. water
1	Tbsp. pinon (pine) nuts (optional)
1	tsp. mild or hot ground red chile (optional)
1/4	c. Parmesan cheese (optional)

Pecos Pesto (Cont.)

Wash and remove stems from basil and cilantro, let dry. Place garlic in blender or food processor until finely chopped. Add basil, cilantro, oil, water and blend some more. Then add pinon nuts, chile and cheese. Blend until nuts have been finely chopped. Place pesto in a bowl, cover and place in refrigerator for several days or in freezer for several months. Serve over pasta, grilled tuna, etc.

Yields 2 1/2 cups
1 Tbsp. = 20 calories

Fruit Butter
(Rancho La Puerta)

2   medium apples, peeled and cored
2   medium pears, peeled and cored
2   c. apple juice
1   2" cinnamon stick
1/2   tsp. vanilla
1/4   medium orange, seeded

Place all the ingredients in a saucepan. Simmer over medium heat for 20 minutes. Put this mixture into a blender and blend until smooth. Chill overnight in the refrigerator. Will keep for up to 4 days in an airtight container.

Yields 2 1/2 cups
1 Tbsp. = 25 calories

PASTA

Whole Wheat Spinach Lasagna
(Rancho La Puerta)

2	lbs. fresh spinach (or 32 oz. frozen leaf spinach, defrosted and pressed to remove water)
6	oz. dried whole wheat or spinach lasagna noodles
1	Tbsp. olive oil
1	small onion, thinly sliced
6	oz. fresh mushrooms, sliced
2	clove garlic, minced
1	tsp. dried basil
1/2	tsp. dried oregano
	pinch of nutmeg
	black pepper to taste
1 1/2	c. lowfat ricotta cheese
3	Tbsp. Parmesan cheese, grated
1	egg, plus 1 egg white
2	Tbsp. parsley, chopped
2 1/2	c. prepared Tomato Sauce (recipe follows)
3/4	c. (2 oz.) low-sodium, lowfat mozzarella cheese

Wash and drain fresh spinach and steam until just wilted. Drain. Press spinach to remove water and chop. Set aside. Bring a large pot of water to a boil. Add the lasagna noodles and cook for 8 to 10 minutes or until tender. Drain noodles and rinse with water to prevent sticking. Preheat oven to 400° F. Heat oil in medium pan. Saute onions and mushrooms over low to medium heat until the onions are soft, about 10 minutes. Add the garlic, herbs and spinach and cook for 5 minutes. Season with the nutmeg and black pepper. In a medium bowl, mix together the ricotta cheese, the grated Parmesan cheese, the egg plus 1 egg white and the parsley. Spread 1 cup of the tomato sauce in a 10" x 8" x 3" baking dish.

Whole Wheat Spinach Lasagna (Cont.)

Layer half of the lasagna noodles, half of the ricotta cheese mixture and all of the spinach-onion mixture. Finish layering with the remaining noodles, ricotta cheese mixture and tomato sauce. Place the mozzarella cheese on top. Bake for 20 minutes in a 350° F oven or until hot and bubbly.

Serves 6
1 serving = 300 calories

Tomato Sauce
(Rancho La Puerta)

12	tomatoes, cored
4	clove garlic
1	tsp. oregano
2	tsp. champagne vinegar
2	c. onions, chopped
1	c. fresh basil
1	tsp. mint leaves, chopped
6	c. vegetable stock (see recipe under Soups)

Simmer all ingredients together for 20 minutes. Blend in a blender until smooth.

Pasta Primavera
(Tucson National Resort)

2	c. carrots, diced
2	c. yellow squash, diced
2	c. onions, peeled and diced
2	c. cauliflower in small florets
2	c. broccoli in small florets
1	c. low-calorie Italian dressing
4	c. whole wheat fettucine noodles (1/2 lb. dry), cooked
1/2	c. Parmesan cheese, grated
3	c. tomatoes, for garnish, diced

Pasta Primavera (Cont.)

Steam all vegetables until crisp-tender. Marinate all the vegetables except the broccoli for several hours in the dressing. Refrigerate all vegetables until cold, including the broccoli. Combine the cooked pasta and Parmesan cheese. Mix well and refrigerate until cold. To serve, combine the cold marinated vegetables, the cold broccoli and cold pasta and mix thoroughly. Garnish each serving with diced tomatoes.

Serves 8
1 3/4 cup serving = 185 calories

Angel Hair Pasta, Field Mushrooms, Roasted Garlic, Tomatoes and Basil
(Sonoma Mission Inn)

1	tsp. extra virgin olive oil
2	oz. field mushrooms, sliced
1/2	tsp. roasted garlic
4	oz. tomatoes, chopped
1/4	tsp. basil
1	oz. chicken stock
2	oz. angel hair pasta, cooked
	pepper to taste

In saute pan, place oil, field mushrooms, garlic, tomatoes, basil and chicken stock. Toss in cooked pasta and serve. Season with pepper.

Serves 1
1 serving = 200 calories

Szechuan Noodles with Peanut Sauce
(Canyon Ranch)

10	oz. dry oriental-style noodles, 4 c. cooked
1 1/2	tsp. dark sesame oil
1	c. Szechuan Peanut Sauce (see recipe under Sauces)
1/2	c. scallion tops, chopped, for garnish
1	red bell pepper, diced, for garnish (optional)
4	scallion flowers for garnish

Cook the noodles al dente* according to package directions. Drain and rinse with cold water. Drain again thoroughly. Combine noodles and sesame oil and toss. Refrigerate until cold. To serve, place 1 cup noodles on each plate. Pour 1/4 cup of the Szechuan Peanut Sauce over the top. Sprinkle with 2 tablespoons of the scallion tops and red pepper if desired. Top each with a scallion flower.

Serves 4
1 1/4 cup serving = 275 calories

* see glossary

Spa Pasta and Chicken
(Camelback Inn Resort, Golf Club & Spa)

1/2	chicken breast
1/4	oz. safflower oil
3	oz. stir fry vegetable mix
1 1/2	oz. chicken stock
1	oz. tamari (see glossary)
1/4	oz. chicken glaze
5	oz. whole wheat pasta

Saute chicken in oil. Add vegetables and chicken stock. Cook until vegetables are tender. Add tamari and chicken glaze and stir until glaze is dissolved. Add pasta to mix, stir and heat until pasta is hot.

Serves 1
1 serving = 450 calories

Ravioli with Wild Mushrooms, Sage and Demi-Glace
(Golden Door)

1/4	lb. shiitake mushrooms, cleaned and quartered
1/4	lb. white mushrooms, cleaned and sliced
8	oz. canned straw mushrooms,* drained
1	oz. dried mixed mushrooms, reconstituted in 1/2 c. warm water and 1/2 c. dry sherry
	vegetable spray
1/2	c. white onions, sliced
1/4	c. carrots, minced
1/4	c. shallots, minced
2	Tbsp. fresh rosemary, chopped or 2 tsp. dried rosemary
3	Tbsp. fresh thyme or 2 tsp. dried thyme
1	Tbsp. fresh sage or 1 tsp. dried sage
2	c. demi-glace or 4 c. chicken stock slowly reduced by half with 1/2 c. low sodium tomato juice
1	pinch ground allspice
1/4	tsp. ground nutmeg
1	tsp. freshly ground black pepper
	salt to taste
72	ravioli, lowfat ricotta filled
	sprig of sage for garnish
	Parmesan cheese, grated
	fresh parsley, chopped

Prepare mushrooms. Heat a large skillet until hot; spray with vegetable spray. Add onions, carrots and shallots. Cook until slightly brown. Add mushrooms, reconstituted mushrooms and liquid. Cook for 4-5 minutes over medium low flame. Add all remaining ingredients and bring to a boil. Reduce heat and allow to simmer until thickened, about 15 minutes. Adjust seasoning. Sauce can also be thickened with 1 teaspoon cornstarch mixed with 3 ounces dry sherry or white wine.

Ravioli with Wild Mushrooms, Sage and Demi-glace (Cont.)

For Ravioli: Bring salted water to a boil and cook ravioli until tender. Drain well and plate. Spoon mushroom sauce over ravioli and garnish with a sprig of sage. Sprinkle with Parmesan cheese and chopped fresh parsley if desired.

Serves 6
1 serving = 282 calories

* see glossary

Crossover Pasta with Morels, Green Beans and Fennel
(The Claremont)

1/2	c. morels,* sliced
1/4	c. olive oil
1/2	c. fennel, diced and blanched*
1/4	c. green beans, sliced
1/4	c. red bell pepper, diced
1	tsp. shallots, minced
1	tsp. garlic, minced
1	Tbsp. rosemary
1	tsp. thyme
1/4	c. chicken stock
6	oz. pasta, cooked and refreshed

Saute morels in 1 tablespoon oil. Remove from pan. Saute fennel, green beans, red pepper, shallots and garlic. Add morels, herbs and chicken stock. Toss remaining oil and pasta with vegetables until heated through.

Serves 2
1 serving = 144 calories

* see glossary

Fresh Pasta
(Vista Clara)

2	c. unbleached all purpose white flour
1	egg
3	egg whites
1/2	tsp. olive oil

Sift flour onto a pastry board and make a well in the center. Break each egg separately into a cup (this is done so if any egg shells fall into the bowl, they can be removed without getting into the dough). Pour eggs into the flour well. Mix the eggs into flour with a fork and work the dough. It will be fairly stiff to begin with, but after 15 minutes of kneading it will become smooth and pliable with little or no bubbles forming over the surface. Roll into a ball and let rest for 20 minutes on a lightly floured pastry board, covered with a bowl or cloth. If you have a pasta machine, this next step will not be necessary. Roll out the dough into a paper-thin, even sheet, using as little pressure on the rolling pin as possible. Sprinkle dough lightly with flour to prevent sticking. Do not roll out dough in a draft or in a room which is too warm or dry as it may make the dough dry too quickly to be rolled out completely. The dough can be cut into the required shapes immediately while it is still fresh, or it can be left to dry.

Serves 4
1 serving = 237 calories

Pasta Primavera with Scallops
(The Hills)

12	oz. whole wheat spaghetti, cooked al dente*
1/2	onion, chopped
1/2	c. vegetable stock
1/4	c. mushrooms, sliced
1/2	c. green pepper, chopped
1/2	c. broccoli, chopped
1	carrot, cut into thin slices
1	tsp. soy sauce
	dash of cayenne pepper
1/4	lb. sea scallops, quartered

Place onions in a large skillet with 1/4 cup of the stock and cook over medium heat until translucent. Add mushrooms, peppers, broccoli, carrots, remaining stock, soy sauce and cayenne. Bring to a boil, reduce heat to low, cover and simmer for about 10 minutes. Stir scallops into the vegetables and cook until scallops are cooked through, 1-2 minutes. Drain spaghetti, place on a plate and spoon the vegetable mixture on top.

Serves 8
1 serving = 66 calories

*see glossary

329

VEGETARIAN RECIPES

Linny's Bean and Cheese Enchiladas with Mock Sour Cream
(Cal-a-Vie)

1	Tbsp. safflower oil
2	large onions, chopped
6	c. button mushrooms, sliced
3	medium tomatoes, peeled and chopped
1	jalapeno chile pepper, seeded and finely chopped
1 1/2	Tbsp. chili powder
1 1/2	Tbsp. ground cumin
2	c. pinto beans, cooked
1	bunch cilantro, chopped
12	whole wheat flour tortillas
1 1/4	c. Mock Sour Cream (recipe follows)
18	black pitted olives, sliced in half
	Enchilada Sauce (recipe follows)
4	oz. mozzarella cheese, grated

Place 1 tablespoon safflower oil in a nonstick saute pan. Saute the onions and mushrooms until limp and soft. Add the tomatoes, jalapeno peppers, chile powder and cumin. Cook 15 minutes until most of the liquid has evaporated. Mix in the cooked beans and half of the cilantro. Place 1/4 cup of the bean mixture in a tortilla. Add 1 tablespoon Mock Sour Cream and 1 sliced olive. Roll up and place in a casserole dish. Ladle 3/4 cup Enchilada Sauce over the top and sprinkle with grated cheese. Bake at 350° F for 20 minutes until hot. To serve, top with 1/2 tablespoon Mock Sour Cream, 1/2 black olive and a sprinkle of cilantro.

Serves 12
1 serving = 305 calories

Enchilada Sauce
(Cal-a-Vie)

1	large onion, chopped
16	medium tomatoes, peeled and chopped
1	large carrot
2	c. tomato juice
1 1/2	Tbsp. chili powder
1 1/2	Tbsp. cumin

In a large nonstick skillet, cook the onion with the tomatoes, carrots and tomato juice. Add the chili powder and cumin. Simmer 20 minutes on low. Puree in a blender until smooth.

Mock Sour Cream
(Cal-a-Vie)

3/4	c. lowfat cottage cheese
1/2	c. lowfat yogurt
2	drops Tabasco (optional)

In a blender mix cottage cheese, yogurt and Tabasco. Blend until smooth like sour cream, turning the blender off and on to mix.

Spicy Ratatouille
(Cal-a-Vie)

1	Tbsp. virgin olive oil
1	Tbsp. minced garlic
1	small onion, chopped
1	red pepper or bell pepper, cut into 1" strips
1	Tbsp. dry oregano
1	Tbsp. Mexican-style chili powder
2	tsp. ground cumin
1/2	tsp. hot chile flakes
4	large tomatoes, peeled and chopped
1	small eggplant, peeled and chopped

Spicy Ratatouille (Cont.)

2   medium size zucchini, cut lenghtwise into 1" strips
2   Tbsp. parsley, chopped

Over medium fire, heat olive oil. Add garlic, onion and peppers. Stir with spatula and add oregano, chili powder, cumin and hot chile flakes. Add tomatoes and let simmer for 3-4 minutes. Stir in eggplant and zucchini. Cover, let simmer for 20 minutes, stirring occasionally. Sprinkle with chopped parsley and serve. Leftovers are also excellent served cold with lemon wedges on the side and a few drops of olive oil.

Serves 8
1 serving = 65 calories

Stuffed Baked Potato
(Cal-a-Vie)

4   large baking potatoes
      safflower oil for rubbing potatoes
1   c. lowfat cottage cheese
1/2   c. plain lowfat yogurt
1   Tbsp. apple cider vinegar (optional)
1/2   c. scallions, chopped
1/2   c. celery, finely diced
      dash of cayenne pepper
4   broccoli buds, steamed
4   thin slices mozzarella, about 2 oz.

Rub potatoes with safflower oil and bake at 375° F for 1 hour and 10 minutes or until potatoes are done. Meanwhile in mixing bowl, mix cottage cheese, yogurt, vinegar, scallions, celery and cayenne pepper. When potatoes are baked, cut 1/2" off upper lid of potatoes and scoop out, leaving about 1/2". Mix with cottage cheese mixture and nearly fill the potatato. Dot with broccoli buds. Top with mozzarella cheese and return to oven for about 15 minutes until golden brown.

Serves 4
1 serving = 269 calories

California Pizza with Whole Wheat Crust and Chevre Cheese

(Cal-a-Vie)

Crust:

2	Tbsp. dry yeast
1 1/2	c. warm water
	pinch of iodized sea salt
1	Tbsp. honey
1	Tbsp. virgin olive oil
2	c. semolina flour
1 1/2	c. whole wheat pastry flour

1-1 1/4 c. unbleached white flour and flour for dusting

In a bowl combine yeast, water, salt, honey and oil and let the yeast activate. Add semolina flour and unbleached white and whole wheat flour to make a firm dough and let proof for 20 minutes in a lightly oiled bowl covered with a kitchen towel. Let rise to double in volume. Punch the dough down and transfer to table dusted with flour. Make 3 even balls. Use 3 pizza pans 12" in diameter. Roll out dough slightly larger than the pan and cover lightly oiled pans with dough and make an edge. Cover with plastic wrap and leave in refrigerator until ready to use. If all the dough is not used for pizza, it also makes excellent rolls.

Topping for One Pizza:

1	6 oz. log of chevre cheese, crumbled
	enough fresh basil leaves to cover pizza
1 1/2	c. tomatoes (12 medium), peeled, seeded, diced and drained for at least 1 hour (preferrably Italian plum tomatoes)
1	bell peppper, cut in thin strips
2	Tbsp. black olives, thinly sliced
3	Tbsp. tomato puree
2	tsp. fresh oregano or 1 1/2 tsp. dry oregano
	ground pepper and a sprinkle of virgin olive oil
1	Tbsp. Parmesan cheese, freshly grated

California Pizza with Whole Wheat Crust and Chevre Cheese (Cont.)

Bake crust in 350° F oven for 10 minutes. Cover with chevre cheese and fresh basil leaves. Spread diced tomatoes over leaves. Arrange bell pepper strips and olives over tomatoes. With a spatula, spread on tomato puree. Sprinkle with oregano, ground pepper, olive oil and Parmesan cheese and bake 30 minutes more.

Serves 8
1 serving = 225 calories

Tofu Lasagne
(Cal-a-Vie)

8	slices zucchini, sliced lengthwise very thin (about 2 medium zucchinis), optional
8	oz. firm tofu, sliced into 8 1 oz. rectangular slices, drained on a towel
2	bunches fresh spinach, washed, rinsed well, steamed, cooled and coarsely chopped
1	c. part skim ricotta cheese
	Tomato Sauce (recipe follows)
4	1/2 oz. slices lowfat mozzarella cheese
2	Tbsp. Parmesan cheese
2	Tbsp. parsley, chopped

Drop zucchini slices in boiling water for 2 minutes. Remove with slotted spoon and drop into ice water to cool. In 4 individual casserole dishes layer 1 slice tofu, 2 slices zucchini and 1/2 cup cooked spinach. Next, scoop 1/4 cup ricotta cheese onto spinach and top with 1/4 cup tomato sauce. Cover with 1 slice tofu. Top with more sauce and 1 slice mozzarella cheese. Bake for 20 minutes in 350° F oven. Top with more sauce and sprinkle with Parmesan cheese and fresh parsley.

Serves 4
1 serving = 290 calories

Tomato Sauce
(Cal-a-Vie)

2	tsp. garlic, minced
1/2	c. yellow onions, minced
2	tsp. olive oil
1	Tbsp. dried basil
1	tsp. dried oregano
5	large tomatoes, peeled and diced (or 1 18-oz. can whole plum tomatoes)
1/2	tsp. black pepper, freshly ground
1	c. tomato puree
2	c. fresh mushrooms, sliced

Gently saute garlic and onions in oil. Add basil, oregano, tomatoes and pepper. Stir in tomato puree and mushrooms. Cover and simmer on low heat 20 minutes or until sauce gets thick.

Miso Stew with Wild Mushrooms, Vegetables and Tofu
(Sonoma Mission Inn)

1	oz. field mushrooms
1	oz. oyster mushrooms
1	oz. shiitake mushrooms
1/2	oz. snap peas
1/2	oz. bok choy, chopped
1/2	oz. bean sprouts
1	Tbsp. light soy sauce
1/4	tsp. miso (see glossary)
1/4	tsp. nori(see glossary)
8	oz. fish stock
1/4	tsp. ginger, minced
1/4	tsp. garlic, minced
2	oz. tofu, diced

Miso Stew with Wild Mushrooms, Vegetables and Tofu (Cont.)

Combine all ingredients except tofu and simmer 5 minutes. Add tofu at end when ready to serve.

Serves 1
1 serving = 100 calories

Southwestern Rice and Beans
(Rocky Mountain Wellness Spa)

1/2	red bell pepper, cut in chunks
1/2	green bell pepper, cut in chunks
1/4	yellow onion, cut in chunks
10	plum tomatoes, peeled, seeded and diced
8	Tbsp. cilantro, chopped
8	Tbsp. fresh oregano
1	Tbsp. cumin
2	Tbsp. chili powder
	dash cayenne
8	cloves garlic, chopped
1/2	c. water
2	Tbsp. no salt tomato paste
2	Tbsp. lemon juice
2	c. beans (kidney, chili, pinto, black), cooked
10	green tomatillos, chopped
3/4	c. red onion, chopped
3	c. brown rice, cooked
3/4	c. cheddar cheese, shredded
4	Tbsp. green onion, chopped

Saute peppers and yellow onion. Add tomatoes, herbs, spices, garlic, water, tomato paste and lemon juice. Stir in beans. Simmer 20 minutes on low. Add tomatillos and red onion. Pour over rice and top with shredded cheese and green onion.

Serves 4
1 serving = 146 calories

With permission from Sheri Stephens

337

Vegetable K-Bobs
(Rocky Mountain Wellness Spa)

8	green bell pepper, cut in chunks
8	zucchini, cut in chunks
8	red onion, cut in chunks
8	eggplant, cut in chunks
	whole mushrooms
8	yellow squash, cut in chunks
8	fresh pineapple, cut in chunks
4	long bamboo skewers
	spray bottle of water
1 1/2	c. brown and wild rice, cooked and seasoned with celery, parsley and scallion
	sauces and dips

Alternate vegetables and fruit on skewers. Put in pan with 1/2" water and cover with foil to steam in 400° F oven about 15 minutes. Remove foil and put under broiler. Spray with water and brown lightly. Serve on top of seasoned rice and serve assorted sauces and dips on the side.

Serves 2
1 serving = 251 calories

With permission from Sheri Stephens

Stuffed Artichoke
(Rocky Mountain Wellness Spa)

2	artichokes, tips cut
1	c. brown rice, cooked
2	Tbsp. carrot, diced
4	Tbsp. celery, diced
2	Tbsp. red onion, diced
4	Tbsp. broccoli, diced
4	Tbsp. cauliflower, diced
1/4	c. soy mozzarella, shredded
2	Tbsp. Basil Pesto (see recipe under Sauces)

Stuffed Artichoke (Cont.)

4   Tbsp. Tomato Basil Sauce (see recipe under Sauces)

Boil artichokes 45 minutes or until done. Cool and remove very center leaves only. Very carefully scrape hair from heart with a spoon. Fill with rice, vegetables, cheese, Basil Pesto and 1/4 cup of the Tomato Basil Sauce. Put in baking pan with a little water on bottom and reheat in oven. Spoon 1/2 cup Tomato Basil Sauce on each plate and set artichoke on top.

Serves 2
1 serving = 190 calories

With permission from Sheri Stephens

Lasagne
(Rocky Mountain Wellness Spa)

2	oz. spinach, cooked and drained
3	oz. yellow squash
1	egg
1	lb. nonfat yogurt, well drained
4	cloves garlic, chopped
1/8	tsp. cayenne
1/8	tsp. fresh nutmeg, grated
1	Tbsp. Basil Pesto (see recipe under Sauces)
2	c. Tomato Basil Sauce (see recipe under Sauces)
9	brown rice lasagna noodles
2	oz. mushrooms, sliced
3	oz. eggplant, sliced thin and diced
	parsley for garnish, diced

Chop spinach and puree yellow squash. Mix with egg, yogurt, seasonings and 1 ounce cheese. Pour 1 cup Tomato Basil Sauce on bottom of pan and top with 3 noodles. Pour half of the yogurt mixture on top. Add 3 noodles and the remaining yogurt mixture. Sprinkle with mushrooms and eggplant. Top with 3 more noodles and 1 cup Tomato Basil Sauce. Bake at 400° F 40 minutes.

Lasagna (Cont.)

Top with rest of shredded mozzarella and diced parsley and continue baking until cheese is melted.

Serves 2-3
1 serving = 126 calories

With permission from Sheri Stephens

Indonesian Stir Fry with Tempeh
(Rocky Mountain Wellness Spa)

1	tsp. sesame chile oil
1	oz. yellow bell pepper, julienned
1	small carrot, diagonal cut
8	asparagus, cut in 1" lengths
5	oz. cauliflower florets
4	oz. snow peas, trimmed
4	oz. soy-rice tempeh*
3	oz. yellow squash, cut in strips
1	oz. white eggplant, cut in chunks
1	oz. bok choy, stem and green leaves also, sliced
1/2	can water chestnuts, sliced
1/2	can bamboo shoots
	Stir Fry Sauce (see recipe under Sauces)

Put sesame chile oil in saute pan. Stir fry pepper, carrots, asparagus. Add cauliflower and snow peas and continue stir frying. Last, add tempeh, squash, eggplant, bok choy, water chestnuts and bamboo shoots. Spray with water periodically. Add Stir Fry Sauce and heat.

Serves 2
1 serving = 189 calories

With permission from Sheri Stephens
* see glossary

Quesadillas
(Canyon Ranch)

4	tsp. corn oil margarine
8	whole wheat flour tortillas
4	c. part-skim mozzarella cheese, shredded (16 oz.)
1/2	c. canned jalapeno peppers, chopped
1/2	c. green onions, chopped
4	c. lettuce, shredded
2	c. tomatoes, diced (about 4)

In a skillet over medium heat, melt 1/2 teaspoon corn oil margarine for each tortilla. Place the tortilla in the skillet and sprinkle 1/2 cup mozzarella cheese evenly over the tortilla. Continue to cook until the cheese is melted. Sprinkle 1 tablespoon each of the jalapeno peppers and green onions evenly over the melted cheese. Fold the tortilla in half and cut into three pie-shaped wedges. Keep warm and repeat process with remaining tortillas. To serve, arrange 3 pieces in a fan pattern on a round plate and garnish with 1/2 cup shredded lettuce and 1/4 cup diced tomatoes.

Serves 8
1 serving = 260

Stuffed Bell Peppers
(Canyon Ranch)

1	c. brown rice
1/2	c. lentils
1 1/2	c. Vegetable Stock, boiling (see recipe under Soups)
1/4	tsp. salt
1/2	tsp. dried leaf thyme, crushed, using a mortar and pestle
8	small bell peppers
1	large onion, finely chopped
1	rib celery without leaves, finely chopped
2	small carrots, finely chopped
2	c. mushrooms, finely chopped

Stuffed Bell Peppers (Cont.)

1/4	c. fresh parsley, minced
6	garlic cloves, minced
1	8 oz. can water chestnuts, diced (2/3 c.)

Combine the brown rice, lentils, boiling Vegetable Stock, salt and thyme in a covered saucepan. Cook over low heat until the rice and lentils are done, about 45 minutes. Add a little more stock if necessary. Meanwhile, cut the tops off the bell peppers. Remove the seeds and inner membranes and rinse well. Set aside. In a large pot, cook the onion, covered, over low heat until soft, stirring occasionally to prevent scorching. Add all remaining ingredients except the bell peppers. Continue to cook until all vegetables are tender. Add cooked grain mixture and combine. Stuff 1/2 cup vegetable/grain mixture into each pepper. Arrange in a baking pan and add water to a depth of 1/4". Bake, covered, in a preheated 325° F oven for 45 minutes. Remove the cover and bake an additional 15 minutes or until the tops are browned.

Serves 8
1 serving = 186 calories

Bean Burritos
(Canyon Ranch)

2	c. pinto beans with broth, cooked (recipe follows)
1 1/4	c. onion, chopped
1	c. tomato, chopped
1/2	Tbsp. cilantro, finely chopped
2	Tbsp. canned green chilies, chopped
1/4	tsp. ground cumin
3/4	tsp. chili powder
4	whole wheat flour tortillas

Place 1 cup of beans with some broth in food processor. Reserve the rest. Puree to a paste consistency. Cook onions and tomatoes over low heat in a covered pan until soft. To the tomato mixture add the cilantro, green chilies, cumin and chili powder. Add the pureed beans and the reserved beans.

Bean Burritos (Cont.)

Cook uncovered over medium heat until warmed thoroughly. Stir occasionally. To serve, spoon 2/3 cup bean mixture onto lower half of tortilla. Fold tortilla like an envelope around the beans.

Serves 4
1 serving = 237 calories

Pinto Beans with Broth
(Canyon Ranch)

1 1/2	c. dry pinto beans
	water
3/4	c. onions, diced
1	tsp. garlic, minced
1/2	tsp. black pepper

Soak beans overnight in plenty of water. Next day, drain the water and cover beans with fresh water in a pot. Add the onion, garlic and black pepper. Bring to a boil. Reduce heat and simmer for 2 1/2 hours, or until beans are tender.

Yields approx. 2 cups
1 cup = approx. 50 calories

Eggplant Lasagne
(The Palms)

	nonstick vegetable cooking spray
1	lb. eggplant, peeled and sliced into 1/8" thick rounds
1	8 oz. can plain tomato sauce (70 calories per c.)
1/4	tsp. leaf basil, crumbled
1/4	tsp. leaf thyme, crumbled
1/8	tsp. black pepper
6	oz. part-skim mozzarella cheese, sliced 1/4" thick
1/3	c. sharp cheddar cheese, shredded

Preheat broiler. Spray broiler pan rack with spray. Arrange eggplant in single layer on rack. Broil 5" from heat 3-5 minutes until golden brown.

Eggplant Lasagne (Cont.)

Turn slices over; broil 2-5 minutes until dried out. Broil remaining eggplant. Lower oven temperature to hot (400° F). Heat tomato sauce, basil, thyme and pepper in small saucepan until boiling. Lower heat and simmer 1 minute. Spoon very thin layer of sauce in 9" x 9" x 2" square baking pan. Layer half the eggplant rounds over sauce. Top with mozzarella. Layer on remaining eggplant. Spoon on remaining sauce. Cover tightly with foil. Bake for 15 minutes. Uncover, sprinkle with cheddar. Bake 5-10 minutes to melt cheese.

Serves 4
1 serving = 187 calories

Lasagne
(The Palms)

6	curly-edge lasagne noodles
1	8 oz. can plain tomato sauce (70 calories per c.)
1/4	tsp. leaf basil, crumbled
1/4	tsp. leaf thyme, crumbled
1/8	tsp. black pepper
1 1/2	c. part-skim ricotta cheese
1	clove garlic, finely chopped
1	egg yolk
1/3	c. part-skim mozzarella cheese, shredded
1/3	c. sharp cheddar cheese, shredded

Cook lasagne according to package directions. Combine tomato sauce, basil, thyme and pepper in small saucepan. Bring to boiling. Lower heat and cook 1 minute. Remove from heat and reserve. Combine ricotta, garlic and egg yolk in small bowl. Combine mozzarella and cheddar cheese on wax paper. Preheat oven to 400° F. Spoon a very thin layer of sauce on bottom of 9" x 9" x 2" baking pan. Arrange 3 strips of lasagne on bottom of pan, turning ends under. Spread ricotta filling down length of pasta strips. Layer remaining lasagne noodles over filling. Cover pan tightly with foil. Bake for 20 minutes. Reheat sauce.

Lasagne (Cont.)

Uncover lasagne. Spoon hot sauce over pasta. Sprinkle with mozzarella and cheddar cheeses. Bake, uncovered, 5 minutes or until cheese melts.

Serves 6
1 serving = 242 calories

Nut Cutlets
(Meadowlark)

1 1/4	c. green pepper, chopped
1 1/4	c. parsley, chopped
5	onions, chopped
1/2	tsp. garlic, chopped
1/2	tsp. seasoning salt
1	tsp. basil
1	tsp. dill weed
1/2	tsp. cayenne
4	Tbsp. oil
1 1/4	c. almonds
1 1/4	c. walnuts
1 1/4	c. cashews
2	c. sunflower seeds
5/8	c. sesame seeds
5/8	c. fresh wheat germ
10	eggs
10	Tbsp. lowfat milk
5	c. lowfat cheddar cheese, grated

Saute vegetables and seasonings in oil. Grind nuts and seeds and combine with the vegetables. Add wheat germ. Beat eggs with milk and add to dry ingredients. Stir until moist and shape into patties. Place on lightly oiled cookie sheet and bake at 350° F for 20 minutes. Sprinkle with grated cheese and bake until cheese is melted.

Serves 20
1 serving = 448 calories

Cheese Cutlets
(Meadowlark)

3	c. cheddar cheese
4	eggs
1/4	c. soy or whole wheat flour
2	Tbsp. green pepper, chopped
4	tsp. celery, finely chopped
4	tsp. onions, chopped
1/4	tsp. salt
1/4	c. oil
4	tsp. sweet basil
4	Tbsp. milk
1/2	c. chopped nuts

Mix all ingredients well and spread onto oiled cookie sheets. Bake for 30 minutes in preheated 350° F oven.

Serves 6
1 serving = 448 calories

Nice and Easy
(Meadowlark)

1	onion, chopped
1	stalk celery, chopped
1	Tbsp. oil
1/4	c. butter
3	c. water
5	Tbsp. tamari*
1	c. brown rice
1/2	c. lentils
3	c. chopped vegetables, your choice, steamed
1	c. lowfat cheddar cheese, grated

Saute onion and celery in oil and butter until onions become nice and brown. Add water and tamari. Bring to a boil and add rice and lentils. Cook until tender, about 45 minutes.

Nice and Easy (Cont.)

Put rice mixture on bottom of casserole dish and put vegetables on top of rice. Sprinkle with cheese and pop into oven until cheese is melted.

Serves 6
1 serving = 318 calories

* *see glossary*

Whole Wheat Crepes with Ratatouille and Goat Cheese
(Marriott's Desert Springs Resort and Spa)

8	whole wheat crepes
8	oz. goat cheese, softened
1	Tbsp. Ratatouille (see recipe under Sauces)
4	oz. lowfat mozzarella, grated
3	oz. baby vegetables, preferably carrots, turnips
1	new potato

Lay 2 crepes on clean surface. Spread 1 ounce goat cheese on each crepe. Add 2 ounces of heated Ratatouille. Roll crepes. Sprinkle 1/2 ounce mozzarella on top of each crepe. Place in oven proof dish. Repeat. Bake for 8 minutes or until warm throughout. Remove onto heated platter. Garnish with vegetables and potatoes.

Serves 4
1 serving = 290 calories

Mexi Rice and Bean Casserole
(National Institute of Fitness)

2	c. brown rice, cooked
2	c. pinto beans, cooked
1	16 oz. can tomato bits and pieces
2	large cloves garlic, minced
1	c. onion, diced
1	c. lowfat cottage cheese
1	4 oz. can green chili peppers, minced
1	c. mozzarella cheese, grated

Mix well all ingredients except cheese. Pour mixture in casserole dish sprayed with PAM. Bake 45 minutes at 350° F. Add cheese and bake another 15 minutes.

Serves 8
1 serving = 156 calories

Lemon Rice
(Golden Door)

1	c. long grain white rice or white basmati rice
2	c. water or stock, either vegetable or chicken
	zest* of 1 lemon
1/4	tsp. ground nutmeg
1/4	tsp. ground cloves
1/2	tsp. ground cinnamon
1/2	tsp. ground cumin
1/2	tsp. ground coriander
1	pinch saffron
	parsley, chopped, for garnish

Rinse and soak rice for 1 hour. Drain. Place water or broth with spices in mixer. Blend well. Add to rice and bring to a boil. Cover and reduce heat to simmer. Cook for 20 minutes or until liquid is absorbed. Garnish with chopped parsley.

Serves 6
1 serving = 123 calories

Western Baked Beans and Rice
(Bermuda Resort)

1/2	c. dry red beans
1/2	c. dry white beans
	water
1 1/2	c. brown rice, cooked (1/2 c. uncooked)
1/4	c. brown sugar
1/2	c. catsup
1/4	c. onion, chopped
1/4	c. barbecue sauce
1	Tbsp. spiced brown mustard
1/4	tsp. allspice
1/4	tsp. cinnamon
1/4	tsp. black pepper

Place red and white beans in large pot. Cover with 2 cups water. Bring water to boil and boil two minutes. Remove from heat. Soak for 1 hour, then drain and rinse beans. Add 2 2/3 cups water and simmer until beans are tender, about 1 1/2 hours. Drain beans. Add rice, brown sugar, catsup, onion, barbecue sauce, 1/4 cup water and seasonings. Mix well. Turn into a 1 quart baking dish. Bake, covered, at 325° F for 1 1/2 hours. Stir well before serving. Serve 3/4 cup. Garnish each plate with green and yellow pepper strips, placed in a star or fan shape. Place an orange twist with parsley in center.

Serves 5
1 serving = 277 calories

Lavosh Roll-Ups
(The Plantation Spa)

1	roll whole wheat lavosh* bread
6	oz. cream cheese
1	Tbsp. soy milk
2	tsp. green onion, chopped
1	tsp. seasoning salt
3	lettuce or spinach leaves
1/2	c. sprouts
1/2	c. carrots, grated
1/2	c. cheese, any kind, grated

Lay bread flat. Blend cream cheese, soy milk, green onion and seasoning salt together until of thick spreading consistency. Spread over entire piece of lavosh. Place lettuce, sprouts, carrots and cheese in middle of bread. Pull tightly toward you and roll, keeping the vegetables in the middle. Slice into mini sandwiches.

Makes 12 mini sandwiches
5 mini sandwiches = 125 calories

* *see glossary*

Spinach-Zucchini Lasagne
(Maui Challenge)

2	lbs. fresh spinach, washed thoroughly and chopped
1	lb. mozzarella, shredded
3	medium zucchini, sliced
1	lb. lowfat ricotta cheese
1	egg
3	Tbsp. parsley, chopped
	white pepper to taste
1	recipe Italian Tomato Sauce (see recipe under Sauces)
	olive oil
1 1/2	boxes spinach/whole wheat lasagne noodles, uncooked
1/2	lb. Parmesan, grated
	black olives, sliced (optional)

Spinach-Zucchini Lasagne (Cont.)

In large stockpot, saute spinach in 1 teaspoon water until wilted. Reserve liquid. Stir in a handful of mozzarella cheese and mix thoroughly. Steam zucchini until just tender. While zucchini is steaming, combine ricotta, egg, parsley and pepper in a bowl. When zucchini is done, drain off water and mix in a handful of mozzarella. Add reserved spinach liquid to Italian Tomato Sauce. Preheat oven to 400° F. Oil an 8" x 12" x 2" pan. Line sides and bottom of pan with uncooked lasagne noodles. Note: This provides for a firmer textured lasagne and retains nutrient value of the noodle. Evenly spread 1/3 of the sauce over noodles, then all of spinach mixture. Sprinkle 1/3 of remaining mozzarella and Parmesan over spinach layer, then all of the ricotta mixture. Place another layer of noodles on top of ricotta, then 1/3 of the sauce. Add zucchini mixture and top with 1/3 of mozzarella and Parmesan cheeses. Finally, add 1 more layer of noodles, sauce and remaining cheese and top with sliced olives. Cover with foil and bake for 1/2 hour. Turn heat down to 350° F and continue baking uncovered for 20-30 minutes until golden and bubbly. Cool for 3-5 minutes before serving.

Serves 8-9
1 serving = 525 calories

Eggplant Parmigiana
(Maui Challenge)

4	lbs. eggplant, sliced in 1/4" rounds
	olive oil
1	recipe Italian Tomato Sauce (see recipe under Sauces)
3/4	lb. mozzarella, shredded
1/4	lb. Parmesan, shredded

Brush both sides of eggplant with olive oil and place on a cookie sheet. Broil in oven until golden, approximately 2-3 minutes each side. Spread on paper towels to absorb excess oil. Oil an 8" x 12" x 2" baking pan.

Eggplant Parmigiana (Cont.)

Alternate eggplant, sauce, mozzarella and Parmesan 3-4 times, until all is used, topping with a generous amount of cheese. Bake uncovered in 350° F preheated oven for 30-40 minutes.

Serves 8
1 serving = 385 calories

Squash Cake
(Vista Clara)

1	c. zucchini, grated
1	c. yellow squash, grated
1/2	c. potatoes, grated
1/2	c. onion, finely chopped
3	egg whites
1	tsp. red chile powder
1	tsp. cilantro, finely chopped
1/2	c. fresh corn, blanched* for 3 minutes and cooled

Combine all ingredients in bowl. Preheat pan and coat with a vegetable spray. Use a 2 ounce measure or a large soup spoon to scoop up mixture and place in pan. Cook cakes for 3 to 4 minutes on each side and serve with entree.

Serves 4
1 serving = 27 calories

* see glossary

352

POULTRY

Barbecued Chicken
(Tucson National Resort)

8   chicken legs
      garlic powder
2   c. barbecue sauce

Place the chicken legs in a baking dish and sprinkle lightly with garlic powder. Cover the baking dish with a lid or aluminum foil and bake in a preheated 350° F oven for 30 minutes. Remove from the oven and cool until the chicken legs can be handled easily. Remove and discard the skin and place the chicken legs back in the dish. Pour 1/4 cup of the sauce over each chicken leg. Cover and bake for 20 minutes more.

Serves 8
1 serving = 135 calories

Chicken Enchiladas
(Tucson National Resort)

3   onions, finely chopped
2   garlic cloves, finely chopped
1   tsp. salt
2   Tbsp. chili powder
1   tsp. ground cumin
1   28 oz. can tomatoes, undrained
2   c. diced cooked chicken
1   c. sharp cheddar cheese, grated
8   corn tortillas, warm

Combine the onion and garlic and cook, covered, over very low heat until soft, stirring frequently to prevent scorching. Add the salt, chili powder and cumin and mix well. Pour the juice from the tomatoes into the pan and then chop the tomatoes and add them to the mixture in the pan. Continue to cook, covered, for 10 minutes. Pour half of the sauce in a bowl. Add the chicken and 1/2 cup of the grated cheese to the remaining sauce in the pan and mix well.

Chicken Enchiladas (Cont.)

Spoon 1/8 of the mixture in the center of each tortilla and roll the tortilla around it. Place the enchiladas, fold side down, in a baking dish. Spoon the remaining sauce evenly over the tops of the enchiladas and then sprinkle 1 tablespoon of the remaining grated cheese over each enchilada. Bake, covered, in a preheated 350° F oven for 30 minutes.

Serves 8
1 serving = 230 calories

Game Hens a l'Orange
(Tucson National Resort)

2	large onions, chopped
4	game hens, cut into halves
	freshly ground black pepper
1	6 oz. can frozen unsweetened orange juice concentrate, thawed
2	c. sherry
1/2	tsp. thyme, crushed, using a mortar and pestle

Spread the chopped onions evenly over the bottom of a baking dish. Arrange the game hen halves, cut side down, on the onions. Sprinkle the game hens with freshly ground black pepper. Bake, uncovered, in a preheated 350° F oven for 20 minutes. Combine the orange juice concentrate, sherry and thyme and mix well. Pour over the tops of the game hens and continue to cook 40 minutes more, uncovered, basting frequently. To serve, remove the game hens from the pan and place on plates, cut side down. Stir the onions thoroughly through the sauce and spoon the sauce over the tops of the game hens.

Serves 8
1 serving = 145 calories

Sautéed Duck Breast with Prickly Pear Sauce
(Loews Ventana Canyon Resort)

2	Tbsp. white sugar
2	Tbsp. vinegar
2	oz. prickly pear juice
7	oz. brown sauce or thick duck stock
	salt and pepper to taste
8	duck breasts
1	Tbsp. prickly pear jelly

Place the sugar in a small saucepan with 2 tablespoons of water. Cook over moderate heat until sugar turns a nice caramel color. Add vinegar and prickly pear juice to the sugar and stand back (sugar will crack and spit). Simmer for 3 minutes. Add brown sauce and simmer again until sauce has a not-too-thick consistency. Strain and keep warm. Season duck breasts with salt and pepper and lay skin side down on a hot saute pan. Cook skin side until crisp; turn and cook meat side until golden brown. (Note: If, at this point the meat is too rare, it can be placed in a 350° F oven for 5 to 8 minutes.) Slice duck breast very thinly. Stir the prickly pear jelly into the sauce until completely incorporated. Ladle 1 1/2 ounces of sauce onto the plates. Shingle the sliced duck onto the sauce, starting with the smallest slices and ending with the largest. Serve with fresh vegetables and wild rice.

Serves 4
1 serving = 350 calories

Free Range Chicken in Garlic and Rosemary
(Cal-a-Vie)

1	whole chicken (about 3 1/2 lbs.)
1	Tbsp. virgin olive oil
1	Tbsp. garlic, minced
1 1/2	Tbsp. whole rosemary
1-2	tsp. fresh ground pepper
4	Tbsp. lemon juice
1/2	c. dry white wine
1/4	c. minced Italian parsley

Debone the chicken breast leaving the wing bone attached and partially remove the skin and fat. Cut breast in 2 pieces. Bone out the chicken leg and cut away the drumstick and thigh. Trim and bone the thigh. Cut away all fat and skin from all pieces. Rub the pieces of chicken with 1 tablespoon olive oil, garlic, rosemary, ground pepper and 1 tablespoon lemon juice. Place in baking dish. Add wine and remaining lemon juice. Cover with plastic wrap and leave in refrigerator for 4 hours. Cover tightly with lid or foil and bake at 350° F for about 35 minutes. Baste several times during cooking. Remove from the oven. It should be very juicy. Cook down pan juices then drizzle over chicken. Sprinkle with minced parsley. Serve with roasted garlic and baby vegetables. Garnish with rosemary sprigs.

Serves 4
1 serving = 325 calories

Pan Sautéed Skinless Breast of Chicken, Saffron Scented Fresh Tomato Relish
(Sonoma Mission Inn)

4	oz. skinless breast of chicken
2	pinches saffron
1/2	c. white wine
1/4	c. red wine vinegar
1/4	c. sugar
1	red onion, finely diced
1	red pepper, finely diced
1	yellow pepper, finely diced
4	lbs. tomato concasse*
	zest* of 1 orange
6	oranges, peeled and segmented
8	oz. tomato juice
	salt and pepper to taste
	steamed vegetables

Using Teflon pan, saute chicken breast, garnish with Saffron Scented Fresh Tomato Relish and fresh steamed vegetables. For Saffron Scented Tomato Relish: Simmer saffron with white wine for 5 minutes. Strain into another pan containing red wine vinegar and sugar. Reduce to syrup consistency. Lightly sauté onion and peppers, retaining color and texture. Combine vegetables, tomato concasse, orange zest (blanched* 1 minute), orange segments and tomato juice. Adjust seasonings. Yields 1 1/2 quarts.

Serves 1
1 serving = 250 calories

* see glossary

Oak Smoked Chicken Breast, Slices of Vine Ripened Tomato on Toasted Rye
(Sonoma Mission Inn)

1	Tbsp. lemon yogurt
	rye bread
3	oz. smoked chicken
2	slices tomato
2	lettuce leaves

Spread lemon yogurt on toasted rye bread. Place smoked chicken, tomato and lettuce on top. Cut in half and garnish with pepperoncini and julienned vegetables.

Serves 1
1 serving = 315 calories

Roasted Chicken Marinated in Middle Eastern Spices, Fresh Thin Sliced Vegetables and Salad Greens
(Sonoma Mission Inn)

1/8	tsp. each cumin, oregano and curry powder
4	oz. skinless, boneless chicken breast, cooked
1	oz. coriander
1	oz. carrots, sliced
1	oz. zucchini, sliced
1	oz. squash, sliced
1	tsp. scallions, sliced
2	oz. plain lowfat yogurt
1	oz. lemon juice
	pinch pepper
2	oz. salad greens

Roasted Chicken Marinated in Middle Eastern Spices, Fresh Thin Sliced Vegetables and Salad Greens (Cont.)

Sprinkle spices over cooked chicken and vegetables. Mix yogurt, lemon juice and pepper. Place greens on plate and arrange dressed chicken and vegetables over greens and garnish with spice mixture around rim.

Serves 1
1 serving = 160 calories

Skinless Petaluma Chicken Breast, Chile Salsa
(Sonoma Mission Inn)

3	tomatoes, medium dice
1/2	red onion, fine dice
1/4	tsp. jalapeno, fine dice
1/8	tsp. cilantro, medium dice
1/2	oz. vinegar
	juice from 1/2 lime
	black pepper to taste
4	oz. skinless chicken breast

Combine all ingredients except chicken and toss gently. Cover and allow to stand to develop taste. Grill chicken breast until done. Cover with salsa. Garnish with fresh vegetables.

Serves 1
1 serving = 165 calories

361

Steamed Savoy Cabbage Rolled with Braised Duck, Thin Sliced Vegetables and Sprouts
(Sonoma Mission Inn)

1/2	oz. broccoli stems, julienned
1/2	oz. carrots, julienned
1/2	oz. green zucchini, julienned
1/2	oz. yellow squash, julienned
1/2	oz. celery, julienned
1/2	oz. wild rice
16	oz. chicken stock
1	tsp. light soy sauce
1	oz. rice wine vinegar
1	large savoy cabbage leaf, steamed
3	oz. braised leg meat of duck, cooked and tossed with 1 tsp. light soy sauce and 1 tsp. rice wine vinegar
1/2	oz. alfalfa sprouts

Place vegetables in pan, add rice and stock and simmer until tender. Finish with light soy sauce and rice wine vinegar. Cool and reserve. To assemble: Place steamed cabbage leaf on table. Put duck meat on top of leaf along with julienned vegetables and sprouts. Bring sides together and roll from bottom to top. Press firmly and cut in half. Garnish with rice timbale.*

Serves 1
1 serving = 325 calories

* see glossary

Oven Roasted Turkey, Apricot Chutney on Whole Wheat
(Sonoma Mission Inn)

1	Tbsp. Thai Lemon Yogurt Dressing (see recipe under Dressings)
2	slices whole wheat bread
3	oz. skinless turkey breast, cooked
2	lettuce leaves
2	slices tomato
1	Tbsp. apricot chutney
	pepperoncini
1/2	c. julienned vegetables, steamed

Spread Thai Lemon Yogurt Dressing on whole wheat bread. Place sliced turkey breast, lettuce and tomato on top. Cut in half and garnish with apricot chutney, pepperoncini and steamed julienned vegetables.

Serves 1
1 serving = 335 calories

Teriyaki Chicken
(The Palms)

1	lb. boneless chicken breast halves, skinned (4 cutlets)
3	Tbsp. low-sodium soy sauce or tamari*
2	Tbsp. dry sherry
2	Tbsp. water
1	tsp. honey
1/2	tsp. fresh ginger, peeled, finely chopped
1	small clove garlic, finely chopped
	nonstick vegetable cooking spray

Make 3 diagonal slices, 1/4" deep, 1/2" apart, over top of each cutlet. Combine soy sauce, sherry, water, honey, ginger and garlic in 11 3/4 x 7 1/2 x 1 3/4" glass baking dish.

Teriyaki Chicken (Cont.)

Add chicken to marinade and turn to coat. Cover and refrigerate for 2 hours, turning occasionally. Preheat oven to broil.

Spray rack in broiler pan with nonstick vegetable cooking spray. Remove chicken from marinade; discard marinade. Arrange chicken, sliced side up, on prepared broiler pan. Broil about 5" from source of heat for about 4 minutes. Turn over and broil 4 minutes longer or until no longer pink in center. Serve immediately.

Serves 4
1 serving = 134 calories

* *see glossary*

Chinese Chicken Salad
(The Palms)

1	tsp. garlic, finely chopped
1	tsp. fresh ginger, peeled, finely chopped
1/2	lb. chicken breast, skinned, boned, cooked and finely shredded
2 2/3	c. celery, sliced 1/4" thick
1 1/2	8 oz. cans water chestnuts, drained and sliced 1/4" thick
3/4	c. green onion, chopped
3	Tbsp. reduced-calorie mayonnaise
2	tsp. low-sodium soy sauce or tamari*
1 1/2	c. mung bean sprouts (4 1/2 oz.)
4	lettuce leaves

Saute garlic and ginger over very low heat in a nonstick pan without oil for 30 seconds or until softened. Reserve. Combine chicken, celery, water chestnuts and green onion in a bowl. Stir in mayonnaise, soy and reserved ginger and garlic. Add sprouts. To serve, arrange 1 lettuce leaf on each of 4 individual salad plates. Mound chicken salad onto lettuce.

Serves 4
1 serving = 167 calories

* *see glossary*

Turkey Kabobs
(The Palms)

3/4   c. unsweetened pineapple juice
1/4   c. low-sodium soy sauce or tamari*
1/4   tsp. fresh ginger, peeled, grated
1   lb. raw turkey breast meat, cut into 16 cubes
8   pieces green bell pepper, each about 1 x 1/4" (3 oz.total)
8   pieces onion, each about 1 x 1/4" (2 oz. total)
4   pieces fresh pineapple, each about 1 x 3/4" (2 1/2 oz. total)

Stir together pineapple juice, soy sauce and ginger in small bowl. Add turkey cubes. Refrigerate, covered, 1 hour. Preheat oven to 375° F. Remove turkey from marinade. Thread 4 cubes turkey, 2 pieces green pepper, 2 pieces onion and 1 piece pineapple onto each of 4 skewers. Arrange skewers in 13 x 9 x 2" metal baking pan. Bake, uncovered, for 10 minutes or until center of turkey is no longer pink.

Serves 4
1 serving = 160 calories

* *see glossary*

Cabbage Rolls
(National Institute of Fitness)

3/4   lb. ground turkey
1/4   c. Jensen's Vegetable Broth and Seasoning
1/3   c. egg white powder or 2 egg whites
2   Tbsp. onion, minced
2   Tbsp. green pepper, minced
       pinch of rosemary, onion powder, white pepper
2   tsp. coriander seed, freshly ground
2   tsp. sage
2   c. cooked rice, oatmeal or leftover bread crumbs
       seasoned bread crumbs
       cabbage leaves

Cabbage Rolls (Cont.)
Blend by hand the above ingredients and roll up inside parboiled cabbage leaves. Place seam side down in a pan and bake for 45 minutes at 350° F. For variety, use sauces for extra flavor. Top with seasoned bread crumbs.

Serves 3
1 serving = 318 calories

Chicken Fettuccine
(National Institute of Fitness)

2	chicken breasts, skinned, boned and cut into small chunks
1/2	c. green onions, chopped
1	tsp. garlic, minced
1 1/2	c. mushrooms, sliced
1/2	c. double strength powdered milk or 1/4 c. powdered nonfat milk mixed with 1/2 c. water
	fettuccine, cooked

Bake chicken breasts at 350° F for 1/2 hour. During this time, saute onions, garlic and mushrooms in pan. Add milk and remaining ingredients. Simmer on low for about 15 minutes. Pour over chicken and bake another 15 minutes. Serve over fettuccine.

Serves 2
1 serving = 467 calories

Stuffed Green Peppers
(Bermuda Resort)

1/4	c. long grain rice, dry
3	large green peppers
1/2	lb. ground turkey
1/4	c. onion, chopped
8	oz. tomatoes, diced
1/2	tsp. granulated garlic
1	tsp. Worcestershire sauce
1/2	jar Prego spaghetti sauce

Stuffed Green Peppers (Cont.)

1/2   c. mozzarella cheese, shredded

Boil rice and set aside. Cut peppers in half lenghtwise, discard seeds and membranes. Cook peppers, uncovered, in boiling water for 5 minutes; invert to drain well. In a skillet cook ground turkey and onion until meat is done and onion is tender. Drain off excess fat. Add tomatoes, cooked rice, garlic and Worcestershire sauce. Stuff peppers with meat mixture. Top with one tablespoon of spaghetti sauce, enough to just cover meat mixture. Sprinkle with mozzarella cheese. Spray a baking pan with nonstick cooking spray. Place peppers in pan. Bake, covered, at 350° F for 30-35 minutes.

Serves 6
1 serving = 183 calories

Four Food Group Casserole
(Bermuda Resort)

3/4   c. macaroni, uncooked
3/4   lb. ground turkey
1/8   tsp. pepper
3/4   c. tomato sauce
1   10 1/2 can tomato soup, undiluted
3-4   drops Tabasco sauce
1/2   c. green pepper, chopped
1/2   c. onion, chopped
1   c. whole kernel corn (frozen, thawed or canned, rinsed well)
1/2   c. lowfat American cheese, shredded

Cook macaroni according to directions, drain and rinse (do not add salt). Brown turkey in large skillet, drain any fat. Add pepper, tomato sauce, soup and Tabasco. Stir in macaroni and vegetables. Place in a 6 quart shallow baking dish. Sprinkle cheese on top. Bake at 350° F 30-40 minutes until bubbly. Divide into 5 equal portions.

Serves 5
1 serving = 273 calories

Chicken Stuffed Spuds
(Bermuda Resort)

3	large baking potatoes
1/2	c. plain nonfat yogurt
1/2	c. nonfat or lowfat cottage cheese
1/4	c. nonfat milk
1	c. chicken or turkey, cooked and diced
1	c. whole kernel corn (canned, rinsed or frozen, thawed)
1	Tbsp. pimiento, chopped
	green onion, minced
1	Tbsp. snipped parsley
1/4	tsp. garlic powder

Wash and scrub potatoes and dry. Pierce gently with fork and bake potatoes until thoroughly cooked at 375° F about 1 hour. Cut baked potatoes in half and scoop out centers. Add yogurt, cottage cheese and milk to potatoes and blend with blender or mixer until smooth. Stir in chicken, corn, pimiento, onion, parsley and garlic powder. Spoon mixture back into potato shells. Place stuffed potatoes in shallow baking pan. Bake at 375° F about 15 minutes, until heated through.

Serves 6
1 serving = 205 calories

Pita Pizza
(Bermuda Resort)

1/2	lb. ground turkey
1/4	black olives, chopped
1/4	c. onion, chopped
1/4	c. green peppers, chopped
1/4	c. tomatoes, chopped
4	pita pockets
	Pizza Sauce (recipe follows)
2	oz. mozzarella cheese, shredded

Pita Pizza (Cont.)

Spray pan with nonstick spray. Brown turkey meat. Pour off excess fat. Saute vegetables until tender. Mix vegetables and meat. Spread 4 oz. meat mixture on each pita pocket. Top each with 1 oz. Pizza Sauce and 1/2 oz. mozzarella cheese. Heat in 350° F oven for 20 minutes.

Serves 4
1 serving = 277 calories

Pizza Sauce
(Bermuda Resort)

1/4	c. tomato puree
2	Tbsp. low-sodium tomato juice
2	Tbsp. water
1/4	tsp. Italian seasonings
1/4	tsp. oregano

Mix all ingredients.

Garlic Chicken and Grapes
(Bermuda Resort)

1	Tbsp. Dijon mustard
1	Tbsp. light soy sauce
1	Tbsp. honey
1	Tbsp. wine
2	cloves garlic, minced
6	boneless, skinless chicken breasts
1	Tbsp. sesame seeds
2	c. seedless red or green grapes, washed

Garlic Chicken and Grapes (Cont.)

Mix together mustard, soy sauce, honey, wine and garlic; set aside. Bake chicken breasts in covered pan at 400° F for 10 minutes; uncover. Pour mustard sauce over chicken. Sprinkle with sesame seeds and return to oven, uncovered. Bake until breasts are no longer pink, about 15 minutes longer. Sprinkle grapes over chicken; bake 5 minutes more.

Serves 6
1 serving = 202 calories

Chicken Enchiladas
(Bermuda Resort)

3	chicken breasts (2 cups shredded)
2	green chiles, cleaned and chopped
1	onion, chopped
1	clove garlic, minced
2	c. tomato juice
1	tsp. basil
1	tsp. cumin
1	tsp. oregano
1	tsp. chili powder
6	corn tortillas
1	c. buttermilk, heated
1/2	c. mozzarella cheese, grated
	tomato and parsley for garnish

Roast chicken breasts at 350° F for 1 hour. Cool and shred. Combine chicken, green chiles, onion, garlic, tomato juice, basil, cumin, oregano and chili powder and simmer 1 hour. Dip tortillas in buttermilk to soften. Fill with chicken mixture and roll. Place in boat or individual baking dish. Sprinkle cheese on enchiladas then pour on remaining milk. Bake at 350° F for 45 minutes or until heated through and cheese is bubbly. Garnish with tomato and parsley.

Serves 6
1 serving = 246 calories

Fillet of Turkey Biscayenne with Green Pasta
(Le Meridien)

	olive oil
1/2	lb. carrots, minced
1	lb. zucchini, minced
2	garlic cloves, minced
1/2	lb. onions, sliced
1	lb. fresh tomatoes, peeled, seeded and chopped
2	Tbsp. fresh parsley, chopped
	fresh thyme
	salt and pepper to taste
	dash cayenne
8	oz. red bell pepper sauce (in deli section)
8	oz. veal stock (cubes found in deli section)
1 3/4	lb. turkey breast, cut into 10 medallions
1 1/4	lb. green linquine
	chervil for garnish

In 2 tablespoons olive oil, quickly saute carrots, zucchini, garlic and onions. Add tomatoes, parsley, thyme, salt, pepper and cayenne. Simmer for 10 minutes. Add red bell pepper sauce and veal stock. Cook for 5 more minutes. Saute turkey medallions in olive oil 1 minute on each side. Cook pasta in boiling water. Put pasta on plate. Top with a turkey medallion and sauce. Garnish with chervil.

Serves 10
1 serving = 610 calories

Crossover Chilled Chicken Breast
(The Claremont)

2	double chicken breasts, skinned
1	tsp. garlic
1/3	c. spinach, washed, steamed and drained
1/3	c. basil, plucked
1	egg white
	pepper to taste
1	Tbsp. lemon juice

Trim tips and edges of breasts so that they are square and flatten them slightly; reserve trim. In food processor, chop garlic, spinach, basil and chicken trim until pureed. Add egg white, pepper and lemon juice. Lay chicken breast out on clear wrap, put spinach stuffing mixture in middle, roll up and seal well in wrap, tying off the ends. Steam for 10 minutes until just done, then cool. Unwrap just before serving.

Serves 2 (4 as appetizer)
1 serving = 245 calories

Barbecued Chicken
(La Costa)

4	2 1/2 oz. chicken breasts, deboned and skinned
	nonstick vegetable spray
1/3	c. onions
1	c. pineapple juice, unsweetened
1/4	c. pineapple, finely chopped
1/2	c. tomato puree, no salt added
1	tsp. barbecue spice
1/4	tsp. black pepper
1/2	tsp. granulated garlic
1/2	tsp. liquid smoke
1	bay leaf
	pinch dry mustard

Barbecued Chicken (Cont.)

1   tsp. vinegar
       pinch ground cloves
1/2   c. catsup, no salt or sugar added

Preheat oven to 400° F. Bake chicken breasts for 20-25 minutes or until tender. Preheat a large skillet to medium-high temperature and spray with vegetable spray. Saute onions until translucent and add pineapple juice. Combine remaining ingredients and add to skillet. Bring sauce to a boil, reduce heat and simmer for 1/2 hour. Remove bay leaf and serve 2 ounces sauce with chicken breast. Serve hot. Remaining sauce may be frozen for later use.

Serves 4
1 serving = 150 calories

Chicken Veronika
(The Hills)

1   chicken breast, halved, boned and skinned
1   Tbsp. cold pressed safflower oil
1/2   Tbsp. unsalted butter
1   red onion, chopped
1   apple, cubed
2/3   c. unsweetened apple juice
       dash of sea salt
       dash of ground nutmeg
2   Tbsp. fresh parsley, minced

Cut chicken breast crosswise into 1/2" strips. Place oil in a large skillet and when pan is warm, add the butter. Place chicken strips in the pan when butter has melted. Cook chicken over medium heat until opaque throughout. Remove from pan with slotted spoon so oil and juice remain in the pan. Add onion and apple cubes to the pan. Stir over medium heat. Add the apple juice and simmer for about 10 minutes or until onions are tender.

Chicken Veronika (Cont.)

Add salt and nutmeg and stir over low heat until the sauce has thickened slightly. Stir in parsley. Serve with steamed brown rice and sauteed bell pepper strips.

Serves 4
1 serving = 114 calories

Spa California Chicken with Chile Pepper Salsa
(Carmel Country Spa)

6   6 oz. split chicken breasts, bone-in
1   c. low-calorie BBQ sauce
2 1/2   oz. Chile Pepper Salsa (recipe follows)
6   large snow peas, steamed al dente*

Marinate chicken breasts in BBQ sauce overnight. Grill chicken until done. Top with Chile Pepper Salsa. Serve with snow peas.

Serves 6
1 serving = 285 calories

* see glossary

Chile Pepper Salsa
(Carmel Country Spa)

1/2   c. each red, green, yellow and orange bell peppers, roasted and peeled, seeded and cut into 1/2" cubes
1/2   c. celery, diced
1/2   c. onion, diced
1/4   c. tomatillos, diced
1/4   c. jalapeno peppers
2   Anaheim chiles, diced
4   serrano chiles, diced
1/4   bunch of cilantro
2   green onions, thinly sliced
1   c. tomato juice
         juice from 1 lime

374

Chili Pepper Salsa (Cont.)

1   Tbsp. chile powder
1/2   Tbsp. ground cumin
1 1/2   Tbsp. granulated garlic or 1 Tbsp. fresh garlic
1   tsp. cayenne pepper
6   drops Tabasco sauce

Combine all ingredients and refrigerate overnight.

FISH & SEAFOOD

Swordfish Almondine with Capers
(Tucson National Resort)

1/3	c. raw almonds, finely chopped
1 1/2	lbs. swordfish steak
	fresh lemon
1/4	c. dry white wine
4	tsp. capers

Toast the almonds and set aside. Wash the swordfish and dry thoroughly. Remove the skin and cut into 3 ounce servings. Squeeze fresh lemon juice all over the fish then pour the wine over the fish. Cover and allow to stand for 1 hour at room temperature. Place the fish in a baking dish and spoon 1/2 teaspoon of capers over each piece of fish. Cover and bake in a preheated 350° F oven for 8-10 minutes or until opaque and easily pierced with a fork. Do not overcook. To serve, sprinkle 2 teaspoons of the toasted almonds over the top of each piece of fish.

Serves 8
1 serving = 140 calories

Veracruz-Style Shrimp
(Tucson National Resort)

2	onions, thinly sliced
3	large tomatoes, peeled and diced
2	4 oz. jars sliced pimientos, undrained
2	canned green chiles, seeded and chopped
1	tsp. capers, finely chopped
2	Tbsp. parsley, finely chopped
1/2	tsp. salt
2	lbs. shrimp

Cook the onions, covered, over low heat until they are soft, stirring frequently to prevent scorching. Add the tomatoes, 1 jar of the pimientos plus the juice from the second jar, reserving the remaining pimientos for garnish.

Veracruz-Style Shrimp (Cont.)

Add all other ingredients except the shrimp and simmer, covered, for 10 minutes. Add the shrimp and cook until it is completely opaque and fork tender, about 5 minutes. Garnish with reserved pimientos.

Serves 8
1 serving = 140 calories

Seared Ahi Tuna with Shiitake Mushrooms and Sauce Naturelle
(Loews Ventana Canyon Resort)

6	6 oz. portions of ahi tuna
2	Tbsp. shallots, ground
2	Tbsp. garlic, ground
2	c. shiitake mushrooms, sliced
1	c. fish stock (recipe follows)
1	bunch parsley
1	Tbsp. fresh thyme

Sear ahi tuna in a very hot non stick saute pan 2 minutes on each side. No butter or oil is needed. Pull tuna out of the saute pan and proceed with sauce. Add shallots, garlic and mushrooms and deglaze* with fish stock. Allow to simmer 2 minutes then put fish stock in the pan and add parsley and thyme. Place fish on plate and pour the pan sauce over the fish. Garnish with fresh thyme.

Serves 6
1 serving = 197 calories

* see glossary

Fish Stock
(Loews Ventana Canyon Resort)

1	lb. fish bones and scraps
1	onion
1	bunch parsley stems
1	stick celery
1	Tbsp. white peppercorns
2	c. cold water

Simmer for 1 hour and strain.

Swordfish Steak with Thai Lemon Yogurt Dressing
(Sonoma Mission Inn)

1/2	tsp. mayonnaise
1	Tbsp. yogurt
1/4	tsp. ginger, peeled and finely chopped
1/4	tsp. garlic, finely chopped
1/8	tsp. cilantro, roughly chopped
1/2	tsp. scallions, thinly sliced
	white pepper
1	tsp. light soy sauce
4	oz. swordfish

Mix all ingredients except swordfish and reserve. Grill swordfish. Garnish with fresh vegetables and the dressing.

Serves 1
1 serving = 165 calories

379

Fillet of Salmon with Summer Fruit Salsa
(Sonoma Mission Inn)

2	oz. each cantaloupe, peach, nectarine and apricot, medium diced
1	tsp. red pepper, finely diced
1/4	tsp. jalapeno, finely diced
1/2	oz. lime juice
1	oz. rice wine vinegar
4	oz. salmon
	black pepper to taste

Gently toss fruit and condiments. Grill salmon (seasoned with pepper) to medium rare. Garnish with fresh vegetables and salsa.

Serves 1
1 serving = 300 calories

Mesquite Grilled Seafood Tossed with Sesame Linguine, Japanese Vegetables, Light Soy and Rice Wine Vinegar
(Sonoma Mission Inn)

1	tsp. snap peas
1	tsp. string beans
1	tsp. bean sprouts
2	oz. sesame linguine, cooked
	Light Soy and Rice Wine Vinegar Dressing (see recipe under Dressings)
6	bok choy leaves
1	oz. squid, cooked
1	oz. scallops, cooked
1	oz. prawns, cooked
1	oz. swordfish, cooked
	heart of celery leaves for garnish

Mesquite Grilled Seafood Tossed with Sesame Linguine, Japanese Vegetables, Light Soy and Rice Wine Vinegar (Cont.)

Toss vegetables and linguine with light soy and rice wine vinegar dressing. Place bok choy leaves around perimeter of plate and mound linguine in the center, then vegetables, then seafood. Garnish with heart of celery leaves.

Serves 1
1 serving = 185 calories

Albacore Tuna with Thin String Beans, Potatoes, Kalamata Olives and Capers
(Sonoma Mission Inn)

2	oz. string beans, cooked
2	oz. potatoes, cooked and sliced
4	Kalamata olives
1/2	tsp. capers
	lemon juice
	chopped parsley
	salad greens
3	oz. tuna
3	tomato wedges

Toss string beans, potatoes, olives and capers with lemon juice and chopped parsley. Place greens on plate and arrange mixed items over them. Put tuna in center of plate and garnish with tomato wedges.

Serves 1
1 serving = 200 calories

Garlic and Gingered Shrimp with Light Soy Wasabi Sauce
(Sonoma Mission Inn)

4	oz. shrimp
4	oz. steamed vegetables
1	tsp. light soy sauce
1/4	tsp. wasabi*
1/4	tsp. garlic, minced
1/4	tsp. ginger, minced
1	Tbsp. rice wine vinegar

Peel, devein and grill shrimp. Toss vegetables with light soy sauce, wasabi, garlic, ginger and rice wine vinegar. Arrange vegetables on plate and serve with shrimp.

Serves 1
1 serving = 135 calories

* see glossary

Grilled Swordfish Steak with Tomato and Red Pepper Vinaigrette
(Sonoma Mission Inn)

	pepper to taste
4	oz. swordfish
2	oz. Tomato and Roast Pepper Vinaigrette (recipe follows)
3	oz. steamed fresh vegetables

Pepper fish and grill to medium, taking care to mark fish nicely on grill. Place on plate so curved edge of fish is against curved edge of plate. Lay tomato and red pepper vinaigrette across middle of fish. Arrange vegetables on rest of the plate.

Serves 1
1 serving = 260 calories

Tomato and Red Pepper Vinaigrette
(Sonoma Mission Inn)

4	red peppers, roasted, peeled and seeded
4	yellow peppers, roasted, peeled and seeded
1	medium red onion, peeled and thinly sliced
27	oz. tomato concasse*, roughly chopped
1	Tbsp. garlic, finely chopped
1/2	Tbsp. shallots, finely chopped
1/2	Tbsp. cumin, finely ground
1/2	oz. oregano, finely chopped
1/2	Tbsp. chili powder
1/2	oz. basil, finely chopped
	salt and pepper to taste

Cut roasted peppers into thin strips. In medium pan, saute red onion until tender. Add tomatoes, garlic and shallots. Bring to simmer and add roasted peppers. Strain off extra juice and reduce this juice to tomato paste. Mix in herbs and spices.
* see glossary

Seared Salmon and Fennel with Gazpacho Vinaigrette
(Sonoma Mission Inn)

4	oz. salmon, pounded, seared and thinly sliced
	pepper to taste
2	oz. fennel
1/4	tsp. olive oil
	Gazpacho Vinaigrette (see recipe under Dressings)

Heat plate under broiler. Using paint brush, smear olive oil over half of plate. Place salmon fillet on plate and season with pepper. Put 2 tablespoons Gazpacho Vinaigrette on fish & garnish with fennel mixed with lemon juice, pepper and fennel sprig.

Serves 1
1 serving = 260 calories

Steamed Giant Artichoke Stuffed with Bay Shrimp and Lemon Juice
(Sonoma Mission Inn)

1	large artichoke
3	oz. bay shrimp
1	Tbsp. celery, finely diced
1	Tbsp. apple, finely diced
1	oz. lemon juice
1	tsp. cilantro
	salad leaves, tomato wedge and sprouts for garnish

Cut tips of artichoke off and boil in lemon scented water. Toss bay shrimp with celery, apple, lemon juice and cilantro. Place shrimp mixture in center of artichoke (after removing inside). Garnish plate with few leaves of salad, wedge of tomato and sprouts.

Serves 1
1 serving = 130 calories

Dungeness Crabmeat and Leaf Spinach with Light Soy and Rice Wine Vinegar Dressing
(Sonoma Mission Inn)

3	oz. leaf spinach
	Light Soy and Rice Wine Vinegar Dressing (see recipe under Dressings)
2	oz. Dungeness crab

Clean and wash spinach thoroughly. Spin dry and chill. Pour dressing over spinach and toss. Place crabmeat on top of spinach.

Serves 1
1 serving = 90 calories

Salmon Carpaccio, Roasted Peppers, American Cavairs
(Sonoma Mission Inn)

1	tsp. blended oil (40% peanut oil, 40% extra virgin olive oil and 20% olive oil)
3	oz. salmon fillet
1/2	tsp. salmon caviar
1/2	tsp. sturgeon caviar
1/2	tsp. trout caviar
1	oz. roasted peppers
	pepper to taste

Spread oil on half sheet of parchment paper. Place salmon to one side of the center of paper then fold opposite side over fish. Gently pound fish with mallet evenly, flattening it. Lift paper and turn over with thin side on plate. Place small amounts of caviars evenly around fish. Place mound of roasted peppers in center; season with pepper, splash with extra virgin olive oil.

Serves 1
1 serving = 160 calories

Sturgeon Oven Roasted in Corn Husks, Fine Diced Marinated Vegetables
(Sonoma Mission Inn)

4	oz. sturgeon
	corn husk
2	oz. fish stock
2	oz. water
1	tsp. red onion, fine dice
1	tsp. yellow squash, fine dice
1	tsp. green squash, fine dice
1	tsp. eggplant, fine dice
1	tsp. red pepper, fine dice

Sturgeon Oven Roasted in Corn Husks, Fine Diced Marinated Vegetables, Cont.)

1   tsp. chives, fine dice
1   oz. red wine vinegar
        white and black pepper to taste

Place seared fish in corn husk and tie with strands of cord. Place in pan with fish stock and water and bake until done at 325° F for 10-12 minutes. Marinate vegetables in red wine vinegar. Place marinated vegetables in ramekin and serve on the side.

Serves 1
1 serving = 200 calories

Grilled Salmon with Yogurt Dill Sauce and Pink Peppercorn
(Marriott's Desert Springs Resort and Spa)

4   oz. salmon fillet
        Yogurt Dill Sauce (recipe follows)
1/2   tsp. pink peppercorn
1/2   tsp. chives
        Mrs. Dash seasoning
1/8   tsp. lemon or lime zest*
1   red potato, steamed
2   oz. baby vegetables, steamed

Grill and mark salmon on grill. Place Yogurt Dill Sauce in saucepan. Bring to a simmer. Pour sauce over fish. Garnish with peppercorn, chives, Mrs. Dash and zest. Serve with potato and vegetables.

Serves 1
1 serving = 314 calories

* see glossary

Yogurt Dill Sauce
(Marriott's Desert Springs Resort and Spa)

1	oz. lowfat ricotta
1	oz. fish stock
1	Tbsp. fresh dill
1	oz. yogurt

Blend ricotta, fish stock and dill until smooth. Fold in yogurt.

Shrimp and Lobster with Mescal Mix
(Marriott's Desert Springs Resort and Spa)

3 1/2	oz. yellow pepper, diced
3 1/2	oz. red pepper, diced
1	tsp. cilantro, chopped
1/2	Tbsp. shallots, chopped
	juice of 1/2 lime
2	oz. white wine
20	threads saffron
3	shrimp
	olive oil
1	oz. Tequila Gold
1	lobster claw
3	assorted baby vegetables (carrots, acorn squash, turnips, etc.), cooked

For Mescal Mix: Mix first 7 ingredients together. Saute shrimp in oil, add half the tequila and flambe.* Add 3 ounces of Mescal Mix, cover and simmer for 2-3 minutes. Place shrimp in center of dish with lobster claw crown and garnish with baby vegetables.

Serves 1
1 serving = 190 calories

* see glossary

Spicy Shrimp with Basil, Ginger and Jalapeños
(Golden Door)

24	large shrimp, peeled and cleaned
1	jalapeño
1	shallot
1	2" cube of fresh ginger
1/2	c. basil leaves
3	cloves garlic
1/4	tsp. black pepper
1/4	c. rice wine vinegar
1	tsp. dark sesame oil
1	Tbsp. low sodium soy sauce

Clean shrimp; slice down back and remove vein. Pat dry. Place all other ingredients in a blender and mix to form a smooth paste. Place shrimp and marinade in a bowl. Mix well and let rest for 2 hours. Grill, broil or saute shrimp over high heat until just pink, about 2 minutes per side.

Serves 6
1 serving = 136 calories

Grilled Talapia with Kiwi Salsa
(Golden Door)

4	kiwi, peeled and cubed fine
3	chives, finely chopped or 1/4 tsp. dried
1	tsp. fresh ginger, minced
1/4	tsp. jalapeño, seeded, finely minced
2	Tbsp. rice wine vinegar
2	Tbsp. olive oil or vegetable spray
	salt and pepper to taste
6	talapia or other sole fillets

Grilled Talapia with Kiwi Salsa (Cont.)

Heat grill. Prepare salsa by mixing first 5 ingredients. Let sit at room temperature for 1/2 hour, minimum. Lightly oil and season fish. Grill for 2 minutes per side. Serve with salsa across center.

Serves 6
1 serving = 32 calories

Cioppino
(The Palms)

2	c. tomato juice
1/3	c. onion, chopped
1/3	c. celery, chopped
1/3	c. mushrooms, sliced
	pinch each of garlic powder, leaf rosemary, leaf oregano, leaf marjoram
5 1/2	oz. cod, boned and cut into 3/4" cubes
1/4	c. dry red wine
4	small shrimp, shelled, deveined and sliced in half lengthwise
2	tsp. Parmesan cheese, grated
6	lemon slices
6	parsley sprigs

Combine tomato juice, onion, celery, mushrooms, garlic, rosemary, oregano and marjoram in medium size saucepan. Cook at medium-low heat for 8 minutes. Add cod and simmer 2 minutes. Add wine. Add shrimp and cook 2 minutes or until shrimp are pink. Sprinkle soup with Parmesan cheese. Ladle into soup cups. Garnish each portion with lemon and parsley sprig.

Serves 4
1 serving = 70 calories

Shrimp and Asparagus
(Le Meridien)

15	medium shrimp
1	c. white wine
1	carrot, diced
1	onion
2	bunches asparagus
1	tsp. mustard
	juice from 2 lemons
1	c. olive oil
	salt and pepper to taste
1	bunch chives, chopped
2	tomatoes, peeled, seeded and diced

Poach shrimp in one quart of water with the white wine, carrot and onion. Clean and peel asparagus. Steam for 4 minutes then put in ice water so asparagus retains its color. Make dressing by mixing mustard and lemon juice, then adding olive oil. Salt and pepper to taste. Arrange asparagus and shrimp on plate. Decorate with chives and tomatoes. Serve dressing on the side.

Serves 5
1 serving = 95 calories

Sea Bass with Cucumbers
(Le Meridien)

3	cucumbers, peeled, seeded and sliced
2	Tbsp. cream
1	lb. tomatoes, peeled, seeded and diced
4	cloves garlic, finely chopped
2	Tbsp. parsley, chopped
3	Tbsp. olive oil
3	lb. sea bass fillet, cut into 10 portions

Sea Bass with Cucumbers (Cont.)

Cook the cucumbers with the cream al dente.* Mix together tomatoes, garlic, parsley and olive oil. Set aside. Put the sea bass on a lightly oiled sheet pan and cook in very hot oven. Keep pink. When sea bass is cooked, put on plate with the cucumbers and garnish with tomato mixture.

Serves 10
1 serving = 176 calories

* see glossary

Tuna Salad
(Spa Cafe*, Cliff Lodge at Snowbird)

1   lb. tuna, water packed and drained
6   stalks celery, chopped
1   red onion, chopped
2   dill pickles, diced
    dash of cayenne
    dash of celery salt
    pepper to taste
    juice from 1/2 lemon (or more to taste)

Mix all ingredients together. Serve over crisp lettuce leaves. Squeeze lemon over salad before serving.

Serves 4
1 serving = 622 calories

*For Members of the Club at Snowbird, a Private Club.

Grilled Ahi Tuna with Papaya Salsa
(The Claremont)

1   Tbsp. olive oil
1   Tbsp. saltless seasoning
1   Tbsp. lime juice
4   5 oz. Ahi tuna fillets, skinless
    Papaya Salsa (recipe follows)

Grilled Ahi Tuna with Papaya Salsa (Cont.)

Combine olive oil, saltless seasoning and lime juice. Brush on tuna fillets. Cook on outdoor grill or broiler. Top with Papaya Salsa.

Serves 4
1 serving = 287 calories

Papaya Salsa
(The Claremont)

1	ripe papaya, peeled, seeded and diced
3	medium garlic cloves, minced
1/2	red onion, peeled and diced
1	large tomato, seeded and coarsely chopped
1/2	c. cilantro leaves
3	Tbsp. lime juice
1	jalapeno pepper, seeded and diced
2	Tbsp. red bell pepper, diced
1	tsp. chili powder

Combine all ingredients in a non-reactive bowl. Toss and let stand for 1 hour. Can be made ahead of time and refrigerated for 24 hours.

Mahi-Mahi Picatta
(Maui Challenge)

4	8 oz. fresh mahi-mahi fillets
2-3	Tbsp. butter
	juice of 1 lemon
4	tsp. nonpareille capers
	capers, lemon zest and lemon wedges for garnish

In large skillet, saute fillets in butter for approximately 4 minutes. Before turning, add lemon juice and capers. Turn fillets and continue sauteing for 3-4 minutes. Serve topped with capers, lemon zest and lemon wedges.

Serves 4
1 serving = 360 calories

Salmon Painted Desert
(Vista Clara)

1 3/4   c. soy milk
3   cloves garlic
1/4   c. goat cheese
1/4   tsp. xantham gum*
2   3 oz. salmon fillets
1   Tbsp. Red Desert Pastel Paints (recipe follows)

Combine soy milk, garlic and goat cheese in saucepan and simmer until cheese has melted. Pour into blender and add gum. Mix until thickened. Note: If you let it simmer long enough (1 hour), you don't need gum. Pour back into saucepan, cover and keep warm. Place salmon in a hot steamer until firm but still pink on the inside, 4 to 6 minutes. Place salmon on a sauced plate. Make a design with the Red Desert Pastel Paints and serve.

Serves 2
1 serving = 252 calories

* available from Spice Trader

Red Desert Pastel Paints
(Vista Clara)

1   tsp. canola or other vegetable oil
2   large cloves garlic, finely chopped
1/2   c. mild red chile powder
3/4   c. water

Heat oil in a small skillet over moderate heat. Add the garlic and saute for about 2 to 3 minutes; do not let it brown. Place half of the red chile powder in skillet, stirring constantly. Add rest of the red chile, while still stirring. Immediately add the water and stir until well blended. Remove skillet from heat and pour mixture into a blender and puree. Pour through a fine sieve. Place in squeeze bottle and in the refrigerator until needed.

Yields 1 1/4 cups
1 Tbsp. = 14 calories

Sweet'n Sour Seafood Brochette
(La Costa)

	nonstick vegetable spray
1/4	c. onion, chopped
1	Tbsp. red pepper, diced
6	oz. pineapple juice, unsweetened
1/8	c. distilled vinegar
1	tsp. lemon juice
1	tsp. cornstarch, mixed with 1 Tbsp. water
4	c. water
3	oz. lobster
1/3	lb. large shrimp, shelled and deveined
3	oz. scallops
4	skewers
1/4	medium pineapple, cut into chunks
1/2	medium bell pepper, cut into 1" squares

In a small saucepan sprayed with vegetable spray, saute onions and red pepper until translucent. Add pineapple juice, vinegar and lemon juice and bring to a boil. Reduce heat and simmer 10 minutes. Add cornstarch mixture to sauce and stir until thickened. Set sauce aside. Bring 4 cups water to a boil. Cook lobster, shrimp and scallops in boiling water 3-5 minutes. Drain. Assemble each skewer using 2 scallops, 2 shrimp, 1 (3/4 oz.) piece of lobster, pineapple chunk and bell pepper square. Serve hot with 2 tablespoons of Sweet'n Sour Sauce.

Serves 4
1 serving = 150 calories

Shrimp Scampi
(Loews Ventana Canyon)

4	Tbsp. butter
4	cloves garlic, chopped
1 1/2	lbs. jumbo shrimp
	salt, pepper to taste
1/2	c. white wine
1	Tbsp. Worcestershire sauce
2	tsp. Dijon mustard
1	Tbsp. fresh parsley, chopped
1/2	lb. mushrooms, sliced
1	tomato, diced and seeded

Melt butter in saute pan. Brown garlic in melted butter. Before garlic turns golden brown, set aside. Saute shrimp for 2 minutes. Add salt and pepper, white wine. Add remaining ingredients. Finish off with a touch of butter.

Serves 4
1 serving = 200 calories

Spa Blackened Catfish
(Carmel Country Spa)

6	6 oz. catfish fillets

Seasoning Mix

3	Tbsp. chile powder
1	tsp. cayenne
1 1/2	Tbsp. granulated garlic
1	Tbsp. powdered butter substitute

Roll fillets in seasoning mix, coating both sides. Cook fillets in very hot iron skillet 4 minutes on each side. Be sure cooking area is well ventilated. Serve with fresh steamed vegetables.

Serves 6
1 serving = 165 calories

Spa Calamari
(Carmel Country Spa)

1	Tbsp. extra virgin olive oil
1	lb. Monterey Squid, cleaned, tenderized and butterflied
1	Tbsp. garlic puree
1/2	tsp. ground white pepper
1 1/2	tsp. white wine
30	asparagus tips, steam blanched al dente*

Heat oil in saute pan to 350°. Add all other ingredients except asparagus and saute until fillets have coiled into a roll, approximately 3-4 minutes. Stuff asparagus tips into calamari rolls and serve with puree of butternut squash and/or spaghetti squash and steamed carrots.

Serves 6
1 serving = 130 calories

* see glossary

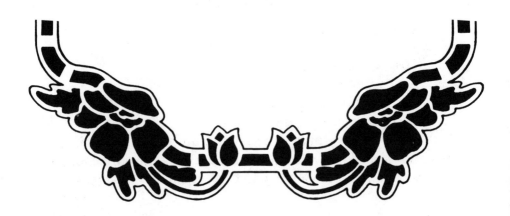

MEAT

Steak au Poivre
(Tucson National Resort)

8	3 oz. steaks (at least 1" thick)
	fresh coarsely ground or cracked black pepper
1	tsp. corn oil margarine
1/2	c. dry red wine
2	Tbsp. brandy

Sprinkle both sides of the steaks generously with the black pepper, pressing it into the surface of the steaks with your hands. Melt the margarine in a large, heavy skillet and then wipe the surface of the skillet with a paper towel to remove the excess. Heat the skillet to very hot before adding the steaks. Cook the steaks over high heat for about 3 minutes per side. Remove the steaks and add the wine and brandy to the skillet. Bring to a boil, stirring constantly. Spoon the wine mixture over the tops of the steaks before serving.

Serves 8
1 serving = 125 calories

French Lamb Chops
(Tucson National Resort)

8	small loin lamb chops, cut 1 1/2" thick and all fat removed
	garlic powder
	freshly ground black pepper
3	c. parsley, finely chopped
3	Tbsp. unprocessed wheat bran
3/4	c. Dijon mustard

Lightly sprinkle both sides of the lamb chops with garlic powder and freshly ground black pepper and place them in a baking dish. Combine the parsley, wheat bran and mustard and mix thoroughly. Spread the mustard mixture evenly over the tops of the lamb chops.

French Lamb Chops (Cont.)
Place in the center of a preheated 500° F oven for 4 minutes.
Turn the oven off but do not open the door for 30 more minutes.

Serves 8
1 serving = 110 calories

Grilled Venison Loin with Cabernet Sauvignon and Prickly Pear
(Loews Ventana Canyon Resort)

3	shallots, chopped
1	bunch fresh thyme
2	Tbsp. black peppercorns
6	juniper berries
4	oz. cabernet sauvignon
4	oz. prickly pear juice
6	oz. venison or beef stock
1	20-24 oz. venison loin
1	oz. butter
	salt and pepper to taste
	salad oil

Place the shallots, thyme, peppercorns, juniper berries, cabernet sauvignon and prickly pear juice in a saucepan and simmer over moderate heat until half of the liquid is gone. Add venison stock and continue to simmer for another 5 minutes. Adjust consistency of sauce with touches of cornstarch and water. Stir in butter, strain sauce and keep warm. Season the venison loin with salt and pepper. Rub with a touch of salad oil and place on broiler or outdoor barbecue. Grill evenly on all sides. Continue cooking for 15 to 20 minutes to achieve desired temperature. (If broiler heat is too high, the meat may be finished in a 350° F oven). Remove meat from oven or broiler and slice thinly. Ladle 1 1/2 ounces of warm sauce on each plate and shingle meat in ascending order according to size of slice.

Serves 4
1 serving = 250 calories

Skirt Steak with Mediterranean Herbs
(Sonoma Mission Inn)

1   oz. zucchini, long thin slices
1   oz. yellow squash, long thin slices
1   oz. green squash, long thin slices
1   oz. eggplant, sliced in rounds
1/8 tsp. Mediterranean herbs*
    pepper to taste
4   oz. skirt steak

Soak vegetables in water (so they do not stick to grill) and then season vegetables with Mediterranean herbs and grill. Season meat with Mediterranean herbs and pepper and also grill. Arrange vegetables on plate with thinly sliced meat. Serve with sourdough toast and tomato salsa.

Serves 1
1 serving = 285 calories

* see glossary

Poached Lamb with California Greens and Balsamic Vinaigrette
(Camelback Inn Resort, Golf Club & Spa)

2   bay leaves
1/2 tsp. thyme
1   tsp. carrots, chopped
1   tsp. onion, chopped
1   tsp. celery, chopped
6   oz. lamb loin
2   c. chicken stock
1   oz. balsamic vinegar
1/4 tsp. shallots, finely chopped
1/4 tsp. garlic, finely chopped
1/2 tsp. lemon juice
1 1/2 oz. safflower oil

Poached Lamb with California Greens and Balsamic Vinaigrette (Cont.)

assorted greens

Place first 5 ingredients in a baking pan. Add lamb. Add enough chicken stock to cover the lamb. Place in preheated 350° F oven for 15 minutes or until internal temperature is 120° F . Cool in poaching liquid. Slice lamb when cool. For vinaigrette, place vinegar, shallots, garlic and lemon juice in a mixing bowl, gently whisking in oil. Pour vinaigrette over greens. Serve with lamb on top.

Serves 1
1 serving = 196 calories

Medallion of Veal with Wild Mushroom Sauce

(Marriott's Desert Springs Resort and Spa)

5	oz. veal loin, pounded thin
1	pinch Mrs. Dash seasoning
2	oz. Madiera sauce
1	oz. wild mushrooms (2 morels and 4 or 5 shiitake slices)
1/2	Tbsp. chives, snipped
1	oz. wild rice, cooked
2	oz. baby vegetables, cooked

Season veal and saute in nonstick pan. Deglaze* pan juice with Madiera sauce. Add mushrooms. Reduce* for about 2 minutes. Arrange veal on platter, top with sauce. Garnish with chives. Serve with rice and baby vegetables.

Serves 1
1 serving = 191 calories

* see glossary

Tournedos of Beef Marco Polo
(La Costa)

4	c. red wine
1/2	c. soy sauce
1	Tbsp. fresh ginger
1	Tbsp. garlic, minced
2	tsp. cornstarch
8	1 1/4 oz. tournedos of beef, cut from tenderloin
4	oz. demi-glace*

Combine red wine with soy sauce, ginger, garlic and cornstarch. Add beef and marinate overnight. Remove tournedos from marinade and grill to desired specificiation. In a saucepan, add remaining marinade and demi-glace. Reduce* by 1/2. Strain sauce. Serve 2 tournedos with 1 tablespoon of sauce.

Serves 4
1 serving = 150 calories

* *see glossary*

VEGETABLES

Grilled Summer Vegetables, Basil and Balsamic Vinaigrette
(Sonoma Mission Inn)

1	oz. eggplant
1	oz. red onion
1	oz. zucchini
1	oz. yellow squash
1/2	oz. red pepper
1/2	oz. yellow pepper
	tri-colored pepper to taste
	Balsamic Vinaigrette (recipe follows)
1	c. salad greens
	Italian parsley sprig for garnish

Slice vegetables into long strips, except peppers, and grill. Roast peppers whole and peel. Season with tri-colored pepper. Cut vegetables into large dice. Place vegetables in bowl and toss with Balsamic Vinaigrette. Put salad greens on plate then mound on the marinated vegetables. Garnish with Italian parsley sprig.

Serves 1
1 serving = 60 calories

Balsamic Vinaigrette
(Sonoma Mission Inn)

1/2	oz. balsamic vinegar*
1	oz. water
1	tsp. red onion, fine dice
	pepper to taste
1/4	tsp. honey
1/2	tsp. olive oil

Mix together all ingredients.
* *see glossary*

Mushroom Meadow
(Meadowlark)

4	medium sized potatoes, baked
	dollop Mushroom Sauce (see recipe under Sauces)
1	c. Guacamole (see recipe under Sauces)
1	c. alfalfa sprouts for garnish

While potatoes are baking, prepare Mushroom Sauce. Keep this simmering on stove. Prepare Guacamole. Slice each baked potato in half, placing them on serving plate. On each potato half, spread some of the Guacamole, followed by a spoonful of the Mushroom Sauce. Garnish the sides of the plate with plenty of alfalfa sprouts.

Serves 4
1 serving = 274 calories

Fresh Green Bean Casserole
(Meadowlark)

3	c. fresh green beans, sliced and steamed
	vegetable oil
1	tsp. butter
1	Tbsp. tapioca flour
1	c. milk
1/2	tsp. salt
1	c. fresh mushrooms, sliced
1/2	tsp. oregano
1	tsp. tamari*
	garlic powder
1/2	tsp. apple cider vinegar
2	eggs plus 1 egg, beaten
1	onion, thinly sliced into rings
1/4	c. wheat germ
1/4	c. sesame seed meal (ground up sesame seeds)
1/4	c. Parmesan cheese, grated

Fresh Green Bean Casserole (Cont.)

Place green beans in oiled casserole. Melt butter in saucepan and stir in tapioca flour. Slowly add the milk, stirring constantly. Add salt, mushrooms, oregano, tamari, garlic and vinegar. Stir mixture well until sauce becomes medium thick. Pour 2 of the eggs over the beans, then add sauce. Soak onion rings in remaining egg for 1 minute. Roll onion rings in wheat germ and sesame seed meal. Place rings on top of casserole. Sprinkle with cheese and bake in preheated 375° F oven for 45 minutes.

Serves 6
1 serving = 175 calories

* see glossary

Vegetable Curry
(The Plantation Spa)

2	Tbsp. salad oil
1	large onion, chopped
1	tsp. herbal salt
2	tsp. curry powder
1/4	tsp. ground ginger
1/4	tsp. cumin
2	bay leaves
2	medium carrots, cut into 2" slices
1/2	lb. green beans, cut to 2" length
1	red or green bell pepper, cut into 1" pieces
1/2	small cauliflower, separated into florets
1/2	lb. broccoli florets
1/2	lb. banana squash, cut into 1" pieces
3/4	c. water

Pour oil into a 5 quart pan and place over medium heat. Add onion and cook until soft, stirring occasionally. Stir in salt, curry powder, ginger and cumin. Cook for 1 minute. Add remaining ingredients. Cover and bring to a boil; reduce heat and simmer until vegetables are just tender.

Vegetable Curry (Cont.)

Remove cover, increase heat and cook for a few minutes to reduce pan juices by one half. Remove bay leaves before serving. Serve with brown rice.

Serves 6
1 serving = 127 calories

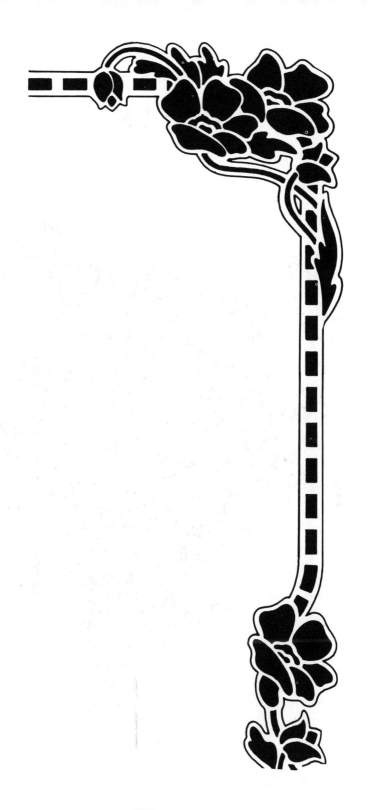

DESSERTS

Lemon Chiffon Shells with Cherry Sauce
(Sonoma Mission Inn)

1 1/2   Tbsp. unflavored gelatin
1/4   c. lemon juice
3   eggs
1/2   c. sugar
1 1/2   tsp. lemon zest*
1 1/2   c. plain lowfat yogurt
         Cherry Sauce (recipe follows)

Dissolve gelatin in lemon juice. Heat slightly to completely dissolve. Whip eggs and sugar on high speed until light and thick. Beat in gelatin and zest. Fold in yogurt. Put in "madeleine" cookie molds and freeze to set. Serve with Cherry Sauce.

To Serve: Run bottom of mold under hot tap water until shells will slide off easily (about 20 seconds). Place 3 shells on plate in star formation. Spoon cherries and sauce into center of shells and allow to flow between them. Shells should not be frozen by serving time.

Serves 12
1 serving = 85 calories

* see glossary

Cherry Sauce
(Sonoma Mission Inn)

1 1/3   c. sour cherry juice from 1 jar of cherries
2   Tbsp. cornstarch
         sour cherries

Strain juice from 1 jar of sour cherries into small pot. Add 2 Tbsp. cornstarch. Heat until it boils and thickens. Remove from heat, cool and add cherries. (Can be sweetened slightly with sugar if desired).

Spa Coffee No Cream Ice Cream
(Sonoma Mission Inn)

3   eggs
6   egg whites
3/4   c. sugar
5   c. nonfat milk
2   c. nonfat evaporated milk
3/4   c. strong decaffeinated coffee
1   c. corn syrup
1   Tbsp. vanilla
1/4   tsp. salt (optional)

   Mix eggs and sugar together in a lare bowl, whisk until combined. Heat milk and evaporated milk in a large sauce pan. Bring milk to a boil, add coffee and mix until dissolved. Add some of the hot milk to the egg and sugar mixture, mix well, then add back to the remaining milk in saucepan. Stir hot milk and egg mixture until thick enough to coat the back of a spoon. Remove mixture from heat and add corn syrup, vanilla and salt. Mix well. Place in an ice bath* until well chilled. Ice cream is then ready to be run through ice cream machine.

Yields 1 gallon
4 oz. serving = 80 calories

* see glossary

Fresh Cut Fruit with Yogurt and Lemon Sauce
(Sonoma Mission Inn)

2   oz. melon
2   oz. grapefruit
2   strawberries
1   oz. kiwi
1   oz. grapes
1/2   tsp. honey

Fresh Cut Fruit with Yogurt and Lemon Sauce (Cont.)

1   tsp. lemon juice
2   oz. natural yogurt
        mint sprig for garnish

Clean and cut all fruit. Mix honey, lemon juice and yogurt. Arrange cut fruit on plate and garnish with mint sprig. Place sauce either in ramekin or over fruit.

Serves 1
1 serving = 125 calories

Butternut Squash Flan
(Cal-a-Vie)

1   butternut squash, about 3 lbs., (2 1/2 - 3 cups), baked
1   tsp. cinnamon
1/2   tsp. ground cloves
1/4   tsp. grated nutmeg
1   tsp. vanilla extract
4   Tbsp. honey
2 1/2   c. lowfat milk, scalded
2   eggs
2   egg whites

Bake squash in a baking pan at 350° F for 1 1/2 hours, turning once. Test for doneness with the tip of a knife. Cut squash in half and scoop out seeds. Peel off skin and puree the pulp in a food processor along with the spices, vanilla and honey. Transfer to mixing bowl. Scald milk. Beat the eggs in a separate bowl. Whip the milk in with the eggs and strain into the pureed squash mixture. Mix well. Pour into 12-15 individual custard baking cups. Place cups on a baking sheet pan and fill pan with 1/4" water. Bake in 350° F oven for 45 minutes or until knife inserted in center comes out clean.

Serves 12-15
1/2 cup serving = 78 calories

413

Banana Orange Parfait
(Cal-a-Vie)

3   c. ice cubes
1/2 c. nonfat powdered milk
6   oz. frozen orange juice concentrate
1   ripe banana
1   Tbsp. orange liqueur
     fruit for parfait glasses: Kiwi, strawberries, peaches and
        other seasonal fruits, sliced

In a food processor combine ice cubes, nonfat powdered milk, orange juice concentrate, banana and orange liqueur. Mix well for about 5 minutes until mixture is smooth and whips up. Fill 12 chilled parfait glasses or large stem glasses with the sliced fruit and the orange-banana mixture. Top with fresh berries. Store in freezer for about 30 minutes or serve immediately.

Serves 12
1 serving = 80 calories

Peach Orange Sorbet
(Cal-a-Vie)

4   ripe, medium size peaches
1 1/2 c. fresh orange juice
1   Tbsp. honey (or 2 pkgs. fructose)
1   Tbsp. orange liqueur
       seasonal fruit for garnish

Drop the peaches in boiling water for 2-3 minutes. Peel peaches under cold running water and cut into wedges, discarding the stone. In blender puree peaches with orange juice, honey and orange liqueur. Transfer to an ice cream maker (sorbetiere) and make sorbet according to manufacturer's directions. Sorbet keeps in freezer for up to 4 hours or serve immediately with garnish such as peach wedge, raspberries or other seasonal fruit.

Serves 8
1 serving = 48 calories

Tofu Cheesecake
(Cal-a-Vie)

For the Crust:

1	pkg. honey graham crackers
2	Tbsp. unsalted butter
1	Tbsp. brown sugar
1	tsp. cinnamon
1	egg white

In a food processor combine the graham crackers, butter, brown sugar, cinnamon and egg white. Process until crumbs form and the mixture holds together when pressed with your fingers. Lightly spray with PAM a 9" pie pan or dish and press the crumbs evenly into the bottom of the pan.

For the Filling:

2	eggs (using 1 yolk and 2 egg whites)
8	oz. very fresh tofu
1/3	c. honey
4	oz. Neufchatel or low-calorie cream cheese
1	Tbsp. lemon juice
1	tsp. vanilla
1	c. fresh berries (strawberries, raspberries or blueberries)

Mix in a blender or food processor until smooth the egg yolk, egg whites, tofu, honey, cream cheese, lemon juice and vanilla. Add the fresh fruit and process until just mixed. Turn into the prepared crust and bake at 350° F for 1 hour. Chill until ready to serve.

Serves 12
1 serving = 135 calories

415

Yogurt Parfait
(Tucson National Resort)

1   qt. nonfat yogurt
1   c. carob sauce
     Place 1/2 cup nonfat yogurt in each of 8 parfait glasses and top with 2 tablespoons of carob sauce.

Serves 8
1 serving = 70 calories

Fruit Torte
(Tucson National Resort)

8   oz. can fruit cocktail, water packed
     water
1   1 oz. envelope diet lemon flavored gelatin
1   c. iced water
6   dietetic lady fingers, split
1   c. prepared whipped topping
     Drain liquid from fruit cocktail into measuring cup and add enough water to equal 1 cup. Set fruit aside. Over heat dissolve gelatin powder into mixture, stirring constantly. Bring to boil. Remove from heat and stir in iced water. Chill until well set. Place well set gelatin in mixing bowl. Beat on high speed until double in volume. Slowly beat in prepared whipped topping and fruit. Line a standard loaf pan with split lady fingers. Spoon mixture over lady fingers. Chill well. Slice into 12 servings.

Serves 12
1 serving = 40 calories

416

Cherry-Berry Sorbet
(Tucson National Resort)

20   frozen dark sweet cherries (unsweetened), still frozen
2   Tbsp. water
1/4   tsp. strawberry extract
   In a blender or food processor combine all ingredients. Process just until smooth. Serve immediately.

Serves 1
1 serving = 50 calories

Banana Sorbet
(Tucson National Resort)

3   firm bananas
2   Tbsp. Calvados (apple brandy)
        fresh mint sprigs for garnish (optional)
   Slice the bananas and place in a plastic bag in the freezer. When the bananas are solidly frozen, place them in a food processor with a metal blade. Add the Calvados and blend until smooth. Scrape the banana mixture into a bowl. Cover tightly and freeze for several hours before serving. Using an ice cream scoop, divide the sorbet into 12 sherbet glasses and garnish with fresh mint.

Serves 12
1/4 cup serving = 40 calories

Tropical Treat
(Tucson National Resort)

1   c. yogurt
2   small bananas, sliced
2   c. crushed pineapple, packed in natural juice, drained
   Combine the yogurt sauce and bananas in a blender and blend until smooth. Pour over the drained crushed pineapple and mix well.

Serves 8
1/2 cup serving = 55 calories

Strawberry Dream
(Tucson National Resort)

1/2   tsp. low calorie strawberry flavored gelatin powder
1/2   c. boiling water
1/4   c. pureed strawberries
1   c. prepared whipped topping

Dissolve gelatin in boiling water. Stir in strawberries. Chill until set. Beat with an electric mixer or egg beater until mixture has doubled in volume. Fold in topping. Spoon into serving dishes and chill for at least 1 hour.

Serves 4
1 serving = 40 calories

Chocolate-Orange Mousse
(Tucson National Resort)

2   egg whites
1/2   tsp. cream of tartar
2   c. prepared whipped topping
2   Tbsp. diet chocolate pudding powder
1/2   c. canned mandarin orange sections, chopped

Whip egg whites with cream of tartar. Set aside. Prepare whipped topping and add pudding and orange sections. Mix well. Fold in beaten egg whites. Chill at least 1 hour prior to serving.

Serves 6
1 serving = 40 calories

Fantastic Fruit Sherbet
(Tucson National Resort)

2   Tbsp. water
1   Tbsp. unflavored gelatin
1   c. buttermilk
2   Tbsp. honey

Fantastic Fruit Sherbet (Cont.)

1 1/2 c. fresh fruit (berries, cantaloupe, peaches, pineapple, bananas)

1 Tbsp. lemon juice

 shredded unsweetened coconut for garnish

Put the water into a small saucepan. Sprinkle gelatin into the water. When gelatin has soaked in, stir over low heat until thoroughly dissolved. Combine buttermilk and honey in a blender or food processor. Add the gelatin and process until thoroughly blended. Add the fruit and lemon juice to the buttermilk mixture and blend until smooth. Pour into freezer trays and freeze. Remove, let thaw slightly and whip in a blender or food processor. Pour back into freezer tray and refreeze. Remove 15 minutes before serving. Let thaw slightly. Whip in a food processor and pour into sherbet glasses. Garnish with shredded coconut.

Serves 10
1 serving = 40 calories

Peaches 'N Creme Mold
(Tucson National Resort)

6 fresh peaches, medium size, peeled and pits removed (12 halves of canned, unsweetened peaches may be substituted)

 sweetener equivalent to 15 tsp. sugar

2 c. water

2 envelopes unflavored gelatin

1 1/2 c. plain lowfat yogurt

1 tsp. vanilla butternut flavor

1/4 tsp. orange or lemon extract

Slice 2 of the peaches in very thin slices. Sprinkle with sweetener equivalent to 3 teaspoons sugar. Set aside. (Note: If peaches are very firm and not too ripe, you may want to cook them in about 1 tablespoon of water for a few minutes, until tender.) Place 1 cup of the water in a small saucepan.

Peaches 'N Creme Mold (Cont.)

Sprinkle gelatin over water and let it soften a few minutes. Heat on low, stirring frequently, until gelatin is completely dissolved. Remove from heat. In a blender container combine yogurt and remainder of unsliced peaches. Blend until smooth. Add gelatin mixture, remaining 1 cup water, remaining sweetener and extracts. Blend until smooth. Stir in sliced peaches. Pour into a 9-cup mold and chill several hours, until firm. Unmold to serve.

Serves 18
1/2 cup serving = 54 calories

Fruit "Amaretto"
(Tucson National Resort)

1	c. nonfat milk
1	egg, lightly beaten
2	Tbsp. fructose
2	tsp. vanilla extract
1/2	tsp. almond extract
4	c. fresh fruit, peeled and sliced (when peaches are available, they are the favorite with this sauce)

Bring milk to a boil in the top of a double boiler. Slowly pour the hot milk into the beaten egg, stirring with a wire whisk. Return the mixture to the double boiler and continue cooking until the custard coats a metal spoon. Remove from heat and cool slightly. Add all other ingredients except the fruit and mix thoroughly. Spoon 2 tablespoons of the sauce over each 1/2 cup of the sliced fruit.

Serves 8
1/2 cup serving = 70 calories

Custard
(Tucson National Resort)

3	eggs plus 2 egg whites, lightly beaten
4	c. nonfat milk
1/3	c. fructose
2	tsp. ground cinnamon
1	Tbsp. vanilla extract

Combine all ingredients in a large bowl and mix well, using a wire whisk. Pour the mixture into a casserole or baking dish and set in a baking pan or another baking dish with warm water to a depth of 2" and bake in a preheated 250° F oven for 2 hours or until the custard is firm in the middle. Cool and refrigerate until cold before serving.

Serves 8
1/2 cup serving = 90 calories

Peach Cobbler
(Rocky Mountain Wellness Spa)

2	fresh peaches
2	c. orange juice
1	tsp. lime juice
2	oz. mango pulp, pureed in blender with orange juice
1/4	tsp. apple pie cinnamon spice
1-2	Tbsp. arrowroot
	Oat Bran Muffins (see recipe under Breads)
	Granola (see recipe under Breakfast)

Blanch* peaches. Peel and dice. Boil orange juice, lime juice, mango and spice. Thicken with arrowroot. Pour on top of crust made from Oat Bran Muffins and raisins. Top with Granola.

Serves 2
1 serving = 103 calories

With permission from Sheri Stephens
* see glossary

421

Chilled Mocha Souffle
(Sonoma Mission Inn)

2	Tbsp. cocoa
2	Tbsp. instant coffee
1/2	c. boiling water
3/4	c. cold water
1	pkg. unflavored gelatin
3	Tbsp. Kahlua
1 1/3	c. instant nonfat dry milk powder
1/2	c. sugar
1/3	c. vegetable oil
1	tsp. vanilla
2	tsp. lemon juice

Combine the cocoa and instant coffee. Mix into 1/2 cup boiling water until dissolved. Add 1/2 cup of the cold water and place container in refrigerator to chill. In a small saucepan or skillet, sprinkle gelatin over the remaining 1/4 cup cold water. Heat gently over low heat until dissolved. Add Kahlua and stir into the cold mocha mixture. In the bowl of an electric mixer, combine the coffee mixture with the powdered milk. Blend until smooth and place in freezer 10 minutes to chill. Beat at high speed until mixture holds peaks, about 5-10 minutes. Gradually add sugar, beating after each addition, then the oil, vanilla and lemon juice. Continue beating until mixture is smooth. Prepare 6 half-cup souffle molds. Make a 1 1/2 inch collar of aluminum foil and tie it with string onto the outside of the souffle dish. Fill molds with the mocha mixture. Refrigerate at least 2 hours or until well set. Remove collars and dust lightly with powdered sugar.

Serves 6
1 serving = 250 calories

Pumpkin Cheesecake
(Canyon Ranch)

2	tsp. corn oil margarine
8	graham cracker squares, crushed
2 1/2	lbs. part-skim ricotta cheese
1	c. granulated sugar
1	egg white
1	tsp. corn oil
1	tsp. nonfat dry milk
3	Tbsp. all-purpose flour
2	tsp. ground cinnamon
1/2	tsp. ground cloves
1	tsp. ground ginger
3/4	c. canned evaporated skim milk
1	Tbsp. vanilla extract
1	1 lb. can mashed pumpkin

Preheat oven to 400° F. Spread margarine evenly over bottom and sides of a 9" spring form pan. Pour graham cracker crumbs into pan, then rotate pan to evenly coat entire inside of pan with crumbs (more crumbs will end up on bottom of pan). Set aside. Combine remaining ingredients in food processor and blend until satin smooth. Pour mixture into prepared crust and bake for 15 minutes. Reduce oven temperature to 275° F and bake an additional 1 1/4 hours. Turn off heat but leave cake in oven for several hours to cool. Remove from oven, cover and refrigerate.

Serves 20
1 serving = 144 calories

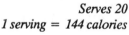

Piña Colada Sorbet
(The Palms)

1 1/2   c. fresh pineapple, cubed
1/2   c. banana, sliced
1/2   c. unsweetened pineapple juice
2   c. ice cubes, coarsely crushed
8   Tbsp. unsweetened coconut (optional)

Arrange pineapple and banana on tray lined with wax paper. Freeze until completely frozen, about 1 1/2-2 hours. Combine pineapple juice, pineapple, banana and crushed ice in blender. Blend until consistency of soft sherbet. Mound into 8 dessert cups. Garnish each with 1 tablespoon coconut, if desired. Note: Add 26 calories per serving if coconut is used.

Serves 8
1 serving = 32 calories

Apple Slices with Creamy Orange Peanut Butter
(The Palms)

1/2   c. plus 2 Tbsp. lowfat cottage cheese
1   Tbsp. orange juice concentrate
1   Tbsp. peanut butter
6   medium apples

Combine cottage cheese, orange juice concentrate and peanut butter in food processor and blend until smooth. Quarter apples and take the core out. Slice thin and frost with 1 tablespoon creamy orange peanut butter mixture.

Serves 12
1 serving = 50 calories

Spa Oatmeal Raisin Cookies
(Camelback Inn Resort, Golf Club & Spa)

2	lb. margarine
14	packets soluable fiber sweetener (available in health food stores)
6	c. apple juice, reduced* to a thick syrup of 1 1/2 c.
1	pt. Egg Beaters or cholesterol free egg product
1	Tbsp. vanilla
22	oz. unbleached bread flour
4	tsp. baking soda
2	tsp. baking powder
8	c. "Quick" oatmeal
3	c. raisins

Cream margarine and sweetener. Gradually add the apple juice and scrape bowl well. Incorporate the Egg Beaters and vanilla and continue to beat well. Combine dry ingredients and add to creamed mixture. Blend well, add oatmeal and raisins. Using a large ice cream scoop, place cookies on a prepared baking sheet (either greased with margarine or lined with parchment paper). These are very large cookies, approximately 4 1/2" in diameter, so be sure to leave plenty of space for them to spread out. Bake at 350° F approximately 20 minutes.

Makes 25-30 large cookies
1 cookie = 200 calories

* *see glossary*

425

Spa Chocolate Chip Cookies
(Camelback Inn Resort, Golf Club & Spa)

1	lb. margarine
7	packets soluable fiber sweetner (available in health food stores)
3	c. apple juice, reduced* to a syrup of 3/4 c.
1 1/4	c. Egg Beaters or cholesterol free egg product
2	tsp. vanilla
31	oz. bread flour
4	tsp. baking soda
4	c. chocolate chips
2	c. chopped nuts

Cream margarine and the sweetener. Gradually add apple juice and scrape bowl well. Incorporate the Egg Beaters and vanilla and beat well. Add dry ingredients and blend well, scrape bowl, add chocolate chips and nuts. Using a large ice cream scoop, place cookies on prepared baking sheet (either greased with margarine or lined with parchment paper). Allow plenty of space for these cookies average about 4 1/2" in diameter. Bake at 350° F for approximately 20 minutes.

Makes 25-30 large cookies
1 cookie = 275 calories

* see glossary

Bread Pudding
(National Institute of Fitness)

6	slices day old bread, cubed
1	Tbsp. cornstarch
1/2	tsp. cinnamon
5	egg whites
2 1/2	c. milk, scalded
2	tsp. butter extract*
1	tsp. vanilla
3	tsp. barley malt sweetener and 12 packets Equal

Bread Pudding (Cont.)

Toss bread with cornstarch and cinnamon. Beat together egg whites, milk, butter extract, vanilla and sweetener. Layer this in a baking dish sprayed with PAM and bake at 350° F for 30 minutes. Top with more cinnamon and serve warm with cream or cold.

Serves 6
1 serving = 333 calories

* see glossary

Strawberry Yogurt Lime Parfait
(National Institute of Fitness)

2	c. nonfat plain yogurt
4	Tbsp. lime juice or amaretto
	strawberries (sweetened with Equal)
1	whole lime for garnish, thinly sliced

Mix yogurt with lime juice or amaretto. Layer yogurt and strawberries in parfait glasses. Garnish with lime slices.

Serves 4
1 serving = 88 calories

Blackberry Bavarian
(National Institute of Fitness)

2	Tbsp. gelatin
1/2	c. water
2	c. berry juice
1/2	c. extra strength powdered milk
1/2	c. lowfat cottage cheese
1	tsp. lime juice
15	packets Equal
1	c. frozen blackberries
	mint sprig for garnish

Blackberry Bavarian (Cont.)

Dissolve gelatin in water. Add to juice and let chill slightly. Combine milk, cottage cheese, lime juice, Equal and blend until creamy. Add berries to chilled juice and fold into cream mixture. Chill and serve with mint garnish.

Serves 6
1 serving = 217 calories

Lemon Boysenberry Upside Down Cake
(Golden Door)

2	c. fresh or frozen boysenberries, thawed
1	tsp. honey
1	Tbsp. fresh lemon zest*
	vegetable spray
2	eggs
2 1/4	oz. granulated fructose or sugar
1/4	tsp. ground cardamom
1	pinch ground nutmeg
1/4	tsp. vanilla
2	oz. sifted all-purpose flour

Puree and sieve 1 cup boysenberries. Combine puree with remaining berries, honey and lemon zest. Spoon berry mixture into 12 small ramekins or souffle dishes that have been lightly sprayed with a nonstick vegetable spray. Whisk eggs, fructose and spices together in a metal mixing bowl over a pan of simmering water until mixture reaches 120° F (hot to the touch). Beat hot mixture until tripled in volume and the bottom of the bowl is cool. Whisk in vanilla and gently fold in flour. Spoon a heaping tablespoon of batter on top of berries. Bake cobblers at 350° F until genoise* is puffy, firm and golden and berry mixture is bubbly.

Yields 12 small or 6 large cakes
1 small cake = 54 calories

* see glossary

Lemon Frost
(Bermuda Resort)

2	egg whites, room temperature
1/2	c. water
1/2	c. nonfat dry milk
2	egg yolks
1/4	c. fructose
1/4	tsp. lemon peel, grated
1/8	tsp. salt
1/4	c. lemon juice
	mint sprigs and very thin lemon slices for garnish

In a small bowl, beat egg whites, water and nonfat dry milk with electric mixer until soft peaks form, about 5 minutes. Scrape bowl frequently to make sure all dry milk dissolves. In separate bowl, beat remaining ingredients until fructose is completely dissolved, about 2 minutes. Gradually fold mixture into the whipped egg whites. Gently spoon into individual dessert dishes and freeze until solid, at least 2 hours. Garnish with mint sprigs and lemon slices before serving.

Serves 6
1 serving = 79 calories

Iced Bittersweet Chocolate Souffle
(Le Meridien)

5	eggs
1	c. sugar
8	oz. cream cheese
1	c. cocoa powder
1	tsp. instant coffee
1	c. meringue (4 whipped egg whites + 1/2 c. sugar)

Whip eggs and sugar until it forms a light mousse. Mix together gently the cream cheese, cocoa and instant coffee. Mix egg mixture and cream cheese mixture together carefully, then add meringue. Put in souffle mold and freeze for 3 hours.

Serves 10
1 serving = 275 calories

Alsation Mirabelle Tart
(Le Meridien)

1	c. flour
1/2	c. butter
1/2	egg yolk
1/2	c. sugar
1	lb. Mirabelles (yellow plums)
3/4	qt. lowfat milk
1	c. almond powder
2	eggs
1	Tbsp. cornstarch
7	oz. cream cheese
2	drops vanilla extract

Mix together flour, butter, egg yolk and sugar for dough. Lay out dough into tart mold. Arrange Mirabelles on dough. Boil milk. Mix together almond powder, eggs, cornstarch, cream cheese and vanilla, then add boiling milk.

Alsation Mirabelle Tart (Cont.)

Cover Mirabelles with custard mixture and cook in 350° F oven for 10-20 minutes.

Serves 10
1 serving = 185 calories

Upside Down Custard with Coffee Sauce
(Le Meridien)

3/4   qt. lowfat milk
3   whole eggs
4   egg whites
1   c. sugar
2   drops vanilla extract
      Coffee Sauce (recipe follows)

Boil milk. Mix other ingredients and pour boiling milk over. Strain through fine mesh. Put in mold and cook in bain-marie.* Pour Coffee Sauce over custard.

Serves 10
1 serving = 210 calories

* see glossary

Coffee Sauce
(Le Meridien)

1/2   qt. lowfat milk
3   Tbsp. fresh ground coffee
4   egg yolks
1   c. sugar

Boil milk with coffee. Strain through paper filter. Mix eggs and sugar and whip until it forms a ribbon. Pour milk over it and stir until it looks like an English cream.

Fruit Charlotte with Tapioca and Pumpkin Sauce
(Le Meridien)

3	c. nonfat milk
2	oz. tapioca
1	c. honey
6	eggs, lightly beaten
1	1 oz. package gelatin, prepared
1/2	c. heavy cream
1	lb. fresh fruit, diced small (apple, mango, pear, pineapple, etc.)
2	oz. raisins, marinated in tea
	zest* of 1 lime
	Pumpkin Sauce (recipe follows)
	mint leaves and strawberries for garnish

Bring milk to a boil. Add tapioca and honey, stir until tapioca is cooked. Add eggs, prepared gelatin, cream and fruit. Pour into a mold and cook in a double boiler in the oven for 10 minutes. Cut Charlotte into individual servings. Pour a small amount of Pumpkin Sauce on a dessert plate and place a slice on each. Decorate with mint leaf and strawberry.

Serves 10
1 serving = 145 calories

* see glossary

432

Pumpkin Sauce
(Le Meridien)

2   c. orange juice
1/2   c. pumpkin puree or canned pumpkin
1/2   c. sugar
      Mix all ingredients together thoroughly.

Warm Apple Tart "Feuillete"
(Le Meridien)

1   c. water
8   oz. flour
1   oz. sugar
     pinch of salt
7   oz. margarine
4   golden apples
1   egg yolk
1   Tbsp. water
1   Tbsp. honey

     Mix water, flour, sugar and salt to form basic dough for Feuillete. On work table, sprinkle flour and roll out dough. Spread margarine on the dough. Fold dough into 3 layers and roll out 3 times. On the third time, roll out to 1/4" thick and cut into 5 circles. Place circles on a sheet pan. Peel apples and cut into very thin slices. Arrange apple slices on dough to look like a flower. Mix egg yolk, water and honey. Brush mixture on apples. Bake tarts at 350° F for 20 minutes until apples have carmelized. Serve warm from oven.

Serves 5
1 serving = 90 calories

433

Strawberry-Papaya Parfait
(Maui Challenge)

1	pint ripe strawberries, sliced
1	large papaya, skinned, seeded and chopped
1 1/2	c. nonfat yogurt
1/2	c. sour cream
1/2	c. honey
2	tsp. cinnamon
1/2	tsp. nutmeg
	strawberries or mint sprig for garnish

Distribute strawberries and papaya alternately in 6 wine glasses or other appropriate serving dishes. Combine yogurt, sour cream, honey, cinnamon and nutmeg until well blended. Pour over fruit. Refrigerate for about an hour before serving. Garnish with a flared strawberry or sprig of mint.

Serves 6
1 serving = 175 calories

Baked Vanilla Custard
(Maui Challenge)

3	eggs
1/4	c. honey
2	c. nonfat milk
1/4	c. nonfat milk powder
1/8	tsp. salt
1	tsp. vanilla extract

Preheat oven to 325° F. Combine all ingredients and beat thoroughly with wisk or electric blender until smooth. Evenly distribute into 6 small custard cups and place in baking dish. Add enough hot water to baking dish to surround cups to a depth of 1". Bake for 40-50 minutes until set. Remove from water bath, cool to room temperature and then chill.

Serves 6
1 serving = 122 calories

Peach Melba
(La Costa)

1/2	c. raspberries, crushed
4	oz. apple juice, unsweetened
2	tsp. grape jelly, unsweetened
1/8	tsp. almond extract
1	tsp. cornstarch
4	peach halves, fresh or canned, in water or juice
4	tsp. plain, nonfat yogurt or low calorie whipped topping for garnish (optional)

Combine raspberries, apple juice, jelly and almond extract in saucepan and bring to a boil. Simmer for 30 minutes. Dissolve cornstarch in 1 tablespoon cold water and add to sauce to thicken. Allow sauce to cool. Place peach halves in 4 sherbet dishes. Spoon 2 ounces of sauce over each peach. Chill. Garnish with yogurt or whipped topping if desired.

Serves 4
1 serving = 40 calories

Baked Apples
(La Costa)

4	small, tart, firm apples
1/2	c. water
1/2	c. apple juice, unsweetened
1/2	tsp. cinnamon
1	stick whole cinnamon
2	whole cloves

Baked Apples (Cont.)

Preheat oven to 375° F. Core baking apples and pare 1" strip of skin from around middle of each apple or pare upper half of each apple to prevent splitting. Place apples upright in a shallow baking pan with a tight lid. Pour liquids and spices around the apples. Cover and bake until tender when pierced with a fork, 30-40 minutes. Serve at once or chill and serve cold.

Serves 4
1 serving = 40 calories

GLOSSARY

AGAR GRANULES: Available in Oriental markets.

AL DENTE: Pasta or vegetables cooked until firm and crunchy, not soft or overdone.

BAIN-MARIE: A hot water bath like a double boiler.

BALSAMIC VINEGAR: Used in Italian dishes. Available in gourmet sections of grocery stores.

BARBECUE SPICES: Any combination of spices placed on meat or vegetables to be barbecued.

BLANCH: To briefly heat foods in a large quantity of boiling water. Sometimes the foods are placed in ice water afterwards to stop the cooking process.

BOUQUET GARNI: Parsley, thyme and bay leaf tied together to flavor a dish as it cooks. Remove before serving.

BUTTER EXTRACT: Found in the spice section of grocery stores.

CHICKEN GLAZE: To give a shiny appearance to chicken, usually using an extract or sauce.

DAIKON: A large white radish used in Oriental dishes. Available in Oriental markets.

DEGLAZE: Pour wine or other liquid into pan in which food has been roasted or prepared in butter or oil (food has been removed and just the pan juices remain).

DEMI-GLACE: Reduced brown sauce.

FENUGREEK: A legume used in India and Africa. Available in health food or specialty stores.

FLAMBÉ: To ignite food with a small amount of heated liquor.

GENOISE: A sponge cake.

ICE BATH: To plunge food into icy water.

KELP: Dried seaweed, found in Oriental markets.

LAVOSH BREAD: Available in health food stores.

LEMON, ORANGE OR LIME ZEST: The grated outer covering of a lemon, orange or lime, use only the skin part, as the white part becomes bitter.

LIQUID AMINOS: Available in health food sections of grocery stores.

LIQUID LECITHIN: Available in health food stores.

MEDITERRANEAN HERBS: A combination of dried rosemary, thyme, sage, parsley and oregano in equal parts.

MIRABELLE: A yellow plum.

MORELS: A wild mushroom used either fresh or dried.

NORI: Thin black sheets of seaweed. Available in Oriental markets.

RED MISO: Fermented bean paste. Available in Oriental markets.

REDUCTION: Boiling until desired thickness and/or quantity is achieved.

RICE TIMBALES: A drum-shaped mold, filled with rice and inverted on the plate. The mold is then removed.

SPIKE: A salt substitute found in the health food sections of grocery stores.

SPIRULINA: Available in health food stores.

STRAW MUSHROOMS: Long stemmed wild Oriental mushroom. Available in Oriental markets

TAHINI: A paste of raw sesame seeds. Can be used as peanut butter. Found in the health food section of grocery stores.

TAMARI: A sauce from soybeans, like soy sauce. Available in Oriental markets.

TEMPEH: A product from the soybean used as a source of protein. Available in health food sections of grocery stores.

TOMATO CONCASSA: Peeled, seeded and chopped tomatoes for a sauce.

WASABI: Japanese horseradish, green in color, usually comes as a paste. Available in Oriental markets.

WHEAT BROWNS: Made by cooking whole wheat berries in pure chicken stock with onions, red and green peppers. This causes the berries to puff up. Before serving, toss slightly in saute pan with a little chicken stock to warm. Use an a healthy alternative to hash browns.

YOGURT CHEESE: Place yogurt in a cheesecloth lined strainer and drain until all the liquid is gone.

YOGURT SAUCE: A blend of 1 cup plain, lowfat yogurt, 1 teaspoon vanilla extract, and 1/2 teaspoon ground cinnamon which yields 1 cup at 15 calories per 2 tablespoon serving.

GEOGRAPHICAL INDEX

HAWAII

MEXICO

NEW MEXICO

UTAH

Index

A

B

C

D

E

F

G

H

I

L

M

N

O

Q

R

S

T

U

V

W

Y

CLIP ART: Dover Publishing Co.

EDITOR: Colleen O'Brien

FRONT COVER: Steve Doty

LITERARY COMMENTS: Tanya Branson

PRINTING: Publishers Press, Inc.

PROOFREADING: Anne Witzleben and Colleen O'Brien

PUBLISHER: The Tastes of Tahoe

All Tastes of Tahoe books are available at special quantity discounts when purchased in bulk by corporations, organizations and special-interest groups. Custom imprinting can also be done to fit special needs. For comments, re-orders, the address of your nearest distributor, or information, please contact:

The Tastes of Tahoe®

P. O. Box 6114

Incline Village, NV 89450

701-831-5182

THE TASTES OF TAHOE®
P. O. BOX 6114
INCLINE VILLAGE, NV 89450
702-831-5182

Please send_____copies of THE TASTES OF CALIFORNIA WINE COUNTRY -NAPA/SONOMA @ $11.95 each

Please send_____copies of THE TASTES OF CALIFORNIA WINE COUNTRY -NORTH COAST @ $11.95 each

Please send_____copies of THE BEST OF THE TASTES OF TAHOE @ $11.95 each

Please send_____copies of THE TASTES OF CRUISING @ $11.95 each

Please send_____copies of TAKE MY BODY AND FIX IT! @ $13.95 each

Add $2.00 postage and handling for the first book ordered and $.50 for each additional book. Enclosed is my check for $_____

Name_____

Address_____

City_____State_____Zip_____

This is a gift. Send directly to:
Name_____

Address_____

City_____State_____Zip_____
Autographed by author. ☐
Autographed to:_____

THE TASTES OF TAHOE®
P. O. BOX 6114
INCLINE VILLAGE, NV 89450
702-831-5182

Please send_____copies of THE TASTES OF CALIFORNIA WINE COUNTRY -NAPA/SONOMA @ $11.95 each

Please send_____copies of THE TASTES OF CALIFORNIA WINE COUNTRY -NORTH COAST @ $11.95 each

Please send_____copies of THE BEST OF THE TASTES OF TAHOE @ $11.95 each

Please send_____copies of THE TASTES OF CRUISING @ $11.95 each

Please send_____copies of TAKE MY BODY AND FIX IT! @ $13.95 each

Add $2.00 postage and handling for the first book ordered and $.50 for each additional book. Enclosed is my check for $_____

Name_____

Address_____

City_____State_____Zip_____

This is a gift. Send directly to:
Name_____

Address_____

City_____State_____Zip_____
Autographed by author. ☐
Autographed to:_____

ABOUT THE AUTHOR

Lake Tahoe's restaurant voyeur, Sonnie Imes, is an impresario of haute cuisine, low cuisine and everything in between - as long as the "tastes" are there.

Under her imprint of "The Tastes of Tahoe," Sonnie has published eleven guidebooks/cookbooks to the best eateries at Lake Tahoe, Reno, California Wine Country, Cruise Ships, and now, her latest "Take My Body and Fix it!."

Sonnie knows whereof she speaks when she reviews a restaurant, cruise ship, or spa for she is a chef herself, both gourmet and down home. She has taught the art of cooking at Sierra Nevada College, produced and directed her own television show on PBS, "A Taste of Tahoe," featuring chefs from area restaurants who prepared gourmet specialties on the air, and paid enough visits to restaurants, cruise ships and spas worldwide, sampling their fare with critical palate, to have developed a discriminating knowledge of what tastes good.

In this latest book, Sonnie sacrificed her body to the nation's health and fitness craze by visiting 24 Western spas and gathered spa recipes. Her only criterion being that the "Tastes" are there.

NOTES

NOTES

NOTES

NOTES

NOTES

NOTES

NOTES

NOTES